CHILD SUPPORT IN A

Child Support
in action

Gwynn Davis, Nick Wikeley and Richard Young
with
Jacqueline Barron and Julie Bedward

·H A R T·
PUBLISHING
OXFORD
1998

Hart Publishing
Oxford
UK

Distributed in the United States by
Northwestern University Press
625 Colfax
Evanston
Illinois
60208–4210 USA

Distributed in Australia and New Zealand by
Federation Press Pty Ltd
PO Box 45
Annandale, NSW 2038
Australia

Distributed in Netherlands, Belgium and Luxembourg by
Intersentia, Churchillaan 108
B2900 Schoten
Antwerpen
Belgium

Hart Publishing is a specialist legal publisher based in Oxford, England. To order
further copies of this book or to request a list of other publications please write to:

Hart Publishing, 19 Whitehouse Road, Oxford, OX1 4PA
Telephone: +44 (0)1865 434459 Fax: +44 (0) 1865 794882
email: hartpub@janep.demon.co.uk
British Library Cataloguing in Publication Data
Data Available

ISBN 1–901362–32–9 (cloth)
1–901362–70–1 (paper)

Typeset in Utopia 10pt
by Hope Services (Abingdon) Ltd
Printed in Great Britain on acid-free paper
by Biddles Ltd, Guildford and Kings Lynn.

Preface

This book offers what we believe is a new perspective on the Child
Support Agency. It is based on a major (or certainly arduous) empirical
research project, for the purpose of which we were granted privileged
access to the Agency's own case files and staff, and were thus able to
monitor case conduct from both the Agency and client perspective. This
means we can compare the accounts of separated parents and their legal
advisers with those of the beleaguered CSA staff who attempted to calculate and enforce child maintenance obligations in those same cases.
The role of the independent child support appeal tribunals is also
explored through detailed case observation and interviews with tribunal
members.

The media picture of the misery visited upon 'absent fathers' is borne
out in part, but even more striking is the evidence of a catastrophic
administrative failure leading to the abandonment of many of the basic
tenets of administrative justice. The reasons for this do not lie primarily
in the perceived unfairness of the formula, but rather in the failure of
those drafting the Child Support Act 1991 to appreciate the impact of
such change upon the rest of our hugely complex benefit structure, and
their failure also to grasp that the problems of inadequate disclosure and
ineffective enforcement—with which courts had grappled for decades—
could not be tackled successfully by a distant bureaucracy.

The work of the Child Support Agency has attracted enormous media
interest, sometimes of the most sensational kind. This presents an unac-
customed difficulty for the socio-legal researcher, who is naturally
drawn to the hidden and obscure. The Child Support Agency is an inno-
vation with which everyone, on some level, is familiar, and upon which
everyone has an opinion. Our task was to conduct a study which would
enable us to go behind media accounts in order to present our own distinctive story. And we do indeed have a story to tell: this has a strong
'human' or dramatic element located within the academic exposition.
We have tried to write simply and accessibly, as befits an account of a
staggeringly bold social experiment.

We employed an essentially qualitative research methodology. That is
to say, we immersed ourselves in individual cases (123 of them) drawn
mainly from the South-West and the West Midlands; we studied these
cases from a variety of perspectives; and we did so over time. This means
incidentally that while our account reflects *all* our research evidence,
any case material is essentially *illustrative*. Qualitative researchers first

inform themselves, and then they inform their readers, but they are never able to present the totality of the evidence: occasionally we offer tables, but comparatively little of what we have to say rests on a numerical breakdown. Equally, when we present case histories we regard these as representative in the sense that they reflect experiences and themes which recur throughout the study. In our presentation of cases we provide pseudonyms and also change certain identifying features.

Throughout the book we use the language of the Child Support Act. Thus we refer to "parents with care" and "absent parents". We may also appear to assume that the former are female and the latter male. This is purely for convenience. Our use of this language is not intended to convey any value judgements or assumptions.

It takes time to write a book, and this one has taken as long as most. We began our research in Spring 1994 and the book will be published in Summer 1998. The Child Support Agency, meanwhile, has been in a state of perpetual revolution. This means that in the detail, and sometimes in more critical aspects, our 'findings' have been overtaken by legislative or administrative change. Indeed it is our understanding that even as we write this Preface (in January 1998) the Labour government is engaged in yet another policy review. We have two things to say about this process of change, and our inability to keep up with it. First, it is inevitable. Secondly, it does not matter—or at least, it does not matter very much. Any major social legislation is a kind of edifice, rather imposing from a distance, which then has to be made to work. After the Lord Mayor's Show comes the dustcart of regulations, and of administrative reorganisation as the original grand design is revealed to be deficient in certain key respects. Trailing along behind the dustcart come the socio-legal researchers, morosely observing. As they do so they are informed by all and sundry that whatever they have to say will be out of date by the time they say it. But academics are not journalists; it is our job to take the long view. All organisations evolve, and, as with the CSA, they may be subject to new rules and procedures. But the fundamentals do not change as quickly as all that, and to date the Agency has not changed its essential character. Even were it to do so, we would still hope that our analysis would contribute to a better understanding of this area of policy and all the difficult issues which have to be faced when contemplating reform on the private maintenance/social security borderline.

We have had a great deal of help in writing the book. Our first debt is to the parents who agreed to be interviewed, often on a repeat basis, about a difficult and painful area of their lives. We are also indebted to the Nuffield Foundation, which funded our study. Thirdly, we are grateful for the co-operation of the Social Research Branch of the Department of Social Security, which gave us access to Agency case files and staff. Thereafter we received unstinting co-operation from managers and child support officers at the Dudley and Plymouth Child Support Assessment Centres, and from field staff. We were indeed treated very generously, and we hope that our account does justice to the perspective of Agency staff as much as it does to the experience of parents. We also wish to express our appreciation for the assistance provided by the Independent Tribunal Service, both by headquarters staff at Salford Quays and by hard-pressed tribunal chairs and wing members. We are also grateful to the Lord Chancellor's Department, which granted access to case files at Birmingham County Court, and to the Birmingham court staff for their assistance. We are similarly indebted to solicitors in Bristol who sought (and generally secured) their clients' agreement to being involved in the research, and who themselves agreed to be interviewed.

Professor David Feldman and Dr Stephen Cretney acted as honest brokers at the formation of the research team. Thereafter we were fortunate to have the assistance of four highly skilled research secretaries: Ann Clarke acted as secretary to the project for the period of the fieldwork; Sara Bladon typed the book, in the course of which she coped magnificently with the additional burdens generated by joint authorship and obsessive editorialising; and Denise Lees and Pat Hammond also gave invaluable support. We are also grateful to Philip Larkin, research assistant in the Faculty of Law at the University of Southampton, for his work on checking proofs.

The research which underpins this book was undertaken by a team of five, Jacqueline Barron and Julie Bedward having been appointed as Research Fellows at Bristol and Birmingham Universities respectively. For the duration of the project we worked closely together, with Jackie and Julie between them undertaking the bulk of the fieldwork. We owe the quality of the research data to their meticulousness both in the conduct of interviews and in subsequent writing up. We were also a team in the sense that we discussed the issues which were raised by the data and shared in refining and dissecting the case material. Jackie and Julie also prepared early drafts of some chapters. Jackie chose to withdraw from the writing process when it became apparent that her approach was in important respects incompatible with that of other team members. In Julie's case the expiry of the research contract, coupled with her new responsibilities, necessarily limited her participation from that point. Jackie's and Julie's contributions were nonetheless critical to the success of the whole project, and to the preparation of this book. Gwynn Davis, Nick Wikeley and Richard Young shared equally in the writing process, in the course of which they agreed about most things and resolved those they did not without bloodshed. Their names, here and on the title page, are listed alphabetically.

GD NW RY

Contents

List of Tables

1

The Birth of the Child Support Agency

1. INTRODUCTION

The Child Support Act 1991 was designed to reinforce personal rather than state responsibility for the maintenance of children. As such it reflected a determination on the part of government to effect a shift in cultural attitudes as well as a desire to rein in benefits expenditure. It has been said that the legislation presumes "that all children are born into a uniformly constituted family which survives, in some form or another, even after the relationship between the adult parties has broken down".[1] Our task was to examine how the Child Support Act worked in practice. If there was failure, we wanted to discover the reasons for it. This necessarily involved exploring the relationship between child support and social security. We also wanted to take into account as many perspectives as possible, notably those of parents, legal advisers, Agency staff, and members of appeal tribunals.

In this first chapter we examine the social and political forces that led to the creation of the Child Support Agency. We begin by providing an overview of the complex multi-institutional framework within which financial issues on relationship breakdown are resolved in England and Wales. We then examine the development of a political agenda for reform, and consider the international context. Thereafter we analyse the legislative process that was to lead to the Child Support Act 1991: we reflect on the White Paper *Children Come First*[2] and the consultation process it initiated; then we examine the parliamentary history of the Child Support Bill. It is our contention that the problems which have beset the Child Support Agency were predictable, indeed were predicted, but received inadequate attention within both government and Parliament.

To understand this fully one needs a historical perspective. For example it has long been recognised that the resolution of financial issues on relationship breakdown is complex and fragmented. The Finer Committee, reporting in 1974, referred to the "three systems of Family

---

[1] Graycar (1989), 86.
[2] Department of Social Security (1990).

Law" which it found to be in operation: the divorce court; the magistrates' court; and the administration by the then Department of Health and Social Security of welfare benefits for separated families.[3] Finer proposed an assimilation of these three systems through the creation of an administrative mechanism for calculating maintenance obligations which would bring together private obligation and public entitlement. Partly because of the cost implications, and partly because of a reluctance to single out the divorcing population for favourable treatment, these proposals did not find favour with successive governments. There was no legislative integration of the welfare benefit system with maintenance obligations imposed by the divorce courts. From the perspective of the courts, and of the legal practitioners in those courts, child support was but one element in a complex mosaic of financial obligations which also included spousal maintenance, the disposition of the matrimonial home, lump sum payments, and the division of other assets, including household property.[4]

The liberalisation of the divorce laws by the Divorce Reform Act 1969 had brought in its train a fundamental revision of the law governing maintenance and property settlement. The Matrimonial Proceedings and Property Act 1970 rationalised and significantly extended the divorce courts' powers to re-allocate resources on family breakdown. The 1970 Act was subsequently consolidated in the Matrimonial Causes Act 1973, and this remains the principal legislation governing the disposal of family assets on divorce. The legislation entrenched the principle of maintenance for the economically vulnerable partner and her children, essentially on a no-fault basis.

Over the past three decades our society has been faced with the problem of reconciling the practice of serial relationships (with or without formal recognition through marriage) with an on-going child maintenance obligation. Some of these tensions were reflected in the passage of the Matrimonial and Family Proceedings Act 1984, amending the 1973 legislation, which required courts to consider the desirability of both parties becoming self-sufficient, and therefore of achieving a 'clean break' between divorcing spouses.[5] In the 1980s courts and lawyers turned increasingly to social security as a means of squaring the circle when faced with inadequate resources to maintain two households out of one income.

In general the private law mechanism had proved ineffective in securing child support for the majority of separated families. As Parker observed, "the 'private' family law system, characterised by its traditional separation from the 'public' sphere of welfare provision and based

---

[3] Committee on One-Parent Families (1974).
[4] Davis, Cretney and Collins (1994).
[5] See Cretney (1986).

on broad discretionary judicial powers, patently produced results which benefited men at the expense of children, women and the State".[6] From the early 1970s the continued growth in the divorce rate (and lone parenthood generally) saw increasing dependence on state benefit. At the same time there was a wealth of evidence, from the UK and overseas, suggesting that women were likely to suffer downward social mobility on divorce.[7] Research in this country demonstrated that maintenance (whether spousal or child-related) constituted a relatively insignificant element in women's incomes following separation.[8] Overall, about a third of divorced women with children were dependent on the State at any one time, and about two-thirds were dependent at some point in the two years following separation. Income Support provided a small, regular income, in contrast to the problems associated with dependence on male partners, either within or following a marriage or cohabitation.[9]

In practice, the critical issue on separation is commonly that of rehousing. With the advent of the "right to buy" in 1980, owner-occupation became the dominant tenure.[10] This had major repercussions in other areas of social policy. Even as separated parents struggled to maintain two households out of their own resources, house price inflation in the early and mid-1980s often created sufficient equity to enable homeowners to sell their property so that both might be rehoused. More and more divorcing couples found themselves "property rich, income poor". Given this background, and the priority accorded to securing a stable home for the children, divorce lawyers came to appreciate that they could utilise the benefits system to maximise the finances of both parents.[11]

A number of other factors contributed to this trend towards welfare benefit planning.[12] First, a parent with care could achieve a full allowance for her mortgage interest payments when in receipt of Income Support, including any extra cost of buying out her ex-partner's share (this last concession ended in 1994). This form of assistance was not available for recipients of Family Credit, so acting as a disincentive to

[6] Parker (1992), 314.

[7] Weitzman (1985). There is, however, an on-going debate as to the extent of the decline in the standard of living for divorced women: see Peterson (1996).

[8] Eekelaar and Maclean (1986).

[9] Davis, Macleod and Murch (1983); Eekelaar and Maclean (1986).

[10] Owner-occupation accounted for 57 per cent of the housing stock in 1981, rising to 68 per cent in 1993 (Carey, 1995). The discussion here is based on the "norm" of owner-occupation, but this should not disguise the fact that relationship breakdown as between joint tenants in the social housing sector has caused immense problems for local authorities and the courts.

[11] For early research evidence of this practice, see Smart (1984), 181–4. A similar tendency towards the maximisation of social security entitlement as part of divorce settlements was evident in Australia before its child support reforms of the late 1980s: Parker (1991), 26.

[12] Bainham (1993), 302.

work for all home-owners other than those few women able to command an income sufficient to meet both their mortgage and child care costs. Secondly, social security legislation imposed no duty on an ex-husband to support his former partner, although the long-standing public law obligation to maintain his children did remain. Thirdly, after some pre-varication the courts accepted that the availability of state benefits could be taken into account in determining the terms of financial settlement on divorce.[13]

Thus, where there were dependent children, a typical arrangement involved the transfer of the home to the parent with care of the children, whilst the non-carer was permitted to pay but nominal maintenance. The study by Davis *et al.*[14] revealed that the legal framework was highly discretionary, inviting bargaining and pressure in respect of all the elements listed above. Commonly, the agreements which the lawyers nego-tiated reflected the priority given to safeguarding the children's right to secure housing, but at the same time they tended to minimise the absent parent's continuing obligation to maintain his children. This was consis-tent with the 'clean break' philosophy which had been given a consider-able impetus by the Matrimonial and Family Proceedings Act 1984. The man (as it usually was) might lose his right of occupation or even of co-ownership of the matrimonial home, but he would commonly be faced with only a modest maintenance requirement. The State, through the welfare benefits system, picked up the bill. Income Support claimants could continue to live in their own homes, perhaps with a substantial mortgage, because their benefit entitlement included the interest on the mortgage as a 'housing cost'.[15]

2. THE DEVELOPMENT OF A POLITICAL AGENDA FOR REFORMING CHILD SUPPORT

In 1985 the government had undertaken a major review of social security policy and expenditure, leading to the Social Security Act 1986. At this time spending on single parents was not portrayed as a major issue. Indeed, the financial difficulties which these parents faced were recog-nised by the inclusion of a lone-parent premium within Income Support, and by the creation of Family Credit which was designed to assist claimants to enter low-paid employment. In the late 1980s the newly-appointed Secretary of State for Social Security, John Moore, initiated an internal review of social security policy on lone parents. Encouraged by lobbying groups on the Conservative right, Moore was reportedly deter-mined to explore the possibility of a more punitive approach to single

---

[13] *Ashley* v. *Blackman* (1988) 2 FLR 278.
[14] Davis, Cretney and Collins (1994).
[15] These rules have since been made considerably stricter: see Wikeley (1995).

parents, including a requirement that separated mothers identify the fathers of their children. This in turn was consistent with arguments advanced by some American commentators who claimed that the growth of single parenthood was creating a new "underclass".[16]

Ministerial speeches throughout this period highlighted the alleged perverse incentives for lone parents to seek access both to state benefits and to local authority accommodation. As far as the latter was concerned, plans to restrict the availability of council housing to single mothers collapsed in the face of concerted opposition from interested bodies.[17] Nonetheless, concern at the growing level of social security spending on lone parents led inexorably to the Child Support Act. In June 1989 John Moore informed the House of Commons Social Services Committee that a government statement on policy towards single parents would be made "in the not too distant future".[18] Shortly thereafter John Moore returned to the back benches but the government's interest in measures to limit state spending on one-parent families was sustained. In a speech to the National Children's Homes, delivered on 17 January 1990, the then Prime Minister, Margaret Thatcher, characterised child abuse, lone-parent families and teenage homelessness as consequences of a weakening in family values. She concluded:

> "But when one of the parents not only walks away from marriage but neither maintains nor shows any interest in the child, an enormous unfair burden is placed on the other. Nearly four out of five mothers claiming Income Support receive no maintenance from the fathers. No father should be able to escape from his responsibility and that is why the government is looking at ways of strengthening the system for tracing an absent father and making the arrangements for recovering maintenance more effective."

The government's creation of a political agenda based on support for "family values" left the Labour Party in a quandary. Opposition to such proposals would easily be portrayed as condoning parental irresponsibility and welfare state profligacy. This accounts for the subdued role played by the Labour Party in the debates on the Child Support Bill.[19] Frank Field[20] was one of the few figures in the Opposition ranks who was prepared to debate the issues.[21] Conscious of the need to develop a viable strategy in time for the next election, the Opposition social security spokesman advocated a policy requiring all fathers to pay some

[16] Murray (1984).

[17] However, this issue resurfaced in the run-up to the Housing Act 1996: see Cowan (1997), ch. 8.

[18] Social Services Committee, Ninth Report, Session 1988–9, *Social Security: Changes Implemented in April 1988*, H.C. 437–II, Minutes, 86.

[19] Garnham and Knights (1994).

[20] Now Minister of State at the Department of Social Security, then a Labour back-bencher who chaired the all-party House of Commons Select Committee on Social Security.

[21] Field (1991).

maintenance for their children regardless of their financial circumstances and irrespective of whether they had been married to the
mother. The shift in focus from the social problems of family breakdown
to the narrower question of family finances led to the supposedly "feckless father" becoming the target for action. The presentation of the
debate in these terms, together with the Labour Party's discomfort,
accounts in part for the relatively easy passage of the Child Support Bill
through Parliament the following year.

Further pressure for change had come with the publication of a study
by the National Audit Office[22] demonstrating that whereas the number
of lone-parent families in receipt of state benefit had increased by 86 per
cent between 1981 and 1988, the proportion receiving regular maintenance had fallen from 50 per cent to 23 per cent. By 1988 only 7 per cent
of the cost of supporting lone-parent families on benefit was recovered
from liable relatives.[23] Reasons for this trend included the use of Income
Support to fund 'clean breaks', and increasing levels of unemployment
amongst separated fathers. The Department of Social Security's failure
to give priority to its liable relative work was also a factor. Periodic crises
in the administration of benefits in local offices in the 1980s led to staff
being reallocated from liable relative work so that they might assist in
clearing the backlog of other work.[24] The Prime Minister meanwhile had
declared that "parenthood is for life" and had outlined plans to establish
the Child Support Agency to assess, collect and enforce maintenance
according to a formula.

3. CHILD SUPPORT: THE INTERNATIONAL CONTEXT

The growth in lone parenthood and single parents' increasing dependence on State benefits was not a peculiarly British phenomenon.[25]
Child support had been tackled in a number of other advanced
economies, particularly the United States and Australia, before it
became a major issue in the UK. In the United States, where enforcement
of child support is a state rather than a federal responsibility, the catalyst
was disquiet over the cost of welfare payments for single-parent families.
The Wisconsin scheme attracted particular attention as it was the model
both for other American states and for the Australian system.[26] In a series
of gradual steps between 1983 and 1987, Wisconsin introduced a formula
for calculating child support while leaving the responsibility for making

---

[22] National Audit Office (1990).
[23] Bradshaw and Millar (1991).
[24] Baldwin, Wikeley and Young (1992).
[25] Millar (1989).
[26] On the Wisconsin scheme, see Garfinkel and Melli (1986) and Garfinkel (1992).

such assessments with the courts. Child support payments were calculated as 17 per cent of the father's gross income for one child, 25 per cent for two children, 29 per cent for three, 31 per cent for four, and 34 per cent for five, with no account taken of the mother's income or the father's net pay. Payment was to have been enforced by deduction from salary, but in practice this was not implemented throughout the state.[27] Problems were compounded by the courts' practice of expressing orders in terms of actual figures rather than percentages, with the result that orders rapidly became out-of-date as incomes increased. The experience of several other American states has been that even where collection rates improved this had little impact upon the standard of living of children in one parent families.[28]

Reform in Australia was driven by two policy goals: to improve the standard of living of children in poverty and to reduce the costs to the taxpayer of supporting single-parent families. In language redolent of later British studies, it was observed that child maintenance was effectively "a voluntary act exercised by relatively few" and that the capacity of absent parents to pay more was "being camouflaged by poor assessment procedures and almost non-existent enforcement mechanisms".[29] The Australian scheme, introduced in two phases in 1988 and 1989, was relatively sophisticated.[30] First, the formula was less crude than either the Wisconsin or the subsequent UK model. Although the level of child support was based on the number of children involved,[31] the formula made allowance for personal living expenses, using social security rates. Furthermore, the custodial parent's other income abated the amount of child support payable once it exceeded a certain threshold. As in Wisconsin, the parent with care was allowed to retain an element of maintenance before benefit entitlement was reduced (in other words there was a 'disregard').[32] The formula was based on the parties' taxable income for the previous year, uprated for inflation by applying a standard indexation measure. The awards were then revised annually. A second distinctive feature of the Australian scheme was that enforcement became the responsibility of a child support agency but, unlike the

[27] Garfinkel (1992), 58.

[28] Krause (1989); Thoennes, Tjaden and Pearson (1991); and Pearson, Thoennes and Anhalt (1992).

[29] Harrison, McDonald and Weston (1987), 94 and 100.

[30] Parker (1991 and 1992); Rhoades (1995).

[31] Under the Australian model, the rates are 18 per cent for the first child, 27 per cent for two children, 32 per cent for three, 34 per cent for four and 36 per cent for five children or more.

[32] This is important in persuading absent parents that child support does indeed benefit the children rather than the Exchequer. Although the 1995 changes to the British scheme made some limited changes in the latter direction, there remains no disregard of maintenance payments for Income Support claimants (Family Credit claimants can receive up to £15 a week before their benefit is affected): see Ch. 3.

subsequent British system, the primary means of collection was through the tax system by automatic deduction from salary. A third feature of the Australian model was that it permitted departures from the formula in certain narrowly defined circumstances. And finally, in an astute political move, the Australian government decided that formula-based assessments would apply only to children born on or after 1 October 1989. In other words the legislation did not apply retrospectively, and pre-existing arrangements were allowed to stand. Again, this aspect of the scheme helped to reduce the level of opposition.[33]

4. *CHILDREN COME FIRST*: THE WHITE PAPER AND RESPONSES

The White Paper *Children Come First*[34] was published on 29 October 1990. It noted that 750,000 lone parents were dependent on Income Support, while only 30 per cent of lone mothers and 3 per cent of lone fathers received regular maintenance for their children.[35] It described the system for calculating and enforcing maintenance as "fragmented, uncertain in its results, slow and ineffective".[36] The problem was therefore characterised in terms of system failure, with no reference to the wider social and economic factors discussed above. The government's proposals were designed to ensure that "parents honour their responsibilities to their children whenever they can afford to do so" and that "a fair and reasonable balance is struck between the liable parent's responsibilities for all the children he or she is liable to maintain".[37]

The timetable allowed a mere six weeks for comments. The government did not publish responses, nor provide a summary of the views received. We were able to secure copies of the submissions made by thirty-one of the eighty-six bodies which responded to the White Paper.[38] An analysis of these revealed remarkable unanimity of opinion. Respondents were agreed on the principle that absent parents should, where feasible, contribute to their children's upkeep. There was also widespread support for the principle of a formula. However, views on the specific formula proposed ranged from scepticism to outright opposition. Particular criticism was directed at its inflexibility, the failure to

[33] See Millar and Whiteford (1993) and Millar (1996) for a valuable comparison of the Australian and UK experiences. The New Zealand reforms, which were retrospective, have faced the same crisis of legitimacy as the UK model: see Atkin (1994).
[34] Department of Social Security (1990).
[35] Department of Social Security (1990), Vol. 1/3.
[36] *Ibid.*, p.i.
[37] *Ibid.*
[38] These organisations are listed in a written answer in Hansard, HC Debs., Vol. 244, col. 247 (26 May 1994). We were unable to trace addresses for 13 respondents; a further 35 failed to reply to our request; 5 could not trace their submission; and 2 had since closed.

make any allowance for property transfers and other forms of financial adjustment, and the failure likewise to recognise the costs incurred by absent parents in travelling to work, maintaining contact with children, and loan repayments.[39]

In addition, many respondents were concerned at the likely impact of the scheme on second families. For example, the Association of County Court and District Registrars, with the benefit of their daily experience of ancillary relief work, argued that the approach to step-children:

> "flies in the face of reality. No-one can stop fathers leaving their first family and starting, or acquiring, another one ... the second family will be reduced to subsistence level and the sins of the father will be visited on the children of his second union . . . we have to say that these proposals will cause poverty and bitterness among many people who do not deserve it."[40]

There was no consensus on the proposed institutional machinery. Only two respondents explicitly supported the idea of a child support agency (these were the National Council for One-Parent Families and Church Action on Poverty). Those opposed, perhaps not surprisingly, tended to be those most associated with existing arrangements (the Magistrates' Association, the Justices' Clerks Society and the Law Society). Several respondents who were non-committal on the issue emphasised the importance of adequate funding for the agency:

> "The substantial caseload for the agency is likely to become unmanageable ... the danger is that one slow-moving agency—the courts—will be exchanged for another—the CSA—at much greater public expense."[41]

A recurrent theme in many of the submissions was opposition to the idea of a reduction in benefit where the mother refused to authorise the Agency to pursue a maintenance claim against the absent parent. This question dominated proceedings in Parliament, effectively diverting attention from other, perhaps more fundamental issues.

5. THE CHILD SUPPORT BILL IN PARLIAMENT

The Child Support Bill was published on 14 February 1991, two months to the day after the closing date for responses to *Children Come First*. Convention dictates that controversial legislation is considered by the Commons first, but the Child Support Bill was introduced in the House of Lords. This may have reflected the perception that it was not a party

---

[39] Some of these factors were partly addressed in changes to the scheme in its first two years of operation.

[40] *Submission of the Association of County Court and District Registrars in Response to Children Come First* (1990), 2.

[41] *Response of the Legal Action Group* (1990), 3.

political issue; equally, it may have been due in part to the Lord Chancellor being one of the sponsoring ministers. Several peers raised doubts about aspects of the proposals. Lord Mishcon, leading for the Opposition, regretted that the Bill was a "legislative skeleton" and questioned whether sufficient account would be taken of clean break orders. The most bitter attack was made by Lord Houghton of Sowerby:

"We must acknowledge that the Bill will cause far more tears, anger, resentment and violence than its authors imagined. It is an intrusion by a new arm of bureaucracy into the most delicate, emotional and difficult aspects of human relationships."[42]

A small band of critics continued to raise objections throughout the Report and Third Reading stages, but they were unable to secure any significant government defeats.[43] As Lord Simon of Glaisdale was to comment, the Bill:

"aroused general hostility in your Lordships' House from the two dozen or so members who took a particular interest in it. No-one except the two ministers in charge of the Bill had anything good to say about it."[44]

Yet the Bill received relatively cursory attention once it reached the Commons. On Second Reading it was given a grudging welcome by Michael Meacher for the Opposition. He declared his party's support for the principle of parental responsibility but described the proposals as "seriously flawed". The Bill was considered in Standing Committee, in which legislation is supposed to be subject to detailed scrutiny, for seven morning sessions, a total of just 17½ hours. The Labour Party raised several of the concerns already ventilated in the Lords but only pushed three of its proposed amendments to a vote, in each case unsuccessfully. The government, however, took the opportunity to secure the Committee's agreement to a further forty-seven separate amendments to the Bill. Many of these were technical and uncontroversial, but the last government amendment reversed the one defeat which they had suffered in the Lords, re-inserting the benefit sanction.[45] The Bill then returned to the floor of the House for its Third Reading, where it was disposed of in a little over 3¼ hours. The Third Reading followed the pattern of the Standing Committee debates: the Government tabled six new clauses and almost one hundred further amendments. Labour supported the Bill reluctantly, while several back-benchers from both main parties expressed reservations about aspects of the proposal. For example, the then Conservative MP Emma Nicholson characterised the involvement of the

[42] Hansard, HL Debs., Vol. 526, col. 812, 25 Feb. 1991.
[43] The House of Lords secured one notable victory when the benefit sanction was rejected, but this was later reversed in the House of Commons.
[44] Hansard, HL Debs., Vol. 531, col. 466, 22 July 1991.
[45] *Standing Committee A*, cols. 208–236, 2 July 1991.

DSS, the CSA and the courts as "a tripartite prescription for chaos, slackness and slowness".[46]

The Bill then returned to the Lords for consideration of the Commons amendments. These were accepted, although not without rancour. The changes comprised twelve new clauses and 135 amendments, with peers effectively receiving only a few hours' notice of their contents. At one stage the proceedings were adjourned to see if the Whips could agree to move the business to another day. This proved impossible, and the Lords continued to process the amendments, although not without further protestations. As Lord Simon complained:

> "It is bad enough that your Lordships should be treated as a sausage machine for government legislation. It would be quite intolerable if your Lordships were required to work the treadmill in order to operate that machine."[47]

The Child Support Act 1991 received the Royal Assent on 25 July 1991. Under section 8 of the Act the divorce court is no longer able to exercise the powers conferred on it by statute to make, vary or revive periodical payments orders in respect of a child whose parents are separated. The powers of the magistrates' courts have been similarly curtailed. Under the provisions of the Act a parent with care of a child may—and if on Income Support, Family Credit, or Disability Working Allowance *must*—apply to the Child Support Agency for a formula-based assessment of child support.

It was inevitable that the Child Support Act would have a massive impact. Although it is only in benefit cases that a parent with care of a child is *required* to make an application to the Child Support Agency, it is impossible to make a binding agreement which prevents parents not on benefit from seeking a child support assessment.[48] In all divorce cases involving children, therefore, a sum calculated in accordance with the child support formula must be taken into account by the court as a 'resource' of the parent with care and as an 'obligation' of the absent parent. In most cases the formula represented a significant increase in the level of child support required of the absent parent. The impact on unmarried parents was equally dramatic: men who in some cases had paid no maintenance for a period of years were suddenly faced with a demand that they pay significant sums.

The Act was typical of much modern social security legislation in that it was essentially 'enabling'—that is to say, a skeleton. The statute did no more than lay the basis for the scheme, giving the Secretary of State wide

[46] Hansard, HC Debs., Vol. 195, col. 536, 18 July 1991.
[47] Hansard, HL Debs., Vol. 531, col. 529, 22 July 1991.
[48] Child Support Act 1991, s.9(4). However, it should be noted that "private" cases (i.e. where the parent with care is not claiming a relevant benefit) are excluded from access to the CSA where there is a written maintenance agreement made before 5 Apr. 1993 or there is a court order for maintenance in force: *ibid.*, s.4(10) and Child Support Act 1995, s.18.

regulation-making powers to provide for its details. The Department of Social Security issued a consultation document on the regulations on 1 November 1991, with a six-week deadline for comments. The principal regulations under the Act were presented to Parliament in June 1992, with minimal changes having been made to their content.[49] Under the procedural rules of the House the regulations were subject to a short debate with no opportunity for amendment: they had either to be accepted or rejected in their entirety. The House had to discuss the regulations without the benefit of the scrutiny report of the Joint Committee on Statutory Instruments, the deliberations of which had been concluded just half-an-hour before the main debate opened. The result was a 1½ hour debate in which most of the criticisms were directed at the proposed benefit sanction. The regulations were also debated in the Lords, when many of the objections canvassed during the passage of the original Bill were ventilated again. For example, Lord Stoddart characterised the regulations as "a bureaucrat's dream and a citizen's nightmare".[50]

The passage of the Child Support Act was an object lesson in how to create bad legislation. With the notable exception of a handful of members of the House of Lords there was no effective scrutiny of the government's proposals, and much parliamentary time was spent processing government amendments to the original Bill.

6. THE RESEARCH PROJECT

The Child Support Agency presented unknown territory for researchers, but earlier work on social security adjudication in local offices had thrown light on some of the issues that were likely to arise.[51] That study revealed that adjudication officers faced a dilemma in seeking to maintain the required standards of accuracy whilst processing claims speedily. The quality of adjudication was also affected by difficulties in obtaining sufficient information from claimants.

Another area of concern was the handling of reviews and appeals. Baldwin, Wikeley and Young had highlighted the importance of the internal review mechanism as a means of redress for claimants. The Agency reviews were set up on a rather different basis, in that anyone wishing to appeal was effectively required to lodge this appeal twice before they could have their case aired before a tribunal. Whether Agency customers would understand this two-tier appeal process was open to question.[52]

---

[49] Garnham and Knights (1994).
[50] Hansard, HL Debs., Vol. 539, col. 351, 16 July 1992.
[51] Baldwin, Wikeley and Young (1992).
[52] See, in particular, Sainsbury (1994a).

The tribunals themselves were a further focus of research interest. Tribunals for the most part adjudicate between the citizen and the State, and it has been observed that social security tribunals are often supportive of appellants and concerned to ensure that they receive their full entitlement.[53] But the child support appeal tribunals were faced with a distinctive challenge. They are, to a large degree, adjudicating between citizens. It remained to be seen what procedures would be developed to take account of this. Another key issue concerned the tribunals' powers to require further disclosure of each party's assets: how effective would they be in this respect? Would they be any more effective than the courts? Would they be *as* effective?

We also wanted to discover how the Child Support Agency influenced the deals struck by lawyers in respect of the various other elements in the maintenance/capital/property 'package'. On the face of it there appeared a rather unwieldy relationship between the provisions of the Child Support Act and the courts' residual role. For example, there are many situations where the Agency has no jurisdiction and the parties still have to resort to the courts. We also wanted to discover what impact the new, administratively-imposed maintenance obligation had upon property adjustment orders in respect of the matrimonial home.

We conceived the research task as being to examine each aspect of the system for determining the support obligation on relationship breakdown: the Agency; appeal tribunals; and lawyers/courts. We regarded these as three arms of a single system which ought to be studied together. We therefore undertook a three-pronged enquiry, conducted from our respective institutions, on two sites (Birmingham and Bristol), the object of which was to explore the relationship between the various elements.

The research primarily involved our monitoring live cases over a period of up to eighteen months. We collected most of our data by means of semi-structured interviews with parents, solicitors, Agency staff, and tribunal chairs and wing members. We supplemented this case-monitoring with more general (non-case-based) discussions with lawyers and Agency staff. Our sample comprised 123 cases drawn from four sources: the Child Support Agency (sixty-five); Birmingham County Court (twenty-two); the Independent Tribunal Service (twenty-one); and Bristol solicitors (fifteen). It included eighty parents with care and fifty-eight absent parents.

The strength of the sample lies in its diversity and in the potential which it afforded for the juxtaposition of different perspectives. The twenty cases in which we were able to talk to both parents, to their solicitors, and to representatives of the Child Support Agency provided us with particularly rich data. We were also able to follow many cases over a

---

[53] Baldwin, Wikeley and Young (1992), 121.

significant period, thus enabling us to question the various actors at different points in the process. The study began in April 1994, with the bulk of the fieldwork being undertaken between July 1994 and September 1995. A fuller account of our methodology is contained in Appendix 1.

7. THE STRUCTURE OF THE BOOK

The heart of the child support scheme lies in the formula, which is examined in Chapter 2. That chapter also considers key issues raised by the formula's implementation. In Chapter 3 we examine the inter-relationship between social security policy and child support. Chapters 4 to 7 are devoted to our research findings on the work of the Child Support Agency. Chapter 4 is concerned with the perspective of those working inside the Agency, while Chapter 5 reflects on the experience of parents. Chapters 6 and 7 deal with the processes of review and appeal against Agency decisions. Chapter 8 is concerned with the impact of the Agency on the work of solicitors and courts, while Chapter 9 explores the Agency's influence on relationships between divorced or separated parents. The concluding chapter, Chapter 10, draws together the themes of the book. The major theme is reflected in the title. For whilst the research on which the book is based was conceived as a study of the child support system in action, the main characteristic of that system has been inaction. The predicted "chaos, slackness and slowness" has indeed come to pass. This book argues that the problems which beset the child support scheme are not teething difficulties; they could have been (and in certain quarters were) foreseen; and they stem from fundamental design weaknesses. There is an urgent need for a further, far-reaching policy review.

2
The Formula

Jeremy Hebden, absent parent in Case 117, commenting on his child support assessment:

"The way they work out the amount, it was Q + C + V. I couldn't understand any of that because there's no legend to it, nothing telling you what the numbers [sic] represent."

Child support officer explaining how assessment has been arrived at for Jeremy Hebden (case 117):

"On the first page of this we do what is called a maintenance requirement, which is how much we think by Income Support rates it takes to look after the child. You take into account the needs of the child, and the amount that IS would allow that child, and the amount of child benefit. Then there's a carer allowance, which is broken down like this: if the qualifying child is under 11, they're allowed it all; if they're 11 to 13, they are allowed 75 per cent; then going on as the child gets older, they get less. So once they're over 16, they're not allowed the carer element at all.

You divide that by the number of AUs—that's the number of APs that the PWC has—in this case, she only has one, so it's not divided. She's also allowed the family premium and the one parent premium. So you add the total of this to the amount the child is allowed, and take away the Child Benefit, because she's getting that anyway. So in this case, the PWC, for that one child, she'd be allowed £66.30.

Now the way the rest of the assessment works is that if the AP couldn't afford to pay that amount, that would then be reduced, but if he can afford to pay more than that, it's increased. She's not considered to have any net income because she's on IS. This is what they calculated his net income to be, which is the net income minus half of the pension. The PWC is not considered to have any exempt income either. The exempt income is how you work out what IS would allow them. It's all based on IS rates. So he'd be allowed his personal allowance, and his housing costs. Now if he had a partner, that housing cost would be fractioned—if he had a partner, he'd only be allowed for 75 per cent of that. If he had any children living in the household, it would be fractioned even more.

So he's only allowed a certain amount, and also if he's got a partner you have to consider if they have children living in the household, whether she's able to contribute towards the children of the household, so they are taken into consideration as well. But in this case he has nobody living with him so he's allowed the full personal allowance and the full housing costs.

With the housing costs, he's allowed both the interest and the capital for the interest on the endowment, whereas when you get over here on to the protected income he's only allowed the interest, because the interest is the thing he has to pay, because if he doesn't pay it the building society will be taking the house back. So the exempt income is then subtracted from the net income, and according to this he should have £181 left. And then you go through this formula, which in this case works out at £181 because he doesn't have any AUs to contribute, so that's the total assessment. To get the available assessable income, you multiply that by half. So we're saying that his available assessable income is £95.71.

This is where it gets complicated. Basically what we are saying is that he can afford to pay the maintenance requirement, and that we should ask him for a bit more, because he has extra money in his pocket. It's just the set formula. We work out how much is the additional element, and in this case it worked out at £7.32, because there's only one child. If there's more children it obviously increases. And it worked out that £73.62 is what we were going to ask him for. But before we ask him for that, we have to consider whether he can really afford to pay it.

This is where you take into consideration everybody in the household. If he had a partner who had children of her own that had come into the household, this is where we take them into consideration, because it's only his natural children with his new partner that are taken into account up to this point. We would also take into consideration income of the other people in the household when we are doing this – not for the assessment, it's already been worked out, but just to make sure that he's enough money in the household to cover all his costs. But as I say, he's only allowed for his interest in this one, and he's allowed for his council tax, because he has to pay that as well, and then we give him £30, just to give him an extra margin for his other bits and pieces, but when we work all this out, it only works out at £149, which means he still has enough money. If you take away the maintenance from his disposable income, he still has £212, and his protected income isn't that, which means he is well within his means to pay that, and that's the way that we work it out."

1. INTRODUCTION

The Child Support Act 1991 established a system of child support which differed from the previous arrangements in two fundamental respects. The first was that maintenance for children was to be calculated according to a statutory, non-discretionary formula. The use of a formula, it was claimed in *Children Come First*,[1] would produce fairer and more consistent results, in that parents would be able to predict their obligations in advance, and people in similar circumstances would pay similar amounts.[2] The formula would also, it was argued, lead to more realistic

[1] Department of Social Security (1990).
[2] For valuable discussion of these issues, see Maclean and Eekelaar (1993) and Maclean (1994a and 1994b).

assessments of child support, which in turn would be periodically uprated through the Agency, thus delivering savings in social security expenditure. Eekelaar has argued that the adoption of a formula necessarily emphasises distributive justice, and so seeks to regulate the distribution of common resources amongst groups of the population to reflect the costs of child-rearing.[3] It is premised on some community-based norm as to how much of a parent's income should be devoted to supporting children. The traditional technique adopted by the courts, which Eekelaar describes as a guided discretionary model of resource allocation, is more concerned with the goal of corrective (or "commutative") justice. This approach takes into account a broader range of circumstances in seeking to arrive at a just solution in the individual case. As we shall see, the implementation of the Child Support Act has led to increasing demands from absent parents for a greater element of corrective justice to be incorporated within the formula.

The second major consequence of the 1991 Act was that this formula-based maintenance was to be assessed and collected by the Child Support Agency, effectively an operational arm of the Department of Social Security. It was symptomatic of the skeletal nature of the 1991 Act that it included very few details of the formula (these followed later in regulations, which are not subject to the same degree of Parliamentary scrutiny as primary legislation), and it made no mention of the Child Support Agency itself. Eekelaar,[4] drawing on international comparisons, has demonstrated how a formula-based system of assessment is compatible with either an administrative or a judicial model. The key difference is that the administrative model offers the prospect of reducing legal costs by withdrawing issues of child maintenance from the courts. A formula-based system is, in principle, easier to operate than a guided discretionary model, enabling decisions to be taken at a relatively junior level within a government bureaucracy. Yet a formula must necessarily become increasingly complex in so far as it attempts to cater for individual circumstances (and so serve the ends of corrective justice). This much is evident from the experience of the social security system, an area in which successive governments have sought to modernise benefit rules only to discover that they remain as byzantine as ever because of the need to reflect the diverse nature of people's lives.

The next part of this chapter outlines the nature of the formula and charts the changes that have been made to it since the scheme came into force in 1993. Thereafter we examine some of the problems raised by the operation of the formula, drawing on the cases in our research sample. We conclude by considering whether these difficulties have been

[3] Eekelaar (1997).
[4] *Ibid.*

addressed by the system of departure directions which was introduced by the Child Support Act 1995 and came into force in December 1996.

2. THE FORMULA IN OUTLINE

At the start of this chapter we gave an extended quotation from a child support officer, explaining how an assessment had been reached in one of the cases in our sample. The clarity of her exposition cannot disguise the complexity of the subject matter. In this section we describe the principal elements of the formula and how they have been modified since its inception. It should be emphasised at the outset that the formula as outlined in the 1991 Act (and elaborated in regulations) remains largely intact as the basis for calculating child support maintenance today; the modifications made in February 1994 and April 1995 amount to no more than fine-tuning.[5] Furthermore, notwithstanding the introduction of departure directions by the Child Support Act 1995, the formula remains the starting point for all cases within the Agency's jurisdiction. The underlying premise of the 1995 Act is that the formula produces fair outcomes in the great majority of assessments, but that provision should be made, in exceptional cases, for departures *from the formula* (rather than for a generalised discretion).

The fundamental principles of the child support scheme are set out in section 1 of the 1991 Act, their stark simplicity standing in marked contrast to the complexity of the formula itself. Section 1 declares that "each parent of a qualifying child is responsible for maintaining that child" and that such responsibility can only be discharged by making payments in accordance with the Act. It then imposes a duty on the absent parent to make such payments once a maintenance assessment has been made. There are four key components of the formula: the maintenance requirement; the parents' respective assessable incomes; the deduction rate; and the absent parent's protected income. The focus of the formula is thus on the income of both parents. So far as expenditure is concerned, the formula allows for actual housing costs and for certain other narrowly defined outgoings, but general living costs are incorporated by reference to the basic (and none too generous) Income Support allowances, rather than to real levels of household expenditure. The formula is therefore not based on a percentage of the absent parent's income, or on the actual costs of raising a child. Indeed, the number of children being supported makes relatively little difference to the amount of maintenance assessed.[6] Each element in the formula needs some further explanation.

[5] See the Table on 24 which summarises the key dates and amendments to the formula since its inception.

[6] The number of children involved only affects the level of the maintenance assessment in the upper income range: see below.

(i) The maintenance requirement

The maintenance requirement represents a figure "which is to be taken as the minimum amount necessary for the maintenance"[7] of the child or children in question. In formulaic terms, this is represented as MR = AG—CB. 'MR' is the maintenance requirement, 'AG' is the aggregate of the potential Income Support entitlement of the caring parent and children, and 'CB' is child benefit.

The value represented by 'AG' comprises the aggregate of three different components of a typical Income Support calculation[8]: personal allowance(s) for each relevant child; part or all of the adult Income Support personal allowance (or "carer element"); and the family premium.[9] In the original scheme the carer element consisted of the whole adult Income Support personal allowance where at least one qualifying child was aged under 16. Although intended as a means of reflecting the cost of caring for a child, this was widely perceived by absent parents as a form of spousal maintenance.[10] Since February 1994 the adult rate has only been included in full where at least one child is under 11. Where the youngest child is between 11 and 14, 75 per cent of the adult rate is counted, and when that child reaches 14, 50 per cent of that rate is taken into account. The constituent elements of 'AG' are set figures which change with the annual uprating of Income Support each April. The maintenance requirement is then arrived at by deducting child benefit from this aggregate figure. However, the maintenance requirement is not the amount of child support payable, nor is it even the minimum or maximum amount. Instead it represents a starting point for the operation of the formula, requiring an absent parent to pay 50 per cent of his assessable income until the maintenance requirement figure has been met, and a lower percentage thereafter.

(ii) The assessable income

The second element in the formula consists of both parents' 'assessable income'. The absent parent's assessable income is defined with deceptive simplicity as "N – E", where 'N' is the net income, and 'E' is the

[7] Child Support Act 1991, Sched. 1, para. 1(1).
[8] For consideration of the Income Support scheme, see Ogus, Barendt and Wikeley (1995), Ch. 11.
[9] At the time of writing this is paid at a higher rate for single parents than couples, following the withdrawal of the separate lone parent premium from the Income Support system in April 1997. As from April 1998 even this special rate was withdrawn for all new lone parent claimants.
[10] See further below.

exempt income.[11] Each of these is assessed according to regulations[12] which are in turn modelled on those for Income Support (the parent with care's net income is calculated on the same basis, although using a different algebraic notation.[13]) Net income is calculated as gross earnings less tax, national insurance, and half of any private pension contributions. Most social security benefits count as income, but a person on Income Support is treated as having no assessable income.[14] Some narrow categories of potential earnings are excluded (e.g. the value of free accommodation provided by an employer), as are some benefits (e.g. Child Benefit).

The period of time over which the assessable income is calculated may be crucial.[15] The "relevant benefit week" must be identified in order to establish the appropriate period. For the applicant, the relevant benefit week is the seven days before the Maintenance Application Form is submitted to the Agency; for the other parent, it is the seven days prior to the Maintenance Enquiry Form being sent by the Agency.[16] Under the original scheme income was assessed over the five weeks immediately prior to the relevant benefit week (or over the previous two months where the person was paid monthly). A degree of flexibility was introduced from April 1995 such that a child support officer may now consider evidence of earnings over any appropriate period starting eight weeks before the relevant benefit week and ending with the date of assessment.[17] Cumulative earnings in that tax year can be considered. If this produces a figure which, in the opinion of the child support officer, does not accurately reflect the person's normal weekly earnings then an alternative period may be used.

The exempt income, like the maintenance requirement, follows the model of Income Support. It comprises the adult single person's Income Support personal allowance, with allowances for natural or adopted children living with that parent, together with certain Income Support premiums and reasonable housing costs. There is no provision for expenses incurred in supporting other dependants (e.g. a new partner and any step children). Nor are child care costs or council tax included in the

[11] Child Support Act 1991, Sched. 1, para. 5(1).

[12] Child Support (Maintenance Assessment and Special Cases) Regulations 1992, SI 1992 No. 1815.

[13] 'C = M – F', where 'C' is the PWC's assessable income, 'M' her net income and 'F' her exempt income: Child Support Act 1991, Sched. 1, para. 5(2).

[14] But this does not exclude an absent parent on benefit from paying child support: see further 23.

[15] See, for example, the case study of Stuart and Doreen Mullins in Ch. 7.

[16] Child Support (Maintenance Assessment and Special Cases) Regulations 1992, S.I. 1992 No. 1815, reg. 1(1).

[17] *Ibid.*, Sched. 1, para. 2.

exempt income, and prior to April 1995 housing costs were apportioned with other adults in the household.[18]

Although abandoning the apportionment of housing costs simplified the assessment process, another change made at the same time further complicated the calculation. This was the inclusion of broad brush allowances for pre-1993 property settlements and high travel to work costs.[19] As regards the former, the assumption is that where a property or capital settlement worth £5,000 or more was made before April 1993, half of the equity counts as property transferred. An allowance of £20 per week is added to the exempt income for transfers between £5,000 and £9,999; £40 is added for £10,000 to £24,999; and £60 is added for settlements over £25,000. Travel to work costs are assessed on a "straight line basis" between home and the place of work, with an allowance of 10 pence a mile for commuting in excess of 150 miles per week. Following the Child Support Act 1995 there is now the alternative possibility of a more generous allowance under the departures system. Although these changes were made in the interests of absent parents, it is noteworthy that the government did not accept the Social Security Committee's recommendation that step-children should be taken into account in calculating exempt income.[20] Once the exempt income is calculated, it is deducted from the net income to arrive at the assessable income, which is the amount calculated as available for child support.

(iii) The deduction rate

The third component in the formula is the "deduction rate". In the 1991 Act this is represented by the letter 'P', which was somewhat unhelpfully defined as "such number greater than zero but less than 1 as may be prescribed".[21] Regulations subsequently attributed the value of 0.5 to 'P'.[22] The next step in applying the formula is to calculate $(A + C) \times P$, or, in plain English, to aggregate the assessable incomes of the parents and divide by two. If the resulting figure is less than or equal to the maintenance requirement (i.e. if the parents are on very low incomes), then the absent parent's liability is limited to a maximum of one half of his assessable income.

[18] See the child support officer's explanation at the start of this chapter as to how this operated.
[19] Child Support (Maintenance Assessment and Special Cases) Regulations 1992, S.I. 1992 No. 1815, Scheds. 3A and 3B.
[20] There is now very limited provision for taking into account step-children under the departures provisions: see below.
[21] Child Support Act 1991, Sched. 1, para 2(1).
[22] Child Support (Maintenance Assessment and Special Cases) Regulations 1992, S.I. 1992 No. 1815, reg. 5(b).

If the figure produced by this calculation is more than the amount of the maintenance requirement, then the absent parent's liability increases. In such a case the liability is assessed by adding together the "basic element" and the "additional element". The basic element is calculated using an equation which takes into account the carer's contribution to the maintenance requirement. Where the parent with care has no assessable income, the absent parent's basic element is simply the full maintenance requirement, which is doubled (because of the 50 per cent rule) in order to arrive at his basic assessable income. The additional element is calculated by applying a multiplier to the so-called additional assessable income. The multiplier is 0.15 where there is one child, 0.20 where there are two children, and 0.25 where there are three or more relevant children.[23] The net result is that the absent parent contributes more by way of child support than he would have done under the first stage in the formula, but in total pays less than 50 per cent of his assessable income in maintenance. A still more complex calculation, but based on the same principles, applies where the parent with care has assessable income of her own.

The liability under the 1991 Act is not open-ended; there is a maximum amount of child support payable. Where the parent with care has no income, maintenance is calculated by adding together the maintenance requirement and a figure representing 1.5 times the amount of the relevant Income Support personal allowances and a family premium for each child.[24] The formula has a number of variants to deal with particular circumstances, e.g. where a parent with care has children with different absent parents, or conversely where children of an absent parent are being looked after by different carers, or where both parents are absent parents. The formula is also subject to variation where there is "shared care", i.e. where the parents are each looking after the child for part of the time.[25]

(iv) Protected income

The fourth and final part of the formula is the 'protected income'. The purpose of this is to ensure that an absent parent's disposable income does not, as a result of paying the child support assessed above, fall below a set level. It is only at this stage that the income and expenses of any new family (e.g. a new partner's income or the presence of a step-

---

[23] Until Feb. 1994 a multiplier of 0.25 was applied in all cases; the effect of the change thus benefits absent parents and particularly those on higher incomes.

[24] Before Apr. 1995 the multiplier in this additional element was 3; the change again worked to the advantage of the better off absent parent.

[25] See further below, and also the case study of Malcolm Bridley in Ch. 5.

child) come into the equation. Thus, contrary to popular conception, a new partner's income cannot increase the maintenance assessment, but the absence of any such income may reduce it. The protected income consists of the amount of Income Support which would be payable to meet the needs of the household. This encompasses: the absent parent and any of his children living with him; any new partner and step-children; housing costs (assessed on a narrower basis than with the exempt income); council tax; and an earnings disregard of £30 a week.[26] The protected income also includes 15 per cent[27] of the difference between the absent parent's disposable income (which includes any partner's income) and the basic protected income. A further safeguard for absent parents, introduced in April 1995, is that no parent is required to pay more than 30 per cent of his net income in child support (or 33 per cent if arrears are included).

(v) Other formula provisions

Before we consider the main features of the formula in the light of our research findings, there are three general provisions relating to the pay-ment of child support which should be mentioned. First, there is a mini-mum amount of child maintenance, which at the time of writing was £5.00 a week. This sum was fixed originally at 5 per cent of the adult Income Support personal allowance but was increased to 10 per cent in the 1995 Budget, with effect from April 1996. Secondly, absent parents who are on Income Support are treated as having a nil assessable income, but in most cases are also required to make the minimum con-tribution of £5.00 a week, technically in lieu of child maintenance, and typically by deduction from their benefit at source. Thirdly, some absent parents are 'zero-rated' in that they are not required to pay any child sup-port at all; these include absent parents in receipt of various disability benefits.

The preceding discussion is necessarily confined to the central issues arising from the use of the formula; readers seeking a detailed under-standing of its intricacies should consult one of the standard works of reference.[28] The complexity of the formula can scarcely be overstated. It causes immense operational problems which are explored further in Chapter 4. We now turn to consider our research findings in so far as they relate to the formula. In the following section we report on parents' per-ceptions of the formula. We then analyse some of the problems inherent in the use of such a rigid system for assessing child maintenance. Finally

[26] Originally £8 a week, until Feb. 1994.
[27] Until Feb. 1994, 10 per cent.
[28] See e.g. Jacobs and Douglas (1997) or Knights and Cox (1997).

Table 2.1   A chronology of the Child Support Act formula

April 1993	• Child Support Act 1991 comes into force
February 1994	• carer element in maintenance requirement reduced for older children • taper for additional element in maintenance assessment reduced from 25% to 15% for one child and 20% for two children • margin in protected income increased from £8 to £30 per week • margin on protected income increased from 10% to 15%
April 1995	• abolition of apportionment of housing costs between partners • introduction of ceiling of 30% of net income as maximum amount of child support • reduction in amount of maximum payable by absent parent paying the additional element • introduction of broad brush allowances for high travel to work costs and certain property or capital settlements • suspension of fees and interest • changes to interim maintenance assessments rules • shift to biennial rather than annual reviews • cap of six months on arrears payable by absent parent where delay by Child Support Agency
December 1996	• Departures system introduced

we consider the extent to which the departures system meets these difficulties.

3. THE FORMULA: PARENTS' PERCEPTIONS

It was clear from our interviews that relatively few parents had a clear understanding of how the formula operated in their case. This is hardly surprising given the way the formula is framed. This bewilderment was typified by the response of Jeremy Hebden (case 117), whose comments open this chapter. It should be borne in mind that his case was, in fact, one of the more straightforward ones in our sample. The inherent complexity and opaqueness of the formula led inevitably to misunderstandings, especially on the part of absent parents, which served both to heighten their sense of grievance and to discourage compliance. A recurrent theme of our interviews with absent parents was the perceived unfairness of the formula. This deeply-held sense of injustice was manifested in opposition both to the principle of a formula-based system and to the specifics of the formula itself.

A minority of absent parents simply refused to accept the legitimacy of the move from discretion to formula as the basis for assessing child maintenance. In many instances they also conspicuously failed to acknowledge the weaknesses of the previous system. For example, Colin Lawrence (case 34) argued that "I think that it is wrong that bureaucratic civil servants make judgements against people without a hearing. It is a matter for the court." Fred Winsford (case 40) drew this comparison with the former system for assessing child maintenance:

> "You discussed the details face-to-face with the magistrates and the clerk of the court, and you were given the impression that at least you had a chance to present your case on a human level. With all its manifest possibilities of error, the magistrates' court was still a good place to make an assessment of the situation, as against this which is mere figures on a form. You are given a number and everything is boiled down to actual money. That's it, full stop. You have so much income and you are allowed so much, so much, so much, without regard to one's personality or lifestyle or aspirations or whatever. It was such an abrupt change, you immediately became insignificant, a victim in many ways."

This rejection of the fundamental principles of the child support scheme was reinforced for some absent parents by what was perceived to be the retrospective nature of the assessment. There were a number of cases in our sample where absent parents had transferred property or capital to their former partner, typically in return for an agreement to pay no spousal maintenance and/or limited child support. For example, Patrick Coles (case 23), who separated in 1990, found his liability to support his youngest daughter increased from a court order of £10 per week to over £70 per week as assessed by the Agency:

> "She had everything. This is why I'm annoyed. I recently found out that all solicitors knew about this Act coming in about five years ago, and the agreement I had in court was that if I gave everything up, just come out of the house with my suitcase, she wouldn't come to me for any money. It was a fixed agreement with maintenance for the children, otherwise I would have stuck out for half the house or something like that. But she had the house, mainly she had the children, all the furniture, the family car, everything. And now they've come out with this law."

The fact that the formula, as originally devised, took no account of such capital or property transfers was symptomatic of the broader policy decision to squeeze discretion out of the assessment process. This was the underlying theme of many comments made by absent parents. They were dismayed that the formula took no account of their actual (as against their notional) living costs:

> "I don't think they consider any of your outgoings, to be perfectly honest with you. From memory, the question was 'How much are you earning?' It didn't appear to make any difference what outgoings I would have." (Philip Hyde, case 49)

> "They don't actually ask you anything about your financial situation as such. They are just interested in what comes in and not what goes out." (Michael Seeley, case 54)

> "I went through them and filled them in and my immediate reaction was, hang on a moment, you want to know everything you want but there is nowhere here for me to tell you about my situation. All they asked you for was your basic salary and your circumstances which they can take money from. Your outgoings were dismissed." (Nathan O'Reilly, case 105)

Joe Nixon (case 48), who works for one of the emergency services, had a weekly take home pay of £252 and had initially been assessed to pay £97 a week for his youngest child, later revised to £90.47:

> "So let's give you a brief resumé: taking out £97 a week, that leaves me £155. Lodging, with some food included, and obviously that varies according to my shift pattern, £60 a week, that drops it down to £95. £10 a week food on duty drops it to £85. My solicitor, and you can't do without, I'm paying on a standing order, I started with £100 up front and £20 a week which has now cost me something in the region of £1,300. That drops it down to £65 a week. The home improvement loans on the matrimonial home amount to £32 a week, gives me £33 in my hand. My wife's insurance policy drops it to £30.50. And the endowment policy which I still pay is £12 a week. That drops it down to £18.50 a week. My petrol is £15 a week. That is £3.50 in my actual hand, real figures. Now how can I tax, insure and run my car, toilet requisites, even coming down to razor blades or a new pair of socks . . . how can I exist on £3.50 a week? Obviously now it has gone down to £90.47 a week . . which gives me then a grand sum of roughly £10.50 a week to live on."

In fact Joe managed to survive by using his principal income to pay bills and debts whilst drawing on occasional wages from a second job, which had not been declared to the Agency, for other expenditure. Even so the pressure imposed by the assessment was sufficient to encourage Joe to enter into a private agreement with his ex-wife to opt out of the Agency's jurisdiction.[29]

Other absent parents complained that the level of maintenance required of them meant that they could not afford to visit their children.

---

[29] See further Ch. 9.

For example, Ivan Barr (case 33), a lorry driver on a net wage of £135 a week whose daughter lived 170 miles away, told us that he could only afford to visit her once a month. Likewise Cliff Shilton (case 57), who lived 220 miles away from his ex-wife, said that he saw his son twice a year:

"I run a car and that's costing me £60 return plus spending. You can't go down and see your son and say 'Hello, I've got nothing for you', so you're talking a good £100 a time, which I can't afford. They're killing relationships that they want to save."

This was a criticism much touted in the media, but it is only fair to observe that absent parents who made this complaint, including Cliff Shilton (above), were not necessarily *paying* an increased level of maintenance at the time we interviewed them. They were indignant in anticipation.

This perception of the unfairness of the formula was not confined to absent parents, although they were the most vocal in their criticisms. Most parents with care did not express an opinion on the way the formula was structured, although a minority were critical, usually where they too had essential outgoings which were not taken into account. The fact that child care costs were excluded was a particular source of grievance. For example, Lynette Bass (case 108) told us:

"As I recall it when the Agency was first set up, it was to make absent fathers responsible for their children. And also one of the secondary aims as far as I am aware was to help remove mothers from benefit. And yet because there is no allowance for child care for working mums built into the legislation, and because of their incompetence and lack of consideration in handling the matter and looking into Perry's finances and trying to get me some money, they are literally nearly forcing me into a situation where I can't afford a live-in nanny; without a live-in nanny I can't work; without working I was homeless. I was literally on the verge, probably on three occasions, I was on the verge of having to leave my job: not wanting to, having to, because I couldn't afford to work."

As we have noted, the formula has been modified in several respects since its introduction in April 1993. For example, the April 1995 changes provide some allowance in the calculation of exempt income for property settlements and for high travel-to-work costs, while the departures system introduced the possibility of allowance being made for the costs of visiting or collecting children. These various modifications have mainly been in the interests of "sharp-elbowed absent parents", as they were described by Baroness Hollis during the debates on the Child Support Act 1995.[30] Not surprisingly the changes were not always welcomed by parents with care. For example, Sharon Dean (case 80), a

[30] Hansard, HL Debs., Vol. 565, col. 116 (19 June 1995).

divorced single parent, used to receive £15 a week in court ordered maintenance. When the Agency became involved the amount increased to £25 a week. As Sharon was claiming Income Support she did not receive any more money. Nonetheless, when, following the February 1994 changes in the level of protected income, her ex-husband's assessment was reduced to £4.99, she was indignant:

> "It makes a mockery of the system because that means that tax payers are subsidising him by £10 a week. That goes on my Income Support. . . . He was paying the £15 quite happily."

For many parents with care, it appeared, the *principle* that the absent father should pay whatever he could afford towards his children's upkeep was as important as the (generally chimerical) financial benefit. Absent parents, on the other hand, took a more pragmatic view.

4. THE FORMULA: FUNDAMENTAL PROBLEMS

The views of parents, and especially absent parents, on the formula have been well ventilated in media coverage of the Child Support Agency. Our findings in this respect were therefore not unexpected. We now turn to some of the more fundamental problems with the operation of the formula. The first of these concerns the formula's inability to reflect the true costs of child care. The second, and perhaps more surprising finding was its failure, in certain cases, to deliver a maintenance assessment which was realistic given the financial resources of the two parents.

(i) The formula and the true costs of parenting

Following separation or divorce children typically live with one parent, usually the mother, with or without contact with the other parent. Such contact may be 'staying contact' with the children staying overnight on a short or long term basis (e.g. weekends or holidays). In a small minority of cases the care of the children is split roughly equally in terms of time spent with each of the two parents. The formula, however, cannot be calibrated to reflect these nuances. It assumes that a parent either has care or is 'absent', and will remain so, whereas we found even within our relatively small sample that this was not necessarily the case. Some people share care of children, some children move between parents, and some parents are both 'absent' (from one child or set of children) and 'caring' (for different children). In one case in our sample in which a female 'absent parent' had care of another child from the same relationship, she had been assessed as having to pay maintenance out of her Income

Support—and was indeed paying it—whereas the other parent had not yet been assessed and was paying nothing out of his earnings.

In terms of the formula, a critical issue is whether the absent parent has day-to-day care, taken as an average over the year, on at least two nights a week (the so-called '104 nights rule'). If he does, the amount payable is adjusted proportionately. Where the shared care is precisely 50:50, the 'parent with care' label is attached to the person holding the Child Benefit book. If the absent parent does not reach the 104 nights threshold, the parent with care is regarded as having sole charge of the child, and so the full assessment remains payable. To paraphrase Mashaw, child residence arrangements exist on a continuum; only the decisions are bipolar.[31]

Where an absent parent satisfies the 104 nights rule, the adjustment to the assessment is on a strict arithmetical basis. This may not reflect the actual apportionment of child maintenance costs. Rob Jason (case 72), whose teenage daughters lived with him three days a week, complained:

> "I have them at weekends and I'm sure the expenditure at weekends is far greater than when they're at school. I don't think that's ever taken into account by the CSA. Children eat a lot and they want to go to the pictures at the week-end, or ice-skating or whatever, and they stay up later at weekends, so they do need a bit more cash."

At first sight the formula's inability to reflect all the nuances of parents' financial arrangements may seem relatively trivial. It does, however, point to a more significant difficulty in that the formula necessarily assumes a direct relationship between the Agency assessment and main-tenance in real life. It is unable to accommodate payment in kind. Laura Chapman (case 43) had left her husband because of his repeated affairs, but had felt compelled to leave their son, Luke, in his care, as at that stage she was only able to afford a one-bedroom flat. No money ever exchanged hands, but Laura had regular contact and paid for many of Luke's clothes, shoes, school trips and other expenses. As her solicitor observed: "What the separation agreement said was that they would make equal contributions towards the cost of looking after Luke, and what that boiled down to was she looked after him for a large proportion of the time, rather than cash actually changing hands". The Maintenance Enquiry Form could not cope with this, as Laura Chapman observed:

> "They do leave a square blank for you to write whatever you feel, your own information, so I sent them two pages of A4. I told them everything I buy, everything I do really, like taking him to the dentist, and having his hair cut, and the fact that I deliberately went out and purchased a two-bedroom house so that my child could come and stay, a house with a garden. So I did tell them. I just have to wait and see what happens."

[31] See Mashaw (1983), 82.

By the end of our research the Agency had still not made an assessment in this case, partly because of an inability to resolve a dispute over the level of shared care. Several male absent parents made similar points. For example, according to Tim Wade (case 56):

> "The form didn't allow me to put in information about the costs that I was incurring in my particular situation of shared care . . . the fact that I was paying both the mortgage and the rates. So I listed all these things, and I also said that I can't enter the fact that I'm paying school fees for Saul, I can't enter the costs I incur on his behalf, which I pay direct. So I listed all those things and said 'The format of the CSA form makes no provision for me to enter these expenses without substantially modifying the form. The form offers no shortage of questions totally irrelevant to my situation. It is clearly designed with errant fathers in mind, that is those who abandon their children to be paid for by the other parent. It makes only cursory provision for shared parenting or for agreed clean break settlements.' "

The payment by an absent parent of the carer's housing costs causes difficulty in this context. Since April 1995 the formula has made allowance for 100 per cent (rather than 70 per cent) of the absent parent's housing costs where he has a new partner. However, these housing costs must relate to the absent parent's home. No allowance is made for cases where an absent parent, having moved out, is continuing to pay the mortgage on the former matrimonial home. This can place absent parents in an acute dilemma, as Lynn Enderby's new partner explained (case 65):

> "You can pay the mortgage and not the CSA, or the other way round. And bearing in mind they won't take the mortgage into account, I had no option really. Also, me and Lynn was paying for a flat, and for five children, paying for my three and Lynn's two, so my money was savagely torn to bits, and you have to make the decision there and then."[32]

Where the absent parent continues to pay the mortgage on the former matrimonial home, and the parent with care is on Income Support, the carer's housing costs will not be met by the Benefits Agency. The fact that the child support formula effectively forces the absent parent to stop making these payments sits uneasily with the government's drive in recent years to limit the extent to which the Income Support scheme meets mortgage interest costs. Indeed, in one case we observed a child support appeal tribunal bending the legislation in order to categorise such mortgage payments as a form of indirect maintenance, the object being to reduce the absent parent's maintenance assessment (case 116).[33]

---

[32] This case is examined in depth in Ch. 9.

[33] This approach seems to be wrong as a matter of law: see unreported Commissioner's decision *CCS/012/95*, holding that such matters are relevant only to the recovery of child support (a matter for the Secretary of State) and not to the assessment itself.

Across the board there is an uneasy fit between the formula and the social realities of parenting. We have already seen that the formula takes step-children into account only at the protected income stage. It also makes no provision for grown-up children living with one parent, regardless of their dependency. For example, when Anthony Gardiner and his wife separated (case 51), their 14-year-old son stayed with her, but their two daughters, aged 19 and 17, remained with him. The elder daughter was in practice reliant upon her father, yet she did not figure as a dependant in either the exempt income or the protected income calculations. The only concession was that, although technically she was a non-dependant in his household, there was no deduction from his housing costs.

(ii) The formula and unrealistically low levels of child support

The previous discretionary system for determining maintenance resulted in child support being set at very low levels. Since 1993 the Child Support Agency has become inextricably associated in the public consciousness with high levels of child support. We met many absent parents who were having difficulty in coming to terms with Agency-imposed maintenance assessments which had been set at more realistic levels (in terms of the true costs of maintaining children) than had previously been the case. In this section, however, we highlight a number of ways in which the formula leads to *lower* levels of child maintenance than might have been ordered by a court.

The main circumstance in which an assessment may be set at an unrealistically low level is that involving a self-employed absent parent. In practice there are three inter-related problems for parents with care who have self-employed former partners. Two of these are procedural in nature: the inefficiency of the Agency in extracting the necessary information from the absent parent in order to make an assessment; and the difficulty of enforcing the assessment once made. These two problems are dealt with later in this book.[34] Here we concentrate on the third problem, which concerns the operation of the formula.

There are special rules governing the assessment of self-employed earnings.[35] From the inception of the scheme the government decided not to use the previous year's accounts and profits as agreed with the Inland Revenue, and it has resisted subsequent recommendations that it

---

[34] See Chs. 5 and 6.
[35] Child Support (Maintenance Assessments and Special Cases) Regulations 1992, S.I. 1992 No. 1815, Sched. 1, Ch. 2.

should revert to this method of calculating income.[36] Although the use of tax accounts would significantly reduce the time taken to arrive at earnings figures, the scope for setting off expenses under Inland Revenue rules would be likely to result in assessments which did not prioritise child support. Instead, the regulations under the 1991 Act were closely modelled on those for Family Credit. But these rules "were designed to allow relatively junior officials to determine quickly the benefit payable to families in need",[37] and so had been applied mainly to small tradesmen and shopkeepers. The self-employed clientele of the Child Support Agency come from a much wider range of society, and although the child support provisions are, in a number of ways, less generous than the tax rules, they still offer considerable scope for creative accounting, particularly in relation to allowances for business expenses.[38]

Although the problems associated with the self-employed became especially apparent in the course of our study, these were not the only cases in which the formula could produce somewhat startling results. For example, the rigid manner in which housing costs are calculated for absent parents may in some cases *over*estimate their real liability, notably where that liability is borne by a new partner. A case in point is that of Sam Milsom (case 73) who was left caring for two teenage children when his wife left him to set up home with a neighbour. Joan Milsom and her new partner had bought a new house, principally on the strength of his income. The application of the formula meant that her child support liability was fixed at the minimum weekly amount (then £2.20). Sam Milsom's solicitor contrasted the CSA assessment with what Sam might have expected in court:

"I think it is very interesting that the formula has come out at a lower figure than the court would have ordered. Mrs Milsom has a part-time job, and she went off with her boyfriend who is, I believe, a police sergeant with a decent salary, about £30,000. So they bought a house straight away with a 100 per cent mortgage on his salary. But under the formula she was entitled to take 70 per cent of that mortgage into consideration—no, that would have been higher than her salary, so she would be limited to the £80 maximum housing costs— but that's still more than she was actually having to pay. That's nonsense!

---

[36] See e.g. Social Security Committee, Fifth Report, Session 1993–4, *The Operation of the Child Support Act: Proposals for Change* (London: HMSO, 1994), para. 41. There is, of course, a major issue relating to confidentiality here, but that did not prevent the last Conservative government bringing forward legislation which enables information held by the tax authorities to be supplied to the DSS to combat social security fraud: Social Security Administration Act 1992, s.122, as amended by the Social Security (Fraud) Administration Act 1992, s.1.

[37] Owen (1994), 1486.

[38] The House of Commons Social Security Committee (1996a) has observed laconically that it does "not believe that the vast majority of self-employed parents shoulder their burdens without demur".

Whereas the court would have had the discretion to order more maintenance. They would have recognised that the house was mortgaged on his income, and they would have asked her to pay a bit more, maybe £10 a week. It's not a great deal of difference, but Mr Milsom does feel aggrieved."

It might be argued that the outcome of the Milsom case is as much a function of the traditional differentials between male and female wages as it is of the child support formula. Joan Milsom's part-time earnings were swallowed up by her mortgage liability,[39] leaving Sam to bemoan the perceived injustice of his wife paying nominal child support while enjoying a comfortable standard of living with her new partner. Sam Milsom was in a minority in being a male parent with care. Other men in our sample, predominantly absent parents, were angered by the Agency's enquiries about their new partner's earnings. Female parents with care, on the other hand, seemed not to regard this as an issue, perhaps because many were used to disclosing such information as part of any claim for means-tested benefits. This suggests that attitudes to the involvement of new partners in a child support assessment are governed not only by financial interests but by the gender of those involved.

Finally, unlike the means-tested social security system, the formula works on the basis of income and not capital. In preliminary interviews before embarking on our field work one senior barrister highlighted the difficulty which the Agency would face in making assessments on a father with an extravagant lifestyle who could legitimately argue that his income was nil. In some cases he might be a discretionary beneficiary under a family trust. Others might be more entrepreneurial:

"I've had one such father who would go to his mother when he wanted it and he'd get a cheque for £100,000 and then what he would do is buy commercial property, renovate it and sell it at a profit. But he's not doing that on a sufficiently regular basis to make it a trade or profession or to bring it within the definitions of income in the Act or regulations. In the case I'm thinking of he is living the life of a millionaire . . . but in terms of the Act he has negligible income."

Under the former court-based system, as our informant commented, "any self-respecting District Judge" would have made a substantial maintenance order, considering the substance of the case and not the form. Our sample did not include an example as flagrant as this, but at least one such has been reported. In *Phillips* v *Pearce*,[40] Johnson J held that he had no power to order provision by way of a lump sum order for the regular support of a child, observing that:

---

[39] Indeed, in principle, following the Apr. 1995 changes, 100 per cent of Joan Milsom's mortgage counted as housing costs.

[40] [1996] 2 FLR 230; see commentary by Priest (1997).

"Most people would think that a mother should have no difficulty in obtaining financial support for her child from a father who lives in a house worth £2.6 million and whose standard of living is illustrated by his three motor-cars worth respectively £36,000, £54,000 and £100,000. In this case the Child Support Agency thought otherwise. In responding to the mother's application it said: 'The child support officer has calculated that the weekly amount payable by the father is nought pounds.' In the circumstances of this case that will seem startling to the point of absurdity. However, it is no fault of the Agency. If blame is to be borne by anyone, perhaps it should be the architects of the child support scheme whose appreciation of the realities of people's differing financial arrangements has been described by one learned author as naïve. As to that I make no comment."

5. THE CHILD SUPPORT ACT 1995: DEPARTURES FROM THE FORMULA

It was assumed that the introduction of the Child Support Act would make maintenance assessments less arbitrary than under the former discretionary regime. In theory parents would know how much they were to receive, or how much they would have to pay. As one solicitor put it to us: "You used to say that if you went to fifty different judges, you would get something like ten different results." So as well as child maintenance being given greater priority, there should have been greater consistency and therefore fairness. Against this there is the argument that a formula can never deliver justice because individual family circumstances vary too much, that variation often being in matters of fine detail. This is how the dilemma was put to us by one District Judge:

"The first parts of the formula are not at all unfair. I think that they're reasonable. It's a logical way of arriving at a figure that ought to be paid. The problem with working out the particular rate at the end of it is that if you are going to have a rigid formula, it can't by definition take account of all the circumstances in which people might find themselves. I think almost that that's an unsolvable problem. I don't know what the answer is if you want the formula. But I'm certain that that's going to cause injustice. I think that if you tried to concoct a formula which tried to do justice in every case, which actually is what the courts try to do, because we look at the individual cases before us, if you tried to work out a formula for that, then it would either be too detailed with pages and pages of regulations, or it would be impossible. I think that it would be impossible."

This view was echoed by many solicitors. In their view it was impossible for a formula to take into account all the quirks of individual financial circumstances, which meant that a degree of injustice would inevitably result. The cure for this unfairness, it was often suggested, was to reintroduce an element of discretion. However it was not always clear whether what solicitors were arguing for was indeed discretion, or for another element to be introduced into the formula—for example, the recognition of marital debts. Such debts could be dealt with either by an extension of the formula or by allowing scope for discretion. Either solution is possible. Of course if one is seeking absolute fairness there is no limit to the factors which might need to be introduced into the formula— or alternatively, there is no limit to the need for discretion. But that in turn works against there being any certainty of outcome, and that certainty is what the Child Support Agency is supposed to provide. It is obvious that a formula—unless impossibly detailed—will create some degree of unfairness even if everyone agrees that it is based on sound principles.

The government's response to these dilemmas was to introduce the Child Support Act 1995. This permits a degree of discretion to be exercised in the application of the formula, but within the constraints of a highly regulated system.[41] Introducing the Bill, Lord Mackay of Ardbrecknish, then Minister of State for Social Security, conceded that the Child Support Agency "has had a less than comfortable time since its inception".[42] Others were less charitable. Lord Simon of Glaisdale, speaking from the cross-benches in the House of Lords, declared that the 1991 Act "has been an unprecedented legislative disaster. It has caused injustice; it has caused hardship; it has caused enormous public expense resulting in administrative chaos."[43] For the Opposition, Baroness Hollis argued: "Having ignored Parliamentary dissent, the government found themselves overwhelmed by extra-parliamentary dissent and have created such a culture of resistance that the Act has become unenforceable."[44]

According to the then Secretary of State for Social Security, "the main purpose of the [1995 Act] is to improve the system of child support so that it has greater acceptability and works better, to streamline the operations and to encourage greater compliance".[45] The most fundamental reform was the creation of a "departures system", enabling the Secretary of State to issue a direction modifying the application of the child support formula in prescribed cases. Yet it would be a mistake to see the system of departures as a return to the discretion previously exercised by the courts. The White Paper made it clear that the government's intention was that "formula assessment should continue to be the norm; that the standard formula assessment should be the starting point even when a departure is allowed; and that departures should not be common".[46]

---

[41] There are obvious parallels here with the "discretionary" social fund in the field of social security provision.

[42] Hansard, HL Debs., Vol. 564, col. 1185 (5 June 1995).

[43] *Ibid.*, col. 1190.

[44] *Ibid.*, col. 1194.

[45] Hansard, HC Debs., Vol. 257, col. 22 (20 Mar. 1995).

[46] Para. 2.4. Similarly, in the Parliamentary debates that followed, Alistair Burt, then the responsible Minister of State, acknowledged that "many of the problems with the

The 1995 Act establishes certain 'gateways' to the departures system[47]; an applicant's case must be one which involves one or more types of special expense before it can be considered for a departure direction. In part these 'gateways' build on the April 1995 adjustments to the method of calculating exempt income. Hence special expenses under the departures system include travel-to-work costs and capital or property transfers. Other criteria for issuing a departure direction break new ground (e.g. 'special expenses' for contact). All the 'gateways' for departures under the 1995 Act are expressed in gender-neutral terms and are in principle open to both absent parents and parents with care. In practice, however, departure directions are most likely to be sought by male absent parents in relation to special expenses and property or capital transfers. Departure directions may also be sought in so-called "additional cases", e.g. where "a person's life-style is inconsistent with the level of his income", or the other parent's housing or travel costs are "unreasonably high". Parents with care might use these provisions to make an application for an upward adjustment of what they regard as an unreasonably low maintenance assessment. However, the limited scope of fact-finding undertaken by the Agency[48] makes it doubtful whether such applications will be successful.

It is also not enough to pass through one of the 'gateways': the Secretary of State must be satisfied that it is "just and equitable" to grant a departure direction.[49] This term is defined by regulations to exclude factors which many separated parents regard as central to their notion of justice. For example, responsibility for the breakdown of the relationship, the formation of new relationships, and the existence or otherwise of contact arrangements are all to be disregarded.[50]

Nonetheless, in principle at least, the departures system may be regarded as "the first major crack in the monolithic structure of child support, since it goes to the very heart of the philosophy of the legislation".[51] 'Departures' represent an admission that the formula, however it is tweaked, cannot meet the demand for a more individualised system of assessment. As Eekelaar has observed: "When an attempt is made to impose child support liability above a certain level, the demands of com-

operation of the child support scheme resulted from the universal application of a set formula for assessing maintenance. The [Act] represents an opportunity to introduce a degree of flexibility so as to address certain special costs which it would be neither right nor realistic to include in the universal formula": Standing Committee E, col. 3 (28 Mar. 1995).

[47] The relevant provisions are now to be found in ss.28A–28H and Sched. 4B of the 1995 Act and in the detailed Child Support Departure Directions and Consequential Amendments Regulations 1996, S.I. 1996 No. 2907.

[48] See further Chs. 4, 5 and 8.

[49] Child Support Act 1991, s.28F(1)(b).

[50] Child Support Departure Directions and Consequential Amendments Regulations 1996, S.I. 1996 No. 2907, reg. 30(2).

[51] Bird (1995), 112–113.

mutative justice become overwhelming".[52] We cannot comment on the departures system in operation, but the tightly regulated framework provides a clear indication of the then government's intention that few of those who seek a direction should be successful.

6. CONCLUSION

Most absent parents, especially those with no experience of claiming benefit, will have been used to giving details of their income and outgoings on any application form involving an assessment of their financial status (e.g. for a mortgage, bank loan, or credit card facility). With child support, however, exempt income is modelled on basic Income Support allowances, with some provision for housing costs. Thus, for the first time, many working people have come face to face with the bleak reality of "what the State says you need to live on" (to quote the rubric on the standard notice of assessment used for Income Support purposes).

In addition, the 1991 Act's characterisation of parental responsibility solely in terms of the payment of maintenance inevitably fails to reflect the huge variety of arrangements made for the support of children following relationship breakdown. The formula can result in perversely low assessments for self-employed absent fathers, and indeed perversely low assessments in other cases which do not fit the standard model. We can only speculate about the effect of the departures system on these problems. In our view the departures provisions, grounded as they are within the existing framework, are likely to assist only at the margins.

[52] Eekelaar (forthcoming).

3

Child Support, Social Security and the Lone Parent Family

White Paper (DSS, 1990), paragraph 2.1:

> "The Government propose to establish a system of child maintenance which will. . . avoid the children and their caring parent becoming dependent on Income Support whenever this is possible and, where it is not possible, to minimise the period of dependence."

Marlene Beamon (case 118) on her reactions to a maintenance assessment which, if paid in full, would take away her entitlement to Family Credit on the next renewal:

> "I want to get off benefit, but I don't want to do it that way, because if I'm off benefit and he stops paying . . . At least the social security is regular, and you can rely on it. It might not be as much as you would like, but at least it's there every week, and I need to be secure. He could give me £30 one week and £10 the next, and that's not good enough. I need to know what's coming in each week."

1. INTRODUCTION

It is axiomatic that it is more difficult for one parent to earn enough to support a child unaided than it is for two parents living together. This is even more the case where the lone parent is the mother (as is the case nine times out of ten), given the gender gap in earnings. Despite equal pay legislation the wage structure still reflects the view that men need a "family" wage.[1] The three principal sources of income open to lone parents are maintenance from the absent parent, State benefits, and their own earnings. In practice, social security benefits (and in particular Income Support) comprise lone parents' primary source of income, followed by earnings. Maintenance comes a poor third.[2] Lone parents' increasing reliance on Income Support, and a corresponding decrease in their labour force participation, has been noted by several commentators.[3]

---

[1] See Bradley (1989); Joshi (1991); Martin and Roberts (1984); and Rees (1992).
[2] Bradshaw and Millar (1991); McKay and Marsh (1994).
[3] Brown (1989); Lewis (1997).

In this chapter we examine the inter-relationship between child support and social security in the context of the lone parent family. Three central themes emerge. The first concerns the question of where the balance should be struck in allocating financial responsibility for children as between their parents and the State. This is a question on which divergent views are held. The second theme concerns the difficulty of creating a social security system which meets basic needs yet provides incentives to work on the one hand and incentives to pay maintenance on the other. This issue of incentives cannot be separated from the various practical problems inherent in administering the payment of private maintenance and State benefits through the medium of two bureaucracies (the Child Support Agency and the Benefits Agency) against a backcloth of constantly changing family circumstances.[4] Thirdly, there is the impact of the Child Support Agency on the financial circumstances of parents with care, and in particular on the finances of lone parents in receipt of Income Support. We also draw on our research data to convey lone parents' perceptions of the role of child support in their lives.

2. THE BALANCE BETWEEN PRIVATE AND PUBLIC SUPPORT FOR LONE PARENT FAMILIES

(i) Lone parents and the principle of maintenance

Most commentators accept that parents have an obligation to support their children according to their means; the debate focuses on the relative priority to be given to child maintenance in light of competing considerations. In theory maintenance can take one of two forms: on-going financial support for a former spouse[5] (not payable to a lone parent who has never been married) or payment for the children of the relationship. In practice orders for spousal maintenance were relatively uncommon even before the Child Support Act. This was consistent with the requirement under the Matrimonial Causes Act 1973, as amended in 1984, to give "first consideration" to the welfare of the children in making orders for financial provision on divorce. However, while this stipulation largely determined the disposition of the family home, it had much less impact on the amounts of child maintenance ordered. As Weitzman observed in the context of the United States, courts practised a "father first" approach in which child maintenance is taken from the residue after the father's needs have been met.[6]

---

[4] See further Chs. 4 and 5.

[5] For an analysis of underlying issues of principle relating to spousal maintenance, see Carbone (1994).

[6] Weitzman (1985).

A more child-centred view is advocated by Eekelaar and Maclean,[7] who contend that the issue of spousal maintenance is properly superseded by the other parent's continuing obligation to any children of the relationship. This principle, they argue, should apply whatever the circumstances surrounding the parents' separation. Eekelaar and Maclean also contend that if this provision is to include recognition of the children's need for a home, and for someone to take care of them, then there must also be some provision for the parent providing that care. Thus in their view there can be "no rational basis for distinguishing the two elements" of child support and spousal maintenance: the child's standard of living cannot be separated from that of the caring parent.[8] This principle was given expression in the Social Security Act 1990 which empowered the Department of Social Security to seek an order requiring the 'liable relative' to make payments not only for the children but also for their carer. This power applied even where the parents had not been married.[9] Nonetheless, in terms of public attitudes there appears to be an acceptance of the continuing financial responsibility of parents for their children, but resistance to any continuing responsibility for an ex-partner, even when he or she is caring for those children.[10]

The question of the absent parent's maintenance liability may of course be complicated by his responsibility for other children. "The traditional approach of British social security policy"[11] has been to allow the absent parent to concentrate his resources on his second family, while paying only a residual amount to the State in compensation for its supporting his children by an earlier relationship. This approach reflects the structure of the benefits system, and in particular the 'cohabitation rule'[12] under which a man who cohabits is expected to support his current partner and any children in their care, irrespective of those children's biological parentage. This approach has now been abandoned in part, as the Child Support Act dictates that parents' obligations to the children of their 'first' family take precedence over any subsequently acquired responsibilities.[13] Nonetheless, the cohabitation rule remains firmly in place.

---

[7] Eekelaar and Maclean (1986).

[8] *Ibid.*, 106.

[9] Wikeley (1990).

[10] Bradshaw and Millar (1991). But as Glendon observes (cited in Carbone (1994), 384–5), the principle that parents must provide for their children may be considered uncontroversial, but to employ that principle to trump parents' sense of their own entitlement is a departure from existing law.

[11] Maclean and Eekelaar (1993), 218.

[12] For details see Ogus, Barendt and Wikeley (1995), 389–93.

[13] Maclean and Eekelaar (1993).

(ii) Squaring the circle: maintenance before the Child Support Act

Research conducted before the introduction of the Child Support Act 1991 revealed that about 70 per cent of maintenance orders were not paid in full.[14] Given the difficulties associated with ensuring adequate and regular maintenance, lawyers relied upon public funds to supplement (and sometimes to supplant) private financial support. The practice of taking into account social security entitlement when setting maintenance levels was given the imprimatur of judicial approval in the case of *Delaney v. Delaney*.[15] There the availability of Family Credit was accepted as justification for the absent parent to pay less maintenance so that he might be free to take on a larger mortgage with his new partner. The case gave explicit judicial recognition to the principle that the father had a right to make a new start, relatively unencumbered by financial responsibility to his first family.[16]

Another aspect of the State's commitment to lone parents reflects the unreliability of many maintenance payments. This led to the introduction of the 'diversion' procedure whereby the Department of Social Security paid a separated parent her benefit in full and collected the spousal or child maintenance itself.[17] Bradshaw and Millar found that 19 per cent of lone parents on Income Support received their maintenance in this way.[18] This arrangement, where it exists, highlights the fact that where the parent with care is in receipt of Income Support any maintenance from the absent parent does not add to the money which she receives. Therefore, from the perspective of the payer, it feels like a tax. It follows that this was not something invented by the Child Support Act 1991, although the higher maintenance demands which followed have thrown it into sharper relief.

The relationship between public and private law discussed above has been reviewed on a number of occasions, most notably by the Finer Committee.[19] The Finer Committee challenged the view of the State as a reserve resource. It proposed a guaranteed maintenance allowance which would be payable to all one-parent families, regardless of their status—though the State would seek recovery from the 'liable relative' wherever this was possible. The guaranteed maintenance allowance would have plugged one of the holes which had developed in the safety net of Beveridge's welfare state. It was never implemented, partly on cost

---

[14] Bradshaw and Millar (1991); McKay and Marsh (1994).
[15] [1990] 2 FLR 457. See also *Ashley* v. *Blackman* [1988] 2 FLR 278.
[16] Hayes (1991).
[17] This was introduced following the report of the Committee on One-Parent Families (Finer Committee) (1974).
[18] Bradshaw and Millar (1991).
[19] See n.17.

grounds and partly because of a principled disinclination to favour the separated over those who remained married, although a modest increase to Child Benefit for lone parents was subsequently introduced.[20]

(iii) Shifting the balance: the Child Support Act 1991

The Child Support Act 1991 marked a new departure, albeit one fore-shadowed by the changes to the liable relative procedure introduced by the Social Security Act 1990. As Sugarman[21] has argued: "For conservatives, the central function of the State with respect to the financial well-being of children arises in what conventionally has been called the 'private law' realm—the imposition and enforcement of bloodline-based child support obligations." The Child Support Act 1991 followed the Finer Committee in attempting to reconcile public and private law, but it did so in a very different way. In particular, it sought to square the circle of competing public law and private law interests *without* the additional state subsidy that Finer had regarded as essential.

This has enabled critics of the legislation to argue that the objective of saving Treasury money came before all other considerations, including the welfare of children.[22] Collier[23] likewise argues that there is no coherent conceptual framework to the legislation: "In the name of Treasury savings a legal reform which might have sought to improve the position of women [and children?] has in fact done little to help those most in need". This characterisation is not unique to the British scheme. Atkin, examining equivalent legislation in New Zealand, argues that notwithstanding the rhetoric of "parental responsibility" it was motivated "more by fiscal exigencies than the needs of women or children".[24] Although, as Atkin puts it, "loaded words such as 'right', 'obligation', 'equity' and 'fair' are used with abandon", the interests of children are defined solely in terms of a monetary formula.[25] Atkin argues that formulaic child support need bear little relationship to the reality of parental responsibility for children.

It is also worth pointing out that whereas higher maintenance can, for some parents with care, reduce or eliminate benefit dependency, it does

---

[20] See Ogus, Barendt and Wikeley (1995), 449. The abolition of one parent benefit, to take effect from June 1998, was announced by the former Conservative administration and is being carried through by the Labour government in the Social Security Act 1998.

[21] Sugarman (1995), 2531.

[22] Garnham and Knights (1994). This argument is given credence by the Child Support Agency's Performance Targets for its first year of operation. These included "Benefit savings of £530 million."

[23] Collier (1994), 386–7.

[24] Atkin (1992), 213.

[25] *Ibid.*, 217.

not follow that the recipient enjoys true independence. Reliance on private maintenance from an ex-partner transfers the economic dependence to a private source. As the Child Poverty Action Group has argued: "It appears that the imperative to reduce dependence on the State has blinded policy-makers to the problems of the increased dependence of women on men."[26]

In the course of our interviews both parents with care and absent parents were critical of the fact that the primary purpose of the legislation appeared to be to save government money. Among features which drew particular criticism were the fact that benefit claimants were forced to apply to the Child Support Agency whilst many non-claimants were told they must wait; the lack of any financial benefit to parents with care on Income Support; and the fact that the Child Support Agency appeared to pursue 'easy targets', namely parents who were already paying maintenance under a court order or a previous agreement with the Department of Social Security, whilst truly 'absent' parents were not pursued. These responses were consistent with the shift in media focus from an initial preoccupation with 'feckless fathers' to a concern that responsible fathers were having to pay too much.[27] Thus Miles Saltford (case 66) told us that he believed in parents paying for their children, but the idea had "got out of hand":

> "Greed clouded their judgement and they thought, 'We could wipe out that entire tier of social security benefits in one go and save ourselves millions of pounds . . .' I fully supported the original idea . . . [but] everybody knows it was Treasury led."

Likewise Robert Howell (case 46):

> "It is now proven beyond a shadow of a doubt that it was not set up to track down absent fathers, because I myself am not an absent father. What the Child Support Agency set out to do was to try to relieve the burden of the social security debt by taking as much as they could off the fathers who do maintain their children. They don't track down very many genuine absent fathers and get money out of them."

Although in *Children Come First*[28] increased child support was certainly identified as a means of reducing reliance on social security, the White Paper also stressed the need to encourage lone parents to take up employment. An increase in maintenance thus shifts the balance to private support while ostensibly enhancing individual choice. Research indicated that where maintenance was paid regularly and reliably the

[26] CPAG, *The Poverty of Maintenance: A Response from CPAG to the White Paper on Maintenance, Children Come First* (1990), 10.
[27] Collier (1994).
[28] Department of Social Security (1990).

lone parent was more likely to enter employment.[29] However, McKay and Marsh pointed out that some of the links between maintenance and employment were probably due to the increased employment opportunities for men and women in higher socio-economic groups: higher earners are more likely to be able to pay realistic levels of maintenance to their ex-partners, who themselves are more likely to be in a position to secure reasonably paid work.

We can conclude that the model of family responsibilities on which the Child Support Act was based largely ignored the interests of second families in favour of a one-dimensional emphasis on reducing the costs to the State of single parenthood. This created further problems. First, as alluded to earlier, there is a fundamental inconsistency between the statutory requirement that parents should take financial responsibility for their biological children, and the Income Support assessment procedures which are based on one adult claiming for the whole household in which he or she resides. Secondly, notwithstanding the operation of the protected income element of the formula, some absent parents have concluded that, once expenses are taken into account, they are worse off in work than out of it. Thirdly, prioritising the absent parent's obligation to his first family may act as a deterrent to re-partnering, when that might have removed another family from State support. As a result of these various factors the intended shift of responsibility from State to private resources was never going to be straightforward.

(iv) The requirement to co-operate

At the heart of the Child Support Act lies the requirement imposed on one group of separated parents, namely those on specified means-tested benefits, to cooperate with the regime. It is fundamental both because of its ideological significance—locating the prime responsibility for child maintenance with parents—and ensuring that benefit savings are made. Equally, there is evidence that many lone parents would prefer not to claim maintenance from the father of their children.[30]

Under social security legislation there has always been a duty on liable relatives to maintain their children, and this was reinforced and widened by the 1990 Act, but prior to the Child Support Act 1991 there was no comparable obligation on the claimant to co-operate with the Department of Social Security in the pursuit of maintenance. In practice the Department did not give priority to liable relative work; the number of staff engaged in these sections was not increased in line with the

---

[29] McKay and Marsh (1994).
[30] Bradshaw and Millar (1991), 80.

increase in claimants; and at times of pressure staff were often rede-
ployed to cope with a backlog in other areas.[31]

A second key difference is that the former liable relative rules applied
only to those on the most basic form of social assistance (Supplementary
Benefit; later Income Support). Under the child support legislation the
recoupment principle also applies to those claiming Family Credit and
Disability Working Allowance.[32] To require single parents claiming these
benefits to make a child maintenance application (whereas those with
private means are under no such compulsion, and some are precluded
from doing so[33]) serves to confirm that the primary purpose of the legislation was to reduce social security expenditure.

According to the Agency's own figures, in February 1997 more than 88
per cent of parents with care on its caseload were in receipt of one of the
prescribed benefits, and nearly three-quarters were on Income
Support.[34] A similar pattern, if not quite so pronounced, was evident in
our own case sample. We identified 109 cases in which there was some
Child Support Agency involvement: sixty applications had been triggered because the parent with care was in receipt of Income Support,
and twenty because of her status as a Family Credit claimant; only
twenty-four were private applications.[35]

Some parents with care whose cases we followed said they had felt
pressured into making a child support claim; more often they were given
the impression that they had no choice.[36] This was Melissa Grace's
account (case 69) :

> "The letter said that by law I had to, and if I didn't they would take me to court.
> That was how I interpreted the letter. I thought I had no choice. Otherwise,
> obviously I would have said 'no, we're fine the way things are . . .' Maybe I mis-
> read the letters, but I certainly didn't get the impression that I was able to say
> to them: 'Goodbye' ".

Although most absent parents resigned themselves to Agency involvement, others engaged in various strategies designed to remove themselves from the scope of the Agency's operations. This is considered
further in Chapter 9.

---

[31] National Audit Office (1991).
[32] There are only about 12,000 disability working allowance claimants, so no further reference will be made to this benefit. The mandatory inclusion of benefit cases does not
extend to parents with care who are in work and claiming housing benefit or council tax
benefit. There may be two reasons for this: first, many are likely to be working for less than
16 hours a week and so claiming Income Support in any event. Secondly, these two benefits are administered by local authorities, making co-ordination even more problematic.
[33] See Child Support Act 1995, s.18.
[34] Child Support Agency, *Quarterly Summary of Statistics*, Feb. 1997.
[35] We have no information on this point for the remaining five cases.
[36] See also Clarke, Craig and Glendinning (1996), 13.

(v) 'Good cause' for refusing to co-operate

Even for those parents who remain part of the Agency's caseload, the requirement to co-operate is not absolute. A parent with care who refuses to authorise the Secretary of State to put in train a child support assessment can either plead exemption on the basis of 'good cause' or accept a reduced benefit direction. The good cause exception applies where the Secretary of State is satisfied that there is a risk that the parent with care or a child living with her will suffer harm or undue distress if the case is pursued. The effect of a reduced benefit direction, at the time of our research, was to reduce the parent with care's Income Support entitlement by 20 per cent of the adult personal allowance for six months, followed by a 10 per cent reduction for the following year. If a parent with care on benefit has given her authority at the outset, withdrawal is only possible if she claims good cause. The regulations do not allow her to opt out and take the benefit penalty at this stage. (On the other hand, if she has made a private application, or has subsequently stopped claiming benefit, she is free to opt out whenever she wishes.)

The principle and scope of the good cause exemption were a major focus of debate during the passage of the Child Support Act 1991.[37] In the first two years of the scheme there was a relatively high success rate for applications for exemption, but since 1995 far fewer cases have been accepted, as indicated in Table 3.1.

Table 3.1 Applications for exemption owing to risk of harm or undue distress[38]

	1993/94	1994/95	1995/96	Apr–Dec 1996
Cases considered	64,792	91,414	112,645	113,411
Good cause accepted	31,699 (49 %)	41,666 (46 %)	38,963 (35 %)	27,918 (20 %)
Cases withdrawn	14,206 (22 %)	11,175 (12 %)	23,595 (21 %)	50,106 (37 %)
Good cause refused	18,857 (29 %)	38,573 (42 %)	50,087 (44 %)	58,387 (43 %)
Benefit penalties	627	17,451	27,478	11,489

[37] See Ch. 1.
[38] Source: Knights and Cox (1997), 87.

The reason for the increased number of cases under consideration is probably because at the beginning of 1995 new procedures were introduced requiring parents with care to sign a separate authorisation that the absent parent could be contacted. But the proportion of cases in which good cause has been accepted has fallen dramatically. One explanation advanced by the Agency for this change was that the new procedure had "increased parents with care's awareness that they do not *have* to co-operate with the Agency, but has led to claims for good cause without good reason."[39] A review of the good cause procedures also cited increasing staff experience.[40] Both explanations suggest that the proportion of rejected claims may rise still further.

Cases are 'withdrawn' where parents with care decide to co-operate with the Agency or where they come off benefit before the good cause issue is decided. Some of these applicants will have found employment or re-partnered; but others will have withdrawn for other reasons—including a wish not to have to claim maintenance from the children's father. Concern about collusion between separated parents—highlighted in the official response to a 1996 departmental study of the good cause procedures—prompted the previous government to increase the severity of the benefit sanction to a 40 per cent reduction in the Income Support personal allowance for a period of three years.[41]

The sampling frame adopted by the Child Support Agency on our behalf was such as effectively to exclude the great majority of good cause applications, but this does not mean that parents with care whom we interviewed did not experience any sense of threat, or indeed actual violence. One parent who clearly felt apprehensive about the Agency's intention to contact her ex-partner was Janice Vaughan (case 27). But she was also worried about losing benefit if good cause were not accepted. She therefore signed the authorisation clause, but sent a covering letter listing her concerns for herself and her son. These concerns were clearly justified: she suffered harassment throughout the research period, was assaulted on at least one occasion, and had to change her phone number because of nuisance calls from her ex-partner. Janice later tried to withdraw the authority that she had somewhat ambivalently given:

> "I don't think they're being fair to me . . . [The Child Support Agency officer] said: 'Well, put it this way, if we don't go after him, then we're going to have to suspend half your money.' And I said: 'Well I'd rather do without half my money than go through the trouble that I'm going through at the moment.' I don't think they take into account who suffers at the end of the day."

---

[39] House of Commons Social Security Committee (1996a), Minutes of Evidence, 6 (original emphasis).

[40] Provan *et al.* (1996), 56.

[41] See House of Commons Social Security Committee (1996b) and Department of Social Security (1996).

This issue was still unresolved at the end of the research period: Janice had had one interview with a Child Support Agency field officer and was awaiting another.

Most reports of the operation of the good cause provision suggest that the issue was handled circumspectly, at least in the Agency's early days, so that there was not the additional threat to lone mothers feared by many critics of the legislation around the time it was enacted.[42] Other accounts were more equivocal.[43] Nonetheless the Agency's success in negotiating this particular minefield may be inferred from the fact that much of the criticism which it received was on the basis that it was too ready to permit fathers who threatened violence to be excused payment of whatever maintenance was assessed. For example, one newspaper article[44] reported a case in which a man who had allegedly threatened to shoot his former partner succeeded in escaping both his obligations to the Agency and a criminal charge (the latter because the Agency refused to support a criminal prosecution on the ground that this would not be consistent with their obligation to have regard to the welfare of the child). Apparently the mother in this case appealed and the tribunal upheld the Agency decision because, as it was stated, "Mr. S. told us that Mrs. W. had reason to be afraid of him."

It is clearly unsatisfactory that a man who threatens to kill his ex-wife can make the Agency abandon the attempt to impose a maintenance assessment upon him. The fact that some men do behave in this way poses a real policy dilemma in which pragmatic and humanitarian considerations are sharply at odds with the Child Support Agency's responsibilities as, in effect, a tax gathering authority. In fact the approach of the Agency in its early years appeared not dissimilar to that adopted by the police and the Crown Prosecution Service in dealing with domestic assault.[45] This may be appropriate in circumstances where the key interests represented are those of the two parties to an intimate relationship. But the State is not normally influenced by these considerations when seeking to extract money owed to it by a citizen. So on what model is the Child Support Agency operating? It is not simply that of the independent arbiter engaged in determining the outcome of a dispute between two citizens. If that were the model then the Agency could abandon a substantial part of its caseload, since many parents would prefer to resolve these matters between themselves. On the contrary, the Agency is a State bureaucracy charged with the responsibility of extracting money from citizens according to a formula. Admittedly the situation is rendered

[42] Provan *et al.* (1996).
[43] Clarke *et al.* (1994); Clarke *et al.* (1996); Glendinning *et al.* (1995); Garnham and Knights (1994); Women's Aid Federation of England (1994); Mullinder (1996).
[44] "Father won't pay? Punish the mother", Polly Toynbee, *Independent*, 21 Oct. 1996.
[45] Cretney and Davis (1995).

complex in that, formally speaking, the parent with care *authorises* the Agency's pursuit of the absent parent (although the reality may well be that she feels she has no choice in the matter). Despite this formal authorisation, it would seem reasonable to conclude that the primary relationship is between the Agency, representing the State, and the citizen from whom it is seeking to extract money. It is questionable in these circumstances whether the Agency should allow itself to be deflected from this task—from what, in practice, has proved its *primary* task—by threats of violence made by that citizen against his former partner. On one view the appropriate response to such threats is for the Agency to advise the woman to inform the police, and for it to inform the man that he had better pay up or face all the enforcement procedures at the Agency's disposal. As it is, the good cause provision invites the Agency to modify its tax gathering instincts and to behave more like the Crown Prosecution Service when faced with a reluctant witness.

This reflects a philosophical incoherence at the heart of the Child Support Act 1991. The legislation was drafted in such a way as to allow personal fear (in effect, the ability to induce such fear) to provide an escape route from the Agency's operations. To pursue the analogy with domestic violence prosecutions a little further, the compellability provision (the court's right to force spouses, or former spouses, to give evidence against a violent partner, upon pain of their own punishment) is seldom employed in practice. This is partly for pragmatic and partly for symbolic reasons,[46] but it is arguable whether those aspects which defeat the application of compellability in the context of prosecutions for domestic assault need apply to the Child Support Agency. Some men will threaten, and some will indeed be violent on the pretext of the woman's co-operation with the Agency, but some men will threaten and be violent in any event. There are remedies for that, and they need to be invoked. The problem with this approach is that there are grave weaknesses in the application of these remedies, so that in practice women are inadequately protected from violent, abusive men.[47] It follows that the decision to permit women not to disclose names and addresses for fear of violence can readily be justified on humanitarian grounds. As we have seen, the issue is also highly charged politically: 'CSA suicides' are bad enough; the first 'CSA murder' would have further threatened public support for the scheme. Nonetheless the good cause provision reflects an ambiguity concerning the core objectives and fundamental character of the Child Support Agency. If the Agency acted primarily to redistribute income between families, and if it intervened at the behest of the parent with care, then that parent would clearly have the right to call a halt to the Agency's operations. But if the Agency has the character of a tax

[46] Cretney and Davis (1997).
[47] Cretney and Davis (1996).

authority—and it has that character in virtually all cases in which one might expect good cause to be invoked—then the good cause provision itself appears somewhat anomalous.

3. CHILD SUPPORT, SOCIAL SECURITY AND THE LOW PAID SINGLE PARENT

(i) Lone parents and welfare benefits

An important question facing developed welfare states is whether single mothers should be regarded primarily as workers in the labour market (and therefore expected to take up employment) or whether they should be entitled to State support because of their child-care responsibilities.[48] The British welfare state is based very much on Beveridge's male bread-winner model, although government policy has shifted at key points throughout this century.[49] Beveridge attached great importance to the unpaid work undertaken by women as wives and mothers, and Britain remains one of few industrialised countries which allows single parents to claim benefits without the need to make themselves available for work.[50] Beveridge was reluctant to allow married women access to benefits in their own right, but treated the family as a unit for social insurance purposes.[51] From this perspective the 'problem' facing lone mothers is the lack of a resident breadwinner.

Today the most important benefits for single parents are Income Support and Family Credit. Income Support is available for those who are not in full-time paid work, currently defined as sixteen or more hours per week.[52] The key to understanding entitlement to Income Support is the claimant's "applicable amount", which consists of personal allowances for each member of the family, various premiums, and (for homeowners) housing costs by way of mortgage interest payments.[53] The treatment of housing costs for owner-occupiers under the Income Support scheme has allowed many lone parents, although unemployed

[48] Lewis (1997).

[49] Millar (1994a and 1994b).

[50] Millar (1989); Bingley *et al.* (1994). The Labour government's "New Deal for Lone Parents" may herald a shift in this policy.

[51] "In any measure of social policy in which regard is had to facts, the great majority of married women must be regarded as occupied on work which is vital though unpaid, without which their husbands could not do their paid work and without which the nation could not continue": Beveridge (1942), para. 107.

[52] The legislative test is strictly "remunerative work", which is defined by the Income Support (General) Regulations 1987 (S.I. 1987 No. 1987), reg. 5, to mean not less than 16 hours a week. An easement applies where one person in a couple claims income-based job-seeker's allowance (the equivalent to Income Support for unemployed people): in this case the other partner can work for up to 24 hours before having to move on to in-work benefits.

[53] The housing costs of those in rented accommodation are met through housing benefit, administered by local authorities.

or working only a few hours a week, to remain in the former matrimonial home.[54]

With very few exceptions, any other income is deducted from the applicable amount to arrive at the amount of weekly Income Support payable. Only the first £15 of a lone parent's weekly earnings is disregarded.[55] There is no allowance for child care or for travel to work expenses.[56] In practice even the earnings disregard may be absorbed by the extra expense of taking on paid work, particularly for lone parents who cannot rely on a partner or relative to share child care. Any maintenance, voluntary or otherwise, is aggregated with the parent's income and so deducted from Income Support entitlement pound for pound.[57]

Family Credit on the other hand provides a tax-free 'top-up' income for those parents in paid employment whose wages are considered too low to support a family. Since 1992 the threshold for eligibility has been set at 16 hours (or more) of paid work a week. This is to encourage the take-up of part-time jobs.[58] Like Income Support, Family Credit has some 'passported' benefits, such as free prescriptions.[59] There are however some important differences, the object of which is to generate incentives to engage in low paid work. First, Child Benefit is not included as income for Family Credit purposes. Secondly, maintenance is subject to a weekly £15 disregard. Thirdly, a child care allowance has been incorporated into the calculation.[60] With these advantages, Family Credit has been much more successful than its predecessor, Family Income Supplement, in improving work incentives.[61]

A further key difference between the two benefits is that whereas Income Support can be adjusted weekly to cope with changes in

[54] However, the rules governing the payment of mortgage interest have been tightened in recent years: see Wikeley (1995).

[55] Knowledge of the Income Support rules, although patchy (Bradshaw and Millar (1991), 30), is still much higher amongst lone parents than in other recipients of Income Support: Shaw *et al.* (1996), 41.

[56] Deductions for these expenses were possible before 1988. A challenge before the European Court of Justice under the EC Equal Treatment Directive concerning the absence of any disregards in the Income Support scheme for these costs failed in *Jackson and Cresswell* v. *Chief Adjudication Officer* [1993] 2 WLR 658.

[57] Before 1979 maintenance paid direct to children was disregarded.

[58] Marsh *et al.* (1997) found that for lone parents working 16–23 hours per week, 45 per cent of their total income is derived from earnings while 29 per cent is made up by Family Credit: "This is a wage subsidy policy in action to a remarkable degree: it is quite close to the position of a whole week's wages for half a week's work" (*ibid.*, 13).

[59] Only Income Support claimants receive free school meals for their children.

[60] Originally set at £40 a week in 1994, and raised to £60 in 1996, the Labour government increased the limit to £100 with effect from 1998 as part of its "New Deal for Lone Parents". This still fails to tackle the problem of the steep rate of withdrawal at certain levels of earnings: see Tait (1997).

[61] The worst effects of the 'poverty trap', which had meant that some families claiming Family Income Supplement suffered 100 per cent marginal tax rates, have been ameliorated, but 645,000 claimants still face a marginal net income deduction rate of 70 per cent or more: Department of Social Security (1997), 57.

circumstances, Family Credit is designed as a 'broad brush' benefit and so is paid at a fixed rate for six months; it is only on a repeat claim that any change in earnings or in child support can be taken into account. This can work to the advantage of the parent with care: if she claims Family Credit just before any maintenance arrives, her assessment, running for six months, will be based solely on her earnings. Polly Fookes (case 119) was in this position: on advice from an officer of the Agency she started work and quickly submitted a Family Credit claim, excluding from the calculations the £75 child support which started coming in (via a deduction of earnings order) shortly afterwards:

> "I was saying, 'I want to go out to work, but I can't afford to work, I can't claim Family Credit because I'll be getting this amount of money from my ex-partner, and I'll only be entitled to £15 a week of it or something like that if I claim Family Credit.' But then somebody from the Child Support Agency actually informed me that if I got a job straight away and got my Family Credit sorted, then as soon as his money started coming in, I would get the three[62] for six months. So that's what I did. I ran out then in November and got a job and his payments started coming in at the end of November. It worked out wonderfully for Christmas!"

On the other hand, this rough and ready approach to benefit eligibility can disadvantage the claimant, especially when arrears of maintenance are taken into account. Caroline Saville (case 74) was hoping that her ex-husband would pay off his arrears in one or two lump sums—well before she next needed to apply for Family Credit:

> "I will get all of it if he actually pays. By the time my Family Credit comes through to claim again, [the arrears] will have gone through the system. You put down the last three amounts paid. If the last three amounts included that £1,000 then my Family Credit would be completely stopped. If the last three amounts are just [the assessed figure] then the £1,000 would not have to be mentioned. . . ."

In fact by the end of our study the arrears were still unpaid and Caroline was receiving just £3.20 a week in child support, well below Family Credit's £15 maintenance disregard. Although relatively well-versed in the intricacies of the benefits system, she had no idea whether she was getting her full entitlement, or what she might expect in future.

(ii) Bridges and barriers to employment

Lone parents typically experience much longer spells on Income Support than do other claimants. Although only about one in six lone

---

[62] In other words, earnings, child maintenance from her former partner, and Family Credit as originally assessed.

parents on Income Support has regular part-time work,[63] the majority report that they want to work.[64] Brown identified three factors which prevent the majority of lone parents from becoming self-supporting.[65] First, full time wages are poor for most women. Secondly, although part time work offers a better fit with family commitments, the hourly rate tends to be even lower. Thirdly, there is a lack of affordable child care.[66]

There are also disincentives built into the social security system. First, it is pointless in cash terms[67] for single parents on Income Support to earn more than the £15 disregard unless they can earn enough to transfer to Family Credit. As Sugarman observes in the context of the United States, the limited disregard renders paid employment "economically irrational for anyone who cannot earn enough to achieve financial independence".[68] The only alternative is not to disclose the extra earnings and so risk action for the recovery of overpayments or even prosecution for fraud.[69] Secondly, lone parents have different requirements for employment from secondary earners in two-parent households; for example, it is counter-productive to come off Income Support for a short-term job. The principal disadvantage is in regard to the payment of mortgage interest.[70] Indeed, housing costs have emerged as a major disincentive for lone parents in owner occupied property. This means that there is no easy bridge from Income Support supplemented by part-time work to full-time work supplemented by Family Credit.[71] Thirdly, and more generally, social security claimants who wish to take up employment face considerable uncertainty and insecurity of income in the first few weeks of work.[72] This problem is especially acute for lone parents.[73]

---

[63] Shaw *et al.* (1996), 42, report that 16 per cent of lone parents on Income Support have part-time jobs, compared with just 5 per cent of those registered as unemployed.

[64] Just 14 per cent said that they did not want a regular paid job (*ibid.*, 82). As the authors note, there is thus little evidence to support the "underclass" thesis that Income Support for lone parents has become a preferred means of raising children. For comparative studies of policies relating to lone parents see Bradshaw *et al.* (1993) and Gornick *et al.* (1997).

[65] Brown (1989), 35.

[66] One study calculated child care costs as nearly one quarter of net weekly earnings for mothers with children under the age of 5: Ward *et al.* (1996).

[67] We recognise that single parents' decisions regarding employment are not solely financial: Weale *et al.* (1984), and Shaw *et al.*, (1996), 69–70.

[68] Sugarman (1995), 2545. The effect of the £15 disregard is to create a "poverty plateau" whereby an increase in hours worked provides a minimal increase in net income: Burghes (1993), 15–19.

[69] Shaw *et al.* (1996), 127.

[70] The linking rules provide that periods of 12 weeks or less when the claimant is not on Income Support do not affect the payment of housing costs in the event of an early return to claiming benefit. Thus a gap of three months off benefit will mean that the qualifying period has to be served again before housing costs are paid.

[71] Land (1994).

[72] McLaughlin *et al.* (1989).

[73] Brown (1989), 38.

(iii) Payment of child support and liaison between the Child Support Agency and the Benefits Agency

The Child Support Agency provides both an assessment and a collection and payment service; benefit claimants receive both services free but, at the time of our fieldwork, private clients were charged fees.[74] Parents with care can choose between two methods of payment of child support: either direct from the absent parent, or via the Agency (the "collection service"). If parents disagree on the payment method the Agency makes the final decision, usually opting for collection if the parent with care so requests.[75] In the early days of the Agency all Income Support and Family Credit claimants were expected to use the collection service, and their child support was paid as part of their benefit; but now they are given the same choice as other parents.

The Child Support Agency suggests that "where possible parents should arrange to make maintenance payments directly between themselves" and adds, somewhat optimistically, that "this is the quickest and often the most convenient method".[76] In the case of direct payment, the Agency has no record of how much maintenance is being paid, and it is left to the parent with care to complain if payments are not forthcoming. As a result, many parents with care prefer payments to be made via the Agency and to have their Income Support paid 'gross'. This ensures a regular income. However, there are practical problems with this procedure. When the parent with care is receiving her Income Support in full, with child support collected by the Agency, she may not know whether maintenance is being paid. This is undesirable for two reasons: it can lead to bad feeling between the parents if the absent parent is paying, but the parent with care is convinced he is not; and if the parent with care is considering employment, her decision may be assisted by knowing how much (and how regularly) maintenance is actually being paid.

Difficulties can also arise when there is a breakdown of communication between the Child Support Agency and the Benefits Agency; or when parents are confused about the method of payment to be employed. This can happen where an absent parent requests direct payment but the parent with care opts for payment via the Agency; or where both parents are happy with direct payment but the Agency decides that the collection

[74] These fees were subsequently suspended from Apr. 1995 to Apr. 1999.

[75] One version of the Helpnotes accompanying the Maintenance Application Form states that the collection service will be provided "if it is chosen by at least one parent". Other versions state simply that parents' preferences will be taken into account. Ultimately the method of payment is a matter for the discretion of the Secretary of State: Child Support (Collection and Enforcement) Regulations 1992 (S.I. 1992 No. 1989), regs. 2 and 3.

[76] *Child Support Agency Maintenance Enquiry Helpnotes*, 31; and *Maintenance Application Helpnotes for Income Support Claimants*, 12.

service should operate. In these cases the absent parent may disregard letters and payment slips from the Agency and carry on paying the parent with care directly. She, in turn, might accept such payments in addition to her benefit. The resulting muddle, which gives a temporary financial advantage to one or both parents, can be almost impossible to sort out.

A case in point was that of Delia Shearer and Gavin Field (case 92). On separating, several years previously, they had agreed that Gavin should pay Delia £40 a week for her younger son, Mark. Delia informed her social security office (in the days before the Child Support Agency) that she was receiving just £20, so the extra £20 was received as cash in hand. In due course the Child Support Agency made an assessment of £23 per week, which they asked Gavin to pay to them. He however ignored this request and carried on with the usual arrangement. Delia's Income Support payments also continued, on the understanding that she was receiving £20 (but no more than that). It was some time before either the Child Support Agency or the Benefits Agency realised that a mistake had been made, but even then nothing was done. Meanwhile Gavin built up over £1,000 "arrears" on his Child Support Agency account, while Delia continued to receive her undeclared bonus (albeit at a slightly lower rate than hitherto). In principle, action should have been taken against Delia for recovery of overpaid benefits, and Gavin's arrears should have been adjusted by the amount of his direct payments, but nobody in the Child Support Agency seemed interested in grasping either of these nettles.[77]

A related problem arises where the maintenance assessment is fixed at a level which disentitles the parent with care from receiving any Income Support. If the assessment is incorrect a substantial overpayment of child support may be made, with little prospect of recovery. Amelia Radcliffe (case 114) found herself in this position. Despite protesting that the original assessment was too high, the absent parent, Nathan Banks, began paying it in full to the Agency. Following an appeal hearing, his assessment was reduced by £20 a week. He asked the Agency to refund the overpayment but was told that, as they had passed the money on, he should "sort it out with Ms. Radcliffe". This issue had still not been resolved by the end of the research period.[78]

---

[77] Recovery of overpayments of Income Support is a matter for the Secretary of State, acting through the Benefits Agency: Social Security Administration Act 1992, s.71.

[78] There is provision for the Secretary of State to require the parent with care to reimburse the absent parent in respect of overpaid child support, but this does not apply where the parent with care is on benefit: Child Support Act 1991, s.41B and Child Support (Arrears, Interest and Adjustment of Maintenance Assessments) Regulations 1991 (S.I. 1991 No. 1816), reg. 10A.

(i) The effect of Child Support Agency involvement

In this section we examine two fundamental issues. First, did the intervention of the Child Support Agency lead absent parents to pay more than they had been paying? And secondly, what was the impact of such payments on the finances of parents with care?

Table 3.2 reveals that the Agency's intervention had a positive impact upon the absent parent's payment levels in thirty-nine cases, no impact in forty-eight cases, and a negative impact in sixteen cases.[79]

Table 3.2 Agency involvement and maintenance payments

No payment before or after Agency involvement	25 (24%)
No payment before Agency involvement; some payment afterwards	13 (13%)
Payment before Agency involvement; paid more afterwards	26 (25%)
Payment before Agency involvement; continued payment at same level afterwards	23 (22%)
Payment before Agency involvement; paid less afterwards	16 (16%)
Total	103 (100%)

As might have been anticipated, a record of previous payment was associated with continued compliance, at least in part. Table 3.3 provides a limited historical perspective on the payment of child support.

We also sought to establish how regularly the absent parent paid whatever sum was ordered by the Agency. We found sixty-one cases in which, following a completed assessment, the absent parent had paid at least some maintenance by the end of the study (76 per cent of cases in which there had been a positive assessment). Among these sixty-one payers, however, only twenty-eight had paid in full as ordered; twenty-eight had paid in part or erratically; and five had paid only following enforcement proceedings. We then matched these data with the relative amount of the assessment compared to previous payments. Table 3.4 shows that absent parents who were assessed as having to pay more than hitherto

[79] This analysis excludes 20 cases in which there was either no Agency involvement or in which the data were not available.

Table 3.3 Previous maintenance and continuing payment of child support

	Assessment less than absent parent previously paying	Assessment more than absent parent previously paying	No payments prior to intervention of the Agency
Child support paid following assessment	9 (90%)	33 (75%)	13 (54%)
Child support not paid following assessment	1 (10%)	11 (25%)	11 (46%)
Total	10 (100%)	44 (100%)	24 (100%)

Table 3.4 Previous maintenance and absent parents' patterns of payment

	Assessment less than absent parent previously paying	Assessment more than absent parent previously paying	No payments prior to intervention of the Agency
Paid in full	8 (80%)	12 (27%)	8 (33%)
Paid in part or erratically	1 (10%)	23 (52%)	4 (16%)
Paid following enforcement	–	4 (9%)	1 (4%)
Paid nothing	1 (10%)	5 (11%)	11 (46%)
Total	10 (100%)	44 (100%)	24 (100%)

were most likely to pay erratically or in part. Absent parents who had paid nothing prior to the advent of the Agency were the group most likely still to pay nothing.

We also considered the impact of the Child Support Agency upon the finances of lone parents. In examining this question the composition of the sample must be borne in mind. As explained above, sixty parents with care were on Income Support at the time of application; twenty were receiving Family Credit; and there were twenty-four private applications. Table 3.5 shows that if Agency involvement was triggered by a benefit claim there was a greater likelihood of some child support being paid.[80] In other words, parents and children who were most likely to ben-

---

[80] In 17 of the remaining 20 benefit cases the Agency had yet to arrive at an assessment; the other 3 were nil assessments. The remaining private cases involved 2 pending and 1 nil assessment.

Table 3.5 *Private/benefit applications and payment patterns*

	Private application	Benefit application
Some maintenance paid	10 (48%)	45 (75%)
No maintenance paid	11 (52%)	15 (25%)
Total	21 (100%)	60 (100%)

efit from payment of child support—the private cases—were least likely to receive it.

This picture was confirmed by other data on the circumstances of the lone parents in our sample. In seventy-three of the 102 cases on which we had the necessary information, the Agency's intervention had had no effect on the carer's net income.[81] The parent with care had gained as a result of Child Support Agency involvement in 21 cases, and had lost money in eight cases. In Table 3.6 this information is broken down by parents' benefit status. It is apparent that benefit claimants were very unlikely (in the short term at least) to see any improvement in their finances. Assuming payments were actually made (on which see Table 3.5), parents with care who had made private applications were much more likely to profit from Child Support Agency involvement, although even amongst this group the majority were still no better off.

Table 3.6 *Private/benefit applications and effect on parent with care*

	Income Support claimant	Family Credit claimant	Private applicant
Net gain	5 (9%)	6 (32%)	10 (40%)
No difference	47 (81%)	12 (63%)	14 (56%)
Net loss	6 (10%)	1 (5%)	1 (4%)
Total	58 (100%)	19 (100%)	25 (100%)

The winners and losers in Table 3.6 are categorised according to their status at the point of the original application. Further analysis of the twenty-one 'winners' reveals that by the end of the study eleven were in full-time work and not claiming benefit, six were working and in receipt of Family Credit, and three were unemployed.[82]

---

[81] In 19 of these 73 cases (17 benefit cases and 2 private applications) the Agency had not made an assessment.

[82] In one case the relevant information was missing.

These findings are consistent with those of Marsh *et al.*[83] who found that Child Support Agency assessments had little impact on the number of lone parents receiving maintenance. The reasons they advance are that most Agency assessments are made on those already paying, or on those who would have paid anyway. Other assessments are made on parents who are not required to pay, or on those who would not have paid anyway and still refuse to do so.

(ii) Lone parents and the role of child support

The relationship between the Child Support Agency and the benefits system is such that in most benefit cases the Agency has no immediate impact on the carer's income. These parents were able to view the whole process with relative indifference. For example, Shirley Noakes (case 97) had two young children, claimed Income Support, and earned £15 per week from a cleaning job; her mortgage interest (which was several hundred pounds a month) was paid by the DSS. She knew that it would be a very long time before she could earn enough to come off benefits. The advent of the Child Support Agency was a non-event as far as she was concerned:

> "We just get the DSS and that's it, really. It won't affect us at all. So in that way I feel detached from it ."

The reaction of Simone Byron (case 8) was rather more complex, demonstrating that child support has symbolic as well as practical significance. Simone also had a part-time job and claimed Income Support, which met her mortgage interest payments. When the maintenance assessment eventually arrived she was furious that her ex-husband was expected to pay so little:

> "£2.30 a week, that's for both children, which I find insulting to say the least . . . [The Agency] is a waste of time as far as I'm concerned . . . It's disgraceful!"

Absent parents, on the other hand, had limited enthusiasm for paying more (sometimes considerably more) child support than previously, only for their ex-partners and children to be no better off . Michael Seeley (case 54) was typical in this respect:

> "Even if I had the money I would not want to pay it through the Child Support Agency because she would not be any better off. That's really what it boils down to. No-one's better off, and I'm worse off. The money is just going straight to the Treasury."

Michael was one of the parents in our sample who negotiated a private deal with his ex-partner in order to escape the clutches of the Agency.

---

[83] Marsh *et al.* (1997), 69. See also Clarke, Craig and Glendinning (1996).

Although that arrangement later broke down, Michael continued to evade payment, and eventually moved abroad—the ultimate avoidance tactic.

5. CONCLUSION

Many lone mothers are reluctant to come off Income Support not because of benefit dependency, so-called, but because they are, with good reason, distrustful of the alternatives. A steady income, albeit at subsistence level, may be preferable to low wages, job insecurity and unreliable child support from a former partner. Then there is the problem of child care costs and, for home-owners, the daunting obstacle of mortgage payments. If the policy objective is to provide single parents with a genuine choice between claiming State benefits and taking paid employment, these two issues have to be addressed. The incoming Labour government's 'New Deal' for lone parents makes some attempt to tackle the former, but neglects the latter problem entirely.

4

Inside the Child Support Agency

"Overall, our standard of service did not reach acceptable levels . . . we apologise to our clients for the difficulties they have experienced because of our shortcomings". (Ros Hepplewhite, Chief Executive of the CSA, 1993–4[1])

"The Child Support Act would have been bound to arouse controversy because of the scope of the social change it brought about, even if the administrative performance of the agency implementing the Act had been impeccable. In the event, the Agency's performance in the first year to eighteen months was dire". (House of Commons Social Security Committee[2])

"This is complete chaos. It might be organised chaos but at the end of the day it is chaos, and you just don't feel it is getting any better." (Child support officer, Dudley CSAC)

"I mean, it's got to get better. It couldn't get any worse." (Child Support Agency field officer)

This chapter presents our findings on the Child Support Agency, its procedures and its problems. We begin by examining what official bodies have had to say about the performance of the Agency. The rest of the chapter is concerned with what we ourselves discovered by following cases through the system and by interviewing Agency staff. First, we examine the Agency's structure, its recruitment and training policies, and the problems staff have faced in trying to keep up with their individual workloads. Secondly, we look at the issue of how work is prioritised. Thirdly, we look at the perennial tension between the objectives of speed and accuracy. Fourthly, we comment briefly on the inability of the Agency to keep assessments up to date as parents' circumstances change. Finally we explore the enforcement strategies adopted by the Agency when absent parents do not pay as required.

1. THE OFFICIAL VERDICT ON THE CHILD SUPPORT AGENCY

The lightning rod for much of the public criticism of the Child Support Agency has been the House of Commons Social Security Committee.

---

[1] *Annual Report 1993/4 and Business Plan 1994/5 of the Child Support Agency* (1994), foreword, London: HMSO.
[2] House of Commons Social Security Committee (1996a).

During its 1995–6 session it undertook an inquiry into the Agency's performance.[3] It acknowledged that the Agency's handling of cases had improved somewhat since its first year, but half of all assessments still contained errors, the time taken to complete assessment was still excessive (contributing to a high level of arrears), and there were serious problems in enforcing maintenance. Overall over £700 million of maintenance was unpaid.

The Committee of Public Accounts also reported on the Agency during its 1995–6 session.[4] It too expressed concern at the continuing high error rate and the unambitious target for reducing this. The Committee also pointed to the Agency's failure to implement its strategy of phasing in additional cases. It commented that the extent to which parents would not co-operate with the Agency (or would actively seek to obstruct it) had not been anticipated.

Further evidence of the Agency's shortcomings has been provided by the Chief Child Support Officer whose independent monitoring team, the Central Adjudication Services, noted that in the first year of the Agency's operation only 14 per cent of monitored assessments were correct both in their calculations and in the final assessment.[5] By the second year the proportion had risen to 29 per cent and the assessment was apparently accurate in cash terms in 43 per cent of the sample cases (compared to just 25 per cent in year one).[6] In many instances child support officers did not have sufficient information to make a correct assessment. They were also applying the law incorrectly. The Chief Child Support Officer observed that "understandable operational pressures resulted in clearance of cases without the necessary information". He commented that this was nonetheless insufficient justification for cutting corners and that child support officers "must endeavour to apply the law correctly".

Reports from the Ombudsman have documented the results of investigation into complaints by members of the public regarding maladministration by the Child Support Agency.[7] His inquiries revealed numerous cases which were marked by significant delay and confusion, erroneous calculations and mistakes over identity. He pinpointed major defects in the planning stage and in the priorities adopted by the child support scheme:

---

[3] *Ibid.*

[4] First Report from the Committee of Public Accounts, 1995–6, *Child Support Agency*, HC 31, 1996, London: HMSO.

[5] *Annual Report of the Chief Child Support Officer, 1993–1994* (1994), London: HMSO, 4.

[6] *Annual Report of the Chief Child Support Officer, 1994–1995* (1995), London: HMSO, 4.

[7] See, in particular, Parliamentary Commissioner for Administration, Third Report, 1995–6, *Investigation of complaints against the Child Support Agency* (1996), London: Stationery Office.

"Maladministration leading to injustice is likely to arise when a new administrative task is not tested first by a pilot project; when new staff, perhaps inadequately trained, form a substantial fraction of the workforce; where procedures and technology supporting them are untried; and where quality of service is subordinated to sheer throughput."[8]

The Agency itself has acknowledged most of these deficiencies in its annual reports. It has also observed that "improvements in performance will take time".[9] Nonetheless in her 1995 report the then Chief Executive of the Agency, Ann Chant, struck a more optimistic note.[10] She admitted that half the Agency's cases were over a year old, and that the older cases were particularly difficult to deal with. However, deferring take-up of new cases would allow this backlog to be cleared and, as cases were now being processed more quickly, she was hopeful that this problem would not recur. New procedures had been introduced to facilitate monitoring of all aspects of the child support process. Her expectation was that such monitoring, combined with better staff training, would greatly improve efficiency.

There are indeed signs that the Agency's standards of administration are improving. The Chief Child Support Officer observed that his 1995–6 annual report contained "sound evidence that the general strength of commitment within the Child Support Agency . . . is starting to have the desired effect".[11] For example, the proportion of maintenance assessments which were accurate in cash terms had risen from 43 per cent in the previous year to 53 per cent. However the Chief Child Support Officer noted in the same report that the number of maintenance assessments which were incorrect had increased from 23 per cent in 1994–5 to 29 per cent in 1995–6,[12] while the incorrect application of the law by child support officers remained a problem.[13] Similarly, the 1996 Report of the Parliamentary Commissioner for Administration, whilst acknowledging that the Agency had made "significant progress", observed that this "has not been far enough or fast enough to avoid a great number of people sustaining injustices as a result of maladministration".[14]

All these reports point to error and delay, and to mounting arrears and uncollected maintenance. All express concern that the Agency is providing a poor service to parents. At the same time there has to date been no

[8] *Ibid.*, p.iii, para. 5.
[9] Annual Report 1993/4 . . ., op. cit, p.1.
[10] *The Child Support Agency, Annual Report and Accounts 1994–5*, HC 596, 1995, 1, London: HMSO.
[11] *Annual Report of the Chief Child Support Officer 1995–6*, (1996), London: Stationery Office, foreword.
[12] *Ibid.*, 2.
[13] *Ibid.*, 6.
[14] Parliamentary Commissioner for Administration, Third Report, 1995–6, *Investigation of Complaints against the Child Support Agency* (1996), London: Stationery Office, p. iv, para.13.

independent research into Agency procedures or the experience of its staff.

The Child Support Agency undertakes a number of administrative tasks, including: contacting and tracing absent parents; collecting information from both caring and absent parents; making decisions on 'good cause' and disputed paternity; assessing liability for maintenance; notifying absent parents and caring parents of the assessments; collecting and passing on child support payments; enforcing payment and taking action to recover arrears; reviewing and revising assessments at intervals or when informed of a change of circumstances; liaising with the Benefits Agency; and preparing and presenting appeals.

In order to carry out this work the Agency has developed a complex structure in which local, regional and central administrative units each play a part in processing cases. The key units of organisation are the six regional Child Support Assessment Centres (or CSACs) which between them cover the whole of Great Britain and Northern Ireland. There is also a network of local field offices—usually based on Benefits Agency premises—which support the work of the Assessment Centres.

Agency staff are a mixture of those who have transferred from the Department of Social Security and new recruits. Many of the former had been liable relative officers. A recurrent theme in discussion with this group of experienced staff was their commitment to the rationale for setting up the Child Support Agency, that is to say parents' responsibility to maintain their children irrespective of relationship breakdown. This ideological commitment was less apparent amongst new recruits. We were told that of the Dudley Assessment Centre's initial staff complement 30 per cent were existing Department of Social Security staff and 70 per cent were new recruits. Of the latter, many were in their first job and ill-equipped to cope with the demands placed upon them, for example the need to talk over the telephone to angry or frustrated parents. One mature entrant referred to a 19-year-old colleague as having "too little experience of life . . . to deal with recalcitrant and difficult men on the other end of the telephone". Some field officers were explicitly critical of the recruitment policies of the Agency:

> "They took on brand-new staff into brand-new centres. They were inexperienced with casework and they were almost all very young. They took on too much initially and they didn't admit that they weren't coping. They need an entirely new approach—and some very experienced managers. But the Benefits Agency was loath to lose good staff and so managers were promoted to the CSA and everyone was full of wonderful ideas." (Field officer, Bristol)

Staff training did not begin until early 1993 and was not completed by the time the Agency began its operations.[15] Field staff had between three and four weeks' training while child support officers working within the Assessment Centres had from four to eight weeks. Those staff whom we interviewed acknowledged that the training had been inadequate, particularly for the new recruits who, with no background in social security, lacked the experience and confidence to tackle the work. As one field officer put it to us:

> "These people who came in, 16- and 17-year-olds, had just got no idea, and that was [the CSA's] first downfall. They had got all these people who had six weeks' training but still could not do the work because they had no backup of experience." (Field officer, Dudley)

A child support officer conceded:

> "With the old cases we didn't really know what we were doing . . . people weren't doing everything according to the procedure, because they didn't really know what the procedures were." (Child support officer, Dudley)

In view of the criticism heaped upon the Child Support Agency one might have expected its staff to evince low morale. In fact the mood was surprisingly buoyant in many instances, although a significant minority of staff did appear to be disillusioned. One customer services manager whom we interviewed attributed low morale, where it existed, to three main factors: dissatisfaction with some of the policies that the Agency was required to implement; the level of complaints from the public; and constant staff changes. We ourselves would add to this list by observing that many staff saw their workload as excessive. To the degree that they could never get on top of their cases this must have contributed to stress levels. Indeed it was a theme of many of our conversations with Agency personnel that the staffing complement had been insufficient to enable the Agency to cope with the throughput of work. As it was put to us by one child support officer:

> "We could see there were going to be major problems [when we started] and I don't know why these weren't foreseen at the drafting stage. It just hasn't been thought out properly. . . . If they had started off slowly, given us more time to get on our feet, sort out everything we were doing, rather than taking on such a huge deluge of cases which we can't handle. . . ." (Child support officer, Dudley)

This account of a comprehensive failure to cope with the initial workload was repeated many times and is perhaps best summed up in the words of one business team manager who told us that the Agency was "an absolute bloody shambles" at the outset. He further observed that it

---

[15] Garnham and Knights (1994), 54.

had "been very difficult to get back on track", and that the long delays in processing cases had damaged customer relations.

The Agency has tried a variety of different ways of managing this workload. Originally each person within a business team had a caseload of his or her own and was supposed to see each case through from start to finish. It then became apparent that many staff could not cope with handling all stages of an application. They had insufficient training in many elements of the procedure, with the result that cases were processed too slowly. The operation of the business teams was accordingly altered. Cases were divided into their constituent elements, each of which was assigned to a different member of the business team. This production line style of working, in which one person carries out a particular task before passing the case down the line, was given the label 'functionalisation'. Breaking down the process into its discrete elements was seen as a means of employing relatively unskilled staff and training them quickly in the particular task that they were to perform. However, as child support officers explained to us, there was a down side to functionalisation:

> "You're just juggling and trying to keep them all up in the air, waiting for one to drop . . . it's hard for us when they're shouting at us, screaming 'Why haven't you dealt with my case?' and it's the first time you've looked at it and you don't know anything about it, and they're blaming you for the inaction of the CSAC." (Child support officer, Dudley)

> "When you have one person dabbling in one part and then it gets passed to another person who has a dabble, and then to another person who has a dabble in another part, some of them will be all right but unfortunately a lot of them aren't going to be spot on. Who do you actually blame? Do you blame the one who pushed the button at the end or the one who pushed the button at the start? It isn't a matter of blame, but how do you put it right? How do you go back and say, 'This was done wrong. How can we put it right?' We can't. While functionalisation got the assessments out and the targets up, because that's what our Parliamentary people actually wanted us to do, it's now found that a lot of the cases have got adverse comments by the Central Adjudication Services." (Child support officer, Dudley)

The implication of this and other similar comments was that functionalisation both increased the number of errors (because individual staff did not 'own' a case) and it also made it harder to trace and correct those errors. Indeed it might make it difficult to trace the case at all. Some of the parents whom we interviewed believed that their files had been lost, although it is equally possible that their cases were subject to one of a variety of possible delays, or else that they could not be located quickly enough for the child support officer concerned to respond to a telephone query. But certainly functionalisation did in some instances contribute to lost files. We were ourselves a factor in discovering this, since in some cases where parents had abandoned any attempt to contact the Agency the fact of a file being missing only came to light because we enquired about that case for research purposes. Andrea Koe (case 57) had returned her maintenance assessment form in August 1993. When we interviewed a child support officer about this case in March 1995, her embarrassment was obvious:

"There is a problem with this case—we can't find it. We did a search yesterday but it didn't come to light. It could be absolutely anywhere in the building . . . all I can tell you is that no assessment has been done yet . . . we last worked on the file last August when the absent parent rang us and wanted to know why we needed his partner's details. That was the last we heard of it. We should have done an IMA [interim maintenance assessment] next . . . the service we provide to some customers is absolutely appalling. For example, this case: if I was treated like this I would go up the wall." (Child support officer, Plymouth)

This and other similar stories reveal that the conveyor belt approach is prone to catastrophic failure. More generally, functionalisation appears to have increased delay at every stage following the initial assessment. Even when action is taken on a case and it is passed to the next section, it may then be many months before it works its way back to the top of another in-tray and receives further attention.

Sir Michael Partridge (then Permanent Secretary at the Department of Social Security) acknowledged that functionalisation is "very much a second-best", but argued that it had to be introduced because of "sheer pressure of work".[16] This is doubtless true in part, but Agency staff believed that functionalisation was introduced in order to respond to political pressure to increase the number of initial assessments, principally with a view to achieving benefit savings.

Various changes have since been made within the broad framework of a task-based system. Originally the division of work was geographical; later it was alphabetical. Later still functionalisation was partially replaced by a system in which one team dealt with cases before assessment and another team dealt with whatever happened thereafter—periodic reviews, change of circumstances reviews, and queries.

It was suggested to us that now that most staff had learned their respective responsibilities and were also becoming more familiar with the operation as a whole it might be possible to revert to the original model under which child support officers had their own caseloads for which they were solely responsible. This, it was argued, offered greater job satisfaction. As one field officer told us:

"Originally we were set up functionally, which meant that each person was doing a set bit of the total process . . . but now, because everyone is bored with doing the same bit of work, we've gone back to alphabetical splits so that we

[16] First Report from the Committee of Public Accounts, 1995–6, *Child Support Agency*, HC 31, 1996, London: HMSO, 14.

do the whole work from start to finish, do a bit of everything. But you'll probably find if you went to different offices that there are different setups. It depends on how many staff there are at each one." (Field officer, Edgbaston)

An alternative approach, piloted at the time of our fieldwork at the Hastings Assessment Centre, is termed CAST (Complete Action Service Team).[17] In this system each case is dealt with by a small team, all of whom will in theory be familiar with it and will therefore be able to respond to customer queries, changes of circumstance, or complaints.

It can be seen from this account that the Agency has yet to settle on an organisational system which allows it to deal efficiently and accurately with its workload and which at the same time provides its staff with reasonable job satisfaction. Whether or not the CAST system will allow this to happen remains to be seen.

A related question is whether any of these systems of case management provides reasonable customer access, thereby contributing to better relations between parents and the Agency. At the moment it is our impression that the impersonality of the work not only creates disillusionment among staff; it also contributes to poor customer relations. It was admitted that because nobody 'owns' a case . . . "people have been treated badly . . . there is not the same incentive [to be courteous] when there is a customer on the phone".

In another sense this lack of case ownership may actually protect Agency staff from the pains associated with having responsibility for difficult customers. We were told that disturbing or threatening phone calls were a major source of stress:

"I had a really vile one this morning . . . with some people there's no getting through to them. They won't let you get a word in edgeways. They're not prepared to listen to what you have to say. They're just determined to have a good old shout and a good old swear." (Child support officer, Dudley)

While the Child Support Agency is often characterised as a faceless bureaucracy, some staff have been deeply affected by their contact with members of the public. It is also worth bearing in mind that for field officers this contact may be face-to-face. They may find themselves conducting a home visit to an angry parent. It is unsurprising therefore that the Child Support Agency has suffered absenteeism and high staff turnover. As it was put to us by one child support officer:

"I've never known such wastage of staff . . . they don't seem to be worried about stress management control, when and why people are leaving, and you get so little support from management . . . we are very disillusioned, it's heartbreaking. I go home at the end of the day with a splitting headache . . . and I just

---

[17] See House of Commons Social Security Committee, (1996a) xxi.

worry about the workload . . . a lot of people have gone off on long-term sick because of the stress, which is one of the problems that doesn't seem to be addressed at all . . . we are always understaffed. We've just lost two members of staff and we're only having a replacement for one of them . . . the business teams are undermanned and this is where the bulk of the work is." (Child support officer, Dudley)

The picture we have painted is one of staff who, with exceptions, perceive themselves struggling against the odds within a highly stressful environment. They are the poor bloody infantry, many of them raw recruits with minimal training, set unreasonable targets and caught in the resulting crossfire of official, media and client criticism.

3. PRIORITIES

Given the widespread concern about the time which the Child Support Agency takes to process cases, the question of how it manages this workload and determines priorities within it is of particular interest. In general the Agency claims to take cases in date order. There are however a number of factors which might override this. Parents who contact the Agency frequently, and express their views determinedly, may receive special treatment. One child support officer told us that "perhaps if a caring parent phones up very distressed with financial problems, they may move it up a bit". Another factor which leads to a case being accorded priority is if one of the parents threatens suicide. Cases which involve disputed paternity may also be taken out of strict chronological order. An officer who worked with special cases told us:

"You have to deal with the woman who is distraught, and as in most places if you shout loudest you're going to get dealt with first." (Child support officer, Dudley)

Another way for parents to jump the queue is to enlist the support of their Member of Parliament. Not surprisingly, the Agency has become sensitive to criticism from Westminster. As an illustration of this, when we visited the Dudley Assessment Centre in the summer of 1995 we noticed that the number of queries from MPs dealt with in the preceding week was displayed on a large wall poster, indicating the high priority that these were afforded. Such cases were sent to a Parliamentary Business Unit to be 'fast-tracked' through the entire process. One child support officer told us that involving an MP was the only way in which a case might be dealt with quickly. It is interesting in this context that the Parliamentary Commissioner for Administration severely criticised the Agency for taking almost ten weeks to respond to an enquiry from a particular Member of Parliament.[18] Ten weeks is a mere blink of an eye in comparison with the delays experienced by many parents in their dealings with the Agency.

The claim that cases are in general dealt with in date order has to be set against our understanding of the various systems which have been tried—and later mostly rejected—as a means of managing the Agency's workload. In considering this one must understand that the child support legislation allows for several different kinds of case review. The first and most straightforward of these is the periodic or 'section 16' review. In the early days of the Agency this was meant to be conducted annually, but it is now meant to be held every two years. Secondly, when parents' circumstances change in any way either of them may request a change of circumstances or 'section 17' review. In addition to these reviews there are a great many other reasons why a case might need attention—for example, the deadline for returning information may have passed. Originally the Assessment Centres employed a system of electronic 'alerts' which were designed to warn staff that a case needed attention. We discovered however that only the accounts and debt management sections continued to adhere to this system. All other sections had abandoned it because it was impossible to keep up with the flow of work. As it was explained to us:

"We were reorganising so much, the cases were just getting shoved in drawers and unless something cropped up, a lot of the time nothing happened on them. At one time we just had thousands upon thousands of field cases piled up awaiting action. We just shifted them around from field team to field team". (Child support officer, Plymouth)

"[The system] would churn out a reminder, but basically that's more or less where it stayed. We did get alerts saying it had been another couple of weeks and nothing had happened . . . but we just weren't actioning the alerts in the end. We started to do everything clerically because there were just too many of them. We were getting so behind, we were getting 100 or 200 alerts . . . we were supposed to clear the alerts in the morning before we continued with any new work, but . . . you just couldn't keep on top so they decided to scrap them all in the end . . . there were hundreds and hundreds and they were just blocking up the system, so every few weeks they'd just scrap all the alerts and start again . . ." (Child support officer, Dudley)

Following this debacle a 'brought forward' system was introduced. Each case was given a date at when the officer responsible was meant to review it. Once again however this proved unmanageable:

"And then they went on to this BF [brought forward] system whereby we're told to put dates on the folders and we just date everything when it has to come

[18] Parliamentary Commissioner for Administration, (1995).

up again . . . then of course we got too many of those and we weren't actioning those either." (Child support officer, Dudley)

"When a file is set up it is given BF [brought forward] dates so that cases are actioned fairly. But we have so many cases for each date that in practice the backlog is likely to be another four weeks." (Child support officer, Plymouth)

Both the 'alert' and the 'brought forward' systems are intended to allow cases to be dealt with in date order and so are designed to be fair in that sense. This was not true however of the system adopted in the business teams from June 1995. This is the so-called 'post-driven' system under which a case is given attention only when one of the parties, or someone acting on their behalf, writes to or telephones the Agency. This means that the Agency has become largely dependent on prompts from outside. As one child support officer explained:

"Then it came down to, as soon as somebody phoned in we'd try to action it if it was urgent. And that's what they've done now. We've got to the stage now where unless they actually write in or contact us, we're not dealing with cases at all. . . ." (Child support officer, Dudley)

An inevitable consequence of this 'system' is that staff deal with clients who want progress to be made on their case, for whatever reason. Some child support officers defended this practice, as in the following:

"Essentially you're only dealing with compliant client cases, the ones who want to have action taken, and who do contact us and get the ball rolling . . . it's a way of breaking it down. We can't deal with everyone, and surely it's best to deal with the ones who want to comply than the ones who don't. Meanwhile the others who aren't, are sitting in the files and they're just accumulating with periodic reviews outstanding etc. They're not being touched." (Child support officer, Dudley)

Needless to say, this post-driven system is fundamentally at odds with the principles upon which the Agency is meant to operate. This was recognised by many staff. As one put it to us: "it shouldn't be that the harder you shout, the more you're dealt with quickly". At the same time the system was defended on pragmatic grounds. Anyone who did not telephone or write would be left "until we have spare capacity from post-driven work". But it is difficult to see how this spare capacity will ever be achieved given that staff continue to be overwhelmed by the amount of post coming in:

"I've got so much post I can't keep on top of it. So that's coming in daily and I've got hundreds of cases that need something doing to them on that basis. At the end of the day there's just too much work for the amount of people who are here. We're not giving a very good customer service because there is just too much work." (Child support officer, Dudley)

The Agency's ambition as we understand it is to revert to working off 'alerts'. But without significantly increased resources it seems unlikely that the Assessment Centres will ever get on top of their workloads to the point where they can return to a date-ordered system. It was quite remarkable to come upon this unheralded abdication of the core principles upon which the Agency, and indeed any administrative authority, is meant to operate. The issue is no longer one of error or inefficiency, but of complete abandonment of the principle of effective case management which must be the *sine qua non* of any administrative authority. The Agency has taken to operating in responsive mode. This is an old story, but it is a story associated with the courts (who are content to do nothing unless asked, and who until very recently have accepted no responsibility for case management) rather than of the major state bureaucracies. To understand how fundamental is this departure from established principle, one only has to consider the consequences were the Inland Revenue to conduct itself in like manner. It does not look like a complete breakdown, but in a sense that is precisely what it is.

4. QUALITY VERSUS QUANTITY

When the Agency first started to take on cases, in April 1993, its priority was to process as many cases as possible. All officers working at the Assessment Centres were given weekly targets. They were encouraged not to spend too much time insisting that parents send in all the required information if they (the officers) believed that an approximation would suffice. In order to save time they would make guesses on the basis of what had been supplied. As one field officer explained to us:

> "Originally we were given lots of discretion because . . . they wanted to get fast, so that all that was laid down was put aside and we did not have to follow those guidelines. Like wage slips . . . instead of having to have the five, we could get away with just four or three. So what they wanted was as much work to be processed as quickly as possible." (Field officer, Edgbaston)

As is by now well known, the error rate was high. Following the highly-critical first report by the Chief Child Support Officer,[19] and the appointment of Ann Chant as chief executive following the resignation of Ros Hepplewhite, the emphasis shifted towards maintaining the quality of assessments. At the time of our fieldwork every assessment had to be checked by a supervisor before being sent out, and a proportion of cases were checked again, randomly, on a weekly basis. Those identified as containing errors were returned for recalculation. This change in emphasis was evident to the staff we interviewed:

[19] *Annual Report of the Chief Child Support Officer 1993–4* (1994), London: HMSO.

"... at first the emphasis was more on quantity, but then they said to us: 'hang on, slow down, even if you get less assessments through, they have got to be right'." (Child support officer, Plymouth)

Despite this obviously desirable shift in the direction of greater accuracy of initial assessment, many thousands of cases must now be riddled with historical errors which will require much time and effort to sort out, if in fact these problems ever come to light at all. The pervasive problem of error can be illustrated by the case of Ralph and Anthea Wigley (case 59), where we have the benefit of accounts from both parents and from the Agency officers dealing with the case.

The Wigley case involved a mistake which was noticed too late for it to be corrected, with expensive consequences for Ralph Wigley. Due apparently to misunderstanding rather than deliberate fraud, Anthea Wigley, the parent with care, wrongly claimed an extra £20 exempt income to cover her 'housing costs'. She therefore contributed less to the maintenance requirement than she should have done. Ralph on the other hand was continuing to pay the mortgage on the former matrimonial home, but was unable to offset this against his income. A careful reading of his first maintenance enquiry form should have brought to light the fact that the mortgage payment his ex-wife claimed to be paying was in fact being paid by him. This point was missed, with the result that Ralph's assessment was about £12 a week more than it should have been for a whole year. Understandably, neither parent fully understood the formula, and Ralph did not consider appealing. By the time the error was uncovered it was too late to correct the first year's assessment. The child support officer dealing with the case said of Ralph Wigley: "He could have appealed, but he didn't within the time limit."

In summary, whilst the new emphasis upon quality of assessment is very welcome, the legacy of the Agency's early days lingers on in multitudinous requests for reviews, in appeals, and in the manifold problems of enforcement.

5. THE MOVING TARGET

Any Agency 'case' may involve a multitude of changing circumstances. There is also the possibility—indeed the likelihood—of one or other parent not complying with the demands of the process. Thirdly, there remains—although this is now biennial rather than annual—an obligation for periodic review. Given the huge backlog of work, the Agency finds itself undertaking reviews which are several changes of circumstance out of date. This is quite bewildering for its customers. As one child support officer explained to us:

"In order to do a change of circumstances, there might be an outstanding periodic review which is going to have to be completed before you can look at the change of circumstance. So they say, 'Well, why are you asking me for details for [a previous year] when I want my change of circumstances for now because my wages have been reduced?' It creates so much trouble, having to take this action because we couldn't keep on top of our work before. We're suffering the consequences now . . . and trying to explain this to somebody is very difficult." (Child support officer, Dudley)

Not surprisingly, parents are puzzled to be asked for details of a situation which has long been superseded. Further problems are caused when they receive communications from the Agency which appear to ignore their most recent letters. For example, Richard Timms (case 60) informed the Agency of his change of circumstances in April 1995, and applied for a review pack. In fact he had not received his original assessment until September 1995—but this did not take into account a change of circumstance of which he had informed the Agency in the previous April. Not unreasonably he did not understand that the section 17 change of circumstances review was still pending. He was therefore aggrieved that his changed circumstances had apparently been overlooked. We came across many such examples of Agency staff and parents being at cross purposes, generally as a result of the Agency having been unable to deal with queries and changes as they occurred.

The subsequent confusion could lead to further delay, with the muddle becoming increasingly difficult to sort out. As one child support officer put it:

"You pick up the case because there's a piece of post that comes in to say that today they are notifying you of a change of circumstances; and when you look in the file you find that there are two outstanding changes of circumstance, two outstanding periodic reviews, so you've got months of work to go back over. You can't action that change of circumstances until you've actioned all the outstanding work. It sometimes can be very difficult to . . . piece it all together and it can take a lot of time . . . but you can tie it all together eventually." (Child support officer, Dudley)

The capacity of an administrative authority constantly to keep under review the circumstances of separated parents so as to ensure a fair level of child support at all times was one of the advantages claimed for the Child Support Agency as compared with court-based procedures. This objective has not been realised.

6. ENFORCEMENT STRATEGIES

The Agency has a number of enforcement powers. Essentially these are applicable in two problem areas: the gathering of information and the collection of money.

If an absent parent fails to provide the information required in order to undertake an assessment, the Agency may make an interim assessment set at one-and-a-half times the maintenance requirement. For most absent parents this represents a punitive level of payment. The objective is to secure the return of the maintenance enquiry form so that a full assessment may be made. It would seem that while such interim assessments are commonly issued, no payment is expected from them. The ineffectiveness of such interim assessments is demonstrated by the Gaines case (case 64). Stuart Gaines did not respond to the maintenance enquiry form and so an interim assessment of £136 per week was imposed in December 1994, with an effective date of the previous August. Stuart's maintenance enquiry form arrived at the Assessment Centre in February 1995. The interim maintenance assessment stayed in force until April 1995 but Stuart paid nothing in this period. Asked to comment on this, a child support officer told us: "Normally we find they're not paying". Not paying and, it would seem, not expected to pay. There was no sanction as far as we could tell.

Once the assessment has been completed one might expect the Agency to focus upon the question whether the sum required is in fact being paid. It would appear that during the first few years of the Agency's life there was an almost complete lack of interest in ensuring payment. Several child support officers whom we interviewed acknowledged this, either explicitly or implicitly. Having, as was inevitable, a difficult relationship with absent parents, the Agency then compounded this by failing to secure maintenance for parents with care, thereby frustrating them as well.

The Agency's approach to collecting money reflects a distinction between collecting arrears and ensuring regular payment henceforward. The Agency—unlike many parents with care—does not appear to attach much significance to the payment of arrears: provided the absent parent demonstrates a commitment to pay maintenance henceforward, arrears may be left in abeyance. However, it is not Agency policy to make this fact clear to parents. On the contrary, the standard letter to absent parents (following assessment) demands payment of the often substantial arrears "within 14 days". No information is provided in this letter about possible payment by instalment; nor is it made clear that any voluntary payment made during the initial period should be deducted from the arrears total. This is an obvious failure in customer relations.

If an absent parent continues to avoid payment of child support, then the case will initially be passed to the debt management section. Their first step is to send out a system-generated warning letter, the '801'. This will be followed by another letter, the '769' which asks for immediate contact "to make an agreement, to start paying a regular amount and something towards your arrears". A 'final demand' which warns of a deduction of earnings order (DEO) then follows. This may be supplemented by telephone calls.

In fact the highly-structured, inflexible system of assessment by formula, which is what the Agency is thought to represent, at this point begins to look remarkably ill-defined and discretionary in character. Indeed its practice is reminiscent of the discretion formerly exercised by liable relative officers of the Department of Social Security. This for example is how one officer working in debt management described how agreements were arrived at in respect of arrears:

> "You have to have the maintenance in as assessed and something towards the outstanding balance. So that's basically a decision made on how much there is outstanding, how much he's earning, who's in his household, what his other expenses may be. And that really is a discretionary decision. There are formulae to follow but at the end of the day you have to look at everything that's concerned and make a decision on that basis . . . you'll accept an offer if it seems reasonable, depending on how much they've got to pay off as well . . . the ideal is that within three years it's actually cleared." (Debt management officer, Dudley)

The further the Agency moves towards enforcing payment, the more discretionary its practice appears. The negotiating stance might differ according to whether the absent parent has shown some willingness to co-operate, or perhaps has made a few payments. Even after an arrears agreement has been made, if the absent parent says that he is having difficulty in paying, particularly if he has a second family, the arrears will be looked at again:

> "You have to stop and think, maybe we shouldn't be making so much of the arrears . . . you really have to be more flexible . . . you've just got to have some discretion." (Debt management officer, Dudley)

Those working in the debt management sections tend to claim that non-payment is dealt with quickly; but, as we shall see, this is not the case from the point of view of the parent with care. It is easy to see why this should be: cases go through various stages, with time allowed at each point for the absent parent to respond. Delay is also a function of allowing staff in debt management to exercise discretion:

> "If someone's actually made a weekly contribution, then you telephone them first and ask about their circumstances and explain why you have to do it . . . you do use a certain amount of discretion. You say, well, he has paid maybe half of the maintenance, maybe you should just contact him and say 'You've got to increase your payments', and if you still don't get a response then you do have to push it a little harder, but you don't go in all guns blazing with a 769 every time. You don't always have to have payment by a certain date either. We always tend to ask them when their next payroll is . . . I don't think anyone says

'I want it next week' unless it's somebody who's weekly-paid—then that's different . . . it's not a case of demanding the money now." (Debt management officer, Dudley)

The next step on from debt management is enforcement. Here again there is scope for discretion, and for further delay. Again the absent parent will be given time in which to respond. Thereafter, if payment is still not forthcoming, a Liability Order will be sought from the absent parent's local magistrates' court. This can give rise to various sanctions, including ultimately an application to commit to prison, but as far as we are aware no Agency enforcement section has sought this ultimate sanction. As one of our informants put it:

"The enforcement section hasn't been up and running that long so we're not at the committal stage with any case. Everyone is very nervous about it." (Enforcement officer, Dudley)

At the time of our fieldwork the Agency's enforcement arm was still very much feeling its way. This was particularly apparent in respect of its pursuit of self-employed absent parents. For example, Phil Morris (case 58) had made no more than token payment over two years. He had also delayed sending in his accounts and other information, although eventually an assessment had been made. Then, before anything was paid, Phil's new partner rang the Agency to inform it of a change in their circumstances. A review pack was sent out in December 1994 but not returned until the following March. No effort had been made to pursue this. The business team took no further action on the change of circumstances review until July 1995, when it called for new accounts to be submitted. At the same time the accounts department had been trying to come to an agreement with Phil about what should be paid. He made various promises of payment, but these were not honoured. By July 1995 the arrears had mounted to over £2,000. Only £400 had been paid since the maintenance assessment some two years previously. The officer dealing with this case acknowledged that the enforcement action had been deficient: the final option, she reflected, was court action, but as the caring parent was not complaining (she was in receipt of Income Support) there was no particular incentive to take this step.

It would seem that these rather tentative enforcement strategies offer little advance on the pre-Agency methods of enforcing maintenance through the courts. But to a degree the position is now worse because of the expectations raised by the introduction of the Agency. The Child Support Act 1991 created the expectation on the part of caring parents that the former partner would be forced to pay for his children. As a consequence some parents have pressed harder for payments to be made, and they have been all the more frustrated when nothing has been forthcoming. At the same time absent parents have shown greater reluctance to cooperate than under the court system because the maintenance assessment imposed upon them has usually been at a significantly higher level. The general strategy appears to be to avoid a deduction of earnings order or a liability order if the *threat* of either of these sanctions can bring results. But the effect of this, as one child support officer conceded, is that "people who are honest and are prepared to pay are being nailed, and people who are trying to get away with it are getting away with it".

It is evident that effective enforcement action can take a long time, and it would seem that the Agency did not realise how essential a part of its operation this would prove to be. At the same time, given the hostile political climate, there is a limit to the kind of enforcement action that the Agency can take: it has to be seen to be taking enforcement seriously, but it is constrained by the media outcry that would doubtless follow any draconian action. As with many other agencies charged with regulating areas of social life,[20] the Agency tends to reject automatic use of its enforcement powers in favour of achieving compliance through negotiation and persuasion. To the parent with care, however, this can seem totally ineffectual.

7. OPTING OUT OF THE CHILD SUPPORT AGENCY

It was originally intended that the Child Support Agency should be responsible for all child maintenance applications from April 1996. It is clear, however, that the government got its sums wrong in calculating how many staff would be required to deal with this level of work. As a consequence some existing Income Support claimants have had their cases deferred, while pre-1993 private cases have been postponed indefinitely. This latter development has reinforced the view that the Agency prioritises cases in which the caring parent is in receipt of state benefit. We have already noted that in the vast majority of cases handled by the Agency the parent with care is on benefit, and Agency staff are aware of the political and organisational imperative to achieve benefit savings through their work. One would expect this consideration to influence child support officers in their discretionary decision-making, and we uncovered considerable evidence of this.

For example, a frequently-encountered practical question is that of what should happen when a caring parent comes off benefit before the Agency has finalised the child support arrangements. In these circumstances the Agency only became involved initially because the caring parent was a claimant. We asked one officer whether she would proceed

---

[20] See the discussion by Bell (1994), 90–2.

with the case once it became effectively a private application. She replied:

> "Yes, because she signed the initial application . . . it's up to us to take note (or not) of benefit ceasing, unless she tells us she no longer wants to proceed. It's a matter of discretion for each individual AO [child support officer]. If we do note it, we can ask her 'Do you want to continue?' but we would only close the case if we have her authority to do so . . . a lot of them don't realise that they can stop, or else they think it's automatic that it will stop when they cease to claim benefit." (Child support officer, Plymouth)

We asked further about the precise circumstances in which a child support officer might ask the parent with care whether she wanted to continue with her application. This particular officer was reluctant to be specific, but suggested that consideration would be given to whether there was any likely hardship to the children and whether maintenance might make a difference to the caring parent's income. She also observed that "she might be better off sticking with the court order—which he is paying—than have a higher assessment that he doesn't pay". If there was any chance that the parent with care might wish to drop the application, she would write to her. This was because "it cuts our workload and counts as a concluded case". That is to say, it improves the Agency's statistical returns.

This willingness to drop cases as soon as the status of the parent with care changes from benefit claimant to private applicant is mirrored within the enforcement section of the Agency. As previously noted, the caring parent is given the chance to object to enforcement action. Many parents with care do indeed ask the Agency not to proceed. Requests of this nature from parents who are not on benefit will invariably be granted, following which the case is classified as 'closed'. Benefit claimants would not be afforded the same freedom of manœuvre since in their case the issue of 'good cause' would need to be investigated. It can thus be seen that the broader political context within which Agency officers conduct their work shapes their discretion in particular cases. Whether consciously or not, private applicants are sometimes treated as almost an unwanted distraction from the Agency's core activity of achieving benefit savings.[21]

8. CONCLUSION

It is clear from the account presented in this chapter that the main promises of the switch to an administrative procedure—efficiency,

---

[21] There was the occasional exception to this pattern; for example, one debt management officer told us that she would prioritise private cases since those were the ones in which the parent with care's income might be affected.

effectiveness, and certainty—have not been fulfilled. In practice the Child Support Agency has been overwhelmed by its caseload, overwhelmed by the difficulties of applying a complex formula to the vastly differing and ever-changing circumstances of separated parents, and overwhelmed by the refusal of many parents to cooperate with it in its work.

The government has recognised the problems faced by the Agency and has authorised various measures designed to promote greater efficiency. Many of the measures contained within the 1995 White Paper were aimed at reducing the Agency's workload and limiting the scope for client grievance.[22] Thus the Agency was permitted to defer taking on cases which involved parents who were not in receipt of Income Support, Family Credit, or Disability Working Allowance. Likewise assessment and collection fees were suspended for two years until April 1997, and have now been further suspended to 1999. The Agency meanwhile is said to be giving priority to those cases in which its intervention is likely to make a real difference to the level of maintenance received.[23] It is also, as we have noted, attempting to move from its fragmented "functionalised" way of handling cases towards a form of team processing under which a group of officers have responsibility for all aspects of a given case.[24]

It is possible that these changes will have the desired effect. Nonetheless one may observe that the constant stream of policy and administrative changes since the Agency was set up has left front-line child support officers feeling unable to cope with the pressure. It has also created further scope for bureaucratic error. Measures to ease the situation can always be expected to make matters worse in the short run.

It can be argued that the policy and administrative changes thus far announced amount to little more than tinkering around the edges of the Agency's operation and that what is really required is more fundamental reform. The Chief Child Support Officer has concluded that the only way to achieve acceptable adjudication standards may be to simplify the formula and thus the decision-making process.[25] There are signs of similar thinking within government, although here the motivation is likely to be more complex. For example, the then Secretary of State for Social Security argued in February 1996 that the rules governing entitlement to benefit should be simplified as part of a drive to achieve a 25 per cent cut in administrative costs within the Department of Social Security.[26] Given

[22] Department of Social Security (1995).

[23] Ann Chant, then Chief Executive of the CSA, Evidence to House of Commons Social Security Committee, (1996a) pp. xvi–xvii.

[24] House of Commons Social Security Committee, (1996a).

[25] *Annual Report of the Chief Child Support Officer 1995–6*, (1996), foreword, Central Adjudication Services, London: HMSO.

[26] Department of Social Security, *Improving Decision-making and Appeals in Social Security*, Cmnd 3328, 1996, London: Stationery Office, 67–8.

that subsequent proposals for reform included within their scope the adjudication and administration of child support,[27] it is fair to assume that simplification of the formula is under consideration. The danger is that the government will once again make over-optimistic assumptions about the ability of the Agency to implement its policies.

[27] *Ibid.*, p. iv.

5

The Child Support Agency from the Perspective of Parents

1. INTRODUCTION

"When you read the forms and the books you obviously think you are going to be assisted, but when you return the form it gets passed through so many departments, and along the line it does get lost. It's a slow process, very slow." (Peter Farrow, new partner of Lynn Enderby, case 65)

"I am very satisfied with how this case has been handled. The maintenance assessment was very quick—both parties cooperated. I'd like to see more of them dealt with this quickly." (Child support officer, commenting on case 65)

We have noted the enormous difficulty faced by the Child Support Agency in attempting to cope with its backlog of work. Understandably, Agency staff have lowered their expectations of the length of time it will normally take them to deal with each stage of processing a case. In the Enderby case, for example, it took just over six months from issuing the maintenance assessment form to the announcement of the child support obligation. To a child support officer this was "very quick"; to the parent and her partner with care it was "very slow".

It is interesting to note in this context that measures of client satisfaction with the Agency, arrived at through a series of annual surveys conducted by Market and Opinion Research International (MORI), reveal a satisfaction score of 61 per cent in 1993[1] but only 44 per cent in 1994.[2] One might have expected that the initial high levels of dissatisfaction would be reduced once early teething problems were overcome; instead the level of dissatisfaction appears to have risen. This may in part be due to the fact that the nature of the samples was different. The 1994 survey had a much higher proportion of absent parents and this is likely to have skewed the results. Another possible explanation, supported by our own case data, is that the longer these cases went on, the less tolerant parents became of what they perceived to be poor service. Thus, even where the Agency did improve its performance (as for example by answering the telephone more promptly) its inability to achieve a settled pattern of

---

[1] Speed, Crane and Rudat (1994), 12.
[2] Speed and Seddon (1995), xiii.

maintenance payments was seen, given the length of time involved, to be fundamentally unsatisfactory.

In assessing parents' response it is important to distinguish between criticisms directed at the principles underlying the creation of the Agency or the formula upon which assessment is based and, on the other hand, bureaucratic failure. In general people are able to distinguish process issues from outcome issues. Most of the criticisms which we encountered related to bureaucratic failure rather than to the principles upon which the Agency was meant to operate. This applied particularly to parents with care. Initial support for the Agency often gave way to dis-illusionment as the months dragged by and no progress was made in the assessment and collection of child support.

In conducting our research it was of course important to attempt some forms of cross-checking. We have therefore placed special weight on cases in which we were able to establish points of cross-reference. In some instances this was achieved by examining copies of correspon-dence with the Child Support Agency (provided by our respondents); in others we were able to compare the account given to us by the parent with care with that of the absent parent. But the stories which we are most confident about re-telling are those in which both parents granted us research access so that we were also able to talk to representatives of the Agency. Nineteen cases fell into this category. We believe that this small sample is indicative of the strengths and weaknesses of the Agency's operation. We did not have any cases in which the Agency had sent the maintenance enquiry form to a parent who had died, or to the wrong person altogether, although we are aware that these things have happened on occasion.[3] Rather, the problems experienced by our respondents are those revealed to be widespread in official accounts and reviews of the Agency's performance: excessive delay; failure to respond to correspondence; miscalculation of maintenance and arrears; inade-quate or inappropriate techniques for collecting and verifying informa-tion; and inadequate enforcement.

2. THE STORY OF MALCOLM BRIDLEY AND SELENA ERICSON (CASE 45)

Malcolm Bridley's five-year marriage to Selena Ericson ended in 1985. They had one daughter, Sheree. At the time of our first contact with Malcolm, in July 1994, Sheree was nine years old. Malcolm told us that his post-separation relationship with Selena had been reasonably ami-cable and that they had been able to co-operate over the care of Sheree. An arrangement had developed over the years whereby he had taken on

---

[3] Parliamentary Commissioner for Administration, (1995), 8 and 13.

an increasing role in caring for her to the point where she now spent an equal amount of time with each parent. Each paid the costs associated with caring for Sheree whilst she resided with them, and each paid some additional money into a joint savings account to cover major purchases.

Selena Ericson's status as a benefit claimant triggered the involvement of the Child Support Agency. Under the formula this became a "shared care" case, and Malcolm was defined as the absent parent on the basis that his ex-wife held the Child Benefit book. He was therefore faced with paying child support to his ex-wife even though he felt he had met his obligations by paying for Sheree during the 50 per cent of time when she lived with him. The perceived injustice of this led Malcolm to pursue various avenues in an attempt to avoid additional payment. Some of these methods (such as attempting to come to a private arrangement with his ex-wife whereby he would hold the Child Benefit book and compensate her for any lost benefits) are dealt with in Chapter 9. Here our focus is on Malcolm's dealings with the Agency. His assessment of the level of service he had received was evocative and damning:

> "They are just bastards, they really are, you can never get anywhere. . . . The revolution in the last ten years in advice-giving organisations is that they make themselves accessible and you can get through to advisers and you can talk with them. At the CSA it's exactly the opposite. They have got so much flak down there to stop you getting through to any managers, they defend themselves so much, you can't get through. So you are a completely disempowered person . . ."

This sweeping condemnation was found, however, to hide a much more complex range of experiences. When Malcolm was asked to be more specific, it became clear that his contact with the Agency fell into six distinct phases.

The first consisted of information-gathering by Malcolm prior to the imposition of any formal assessment. This "groundwork", as he described it, was prompted by a telephone call from his ex-wife in April 1994 explaining that she had been asked to authorise Agency intervention and that therefore Malcolm should expect to be approached. He consulted various advice agencies and action groups but found the most useful source of information to be the Agency itself. As he explained:

> "The CSA itself has given me important information. They have explained the rules . . . the best advice I got was from the CSA because I got factual stuff. But clearly the CSA can't advise me to break the rules . . . I phoned the helpline in London and the local one in Bristol . . . I phoned them up and went to meet them and talked with them. This was all on an anonymous basis . . . The CSA I found, when I was making an anonymous enquiry, very helpful."

The second phase began when Malcolm received his maintenance enquiry form in mid-June 1994. Again he was complimentary rather than critical at this point. He found the forms and associated notes of guidance easy to understand, and had no complaints about his treatment by Agency staff when he had telephoned again "just to check some of the rules, details of the form, more procedural issues . . . and also to ask them some further questions: how can I make an appeal, etc." He had told them that he might exceed the seven day deadline imposed for return of the form ". . . and they were happy with that".

It was at this point that things started to go wrong. There was a three month delay before Malcolm received his notice of assessment in mid-September 1994. During this time Malcolm pressed for progress to be made on his case as he wanted to know where he stood in terms of his financial commitments. He also wrote to his MP to query the application of the formula to the special circumstances of his case. She had passed on his five-page letter to the government minister with responsibility for child support. His repeated requests for information brought home to him the compartmentalised nature of the Agency. When we interviewed him in mid-September 1994 his complaints were legion:

"The government minister who is in charge of the CSA can't find my case. I filled out a 35 page document giving more details about me than anybody has had in my life before, and they can't find it! And they can't find it because it goes to the local office and then eventually it goes to Plymouth and before it goes to Plymouth it doesn't get put on the computer and given a number. Up to that point they file it under the person with care's name. Now it is not beyond the wit of information technology to link the two things up. It just astonishes me that I wrote my name and address and everything and sent that, and they are assessing me . . . but they can't find my file. They have found it now because I helped them to find it. I chased the buggers up, nobody else did. And my file has been on somebody's desk for two weeks, doing nothing, just sitting there . . . "

Malcolm's complaints about the Agency appeared to stem primarily from his sense that the rules to be applied were rigid and flawed: "I do really get frustrated in this society when I'm subject to a law to which I cannot find any appeal or any redress. To me, there is a fundamental erosion of a civil right . . . The law makes no accommodation for shared parenting—in our situation, exactly shared care." In truth, many of Malcolm's complaints about Agency staff were about the rules rather than their treatment of him. For example:

"They [CSA staff] are the most uncooperative bunch of people. They're very nice—but you try to get to anyone in authority and you're almost wasting your time. There are questions I want answered, but the front people are no use, they are polite, they're OK, but they're just giving me the stock answers. . . ."

The answer to this of course is that employing a formula to determine child support obligations was always intended to produce "stock answers". Nonetheless Malcolm clung to the belief that there must be some way around the rules if only he could get through to the right person, someone with authority.

> "So you then have to try to get past them [i.e., the 'front people']. I can only start to get past them because I have learnt the names of some managers. I've even got their phone numbers, and so I just say, 'Can I speak to so and so?' That sometimes works. Or I say, 'I'm not putting the phone down till you pass me on.'"

When asked whether he had found the managers more helpful, the pyrrhic nature of these procedural victories became clear.

> "I spoke to one who was helpful, but hasn't actually done anything. She sounded helpful. They always sound helpful, but no action it seems. . . . Again it's Kafka-esque. You go into another room , they are nice to you, you go into another room, but nothing ever happens, and no questions ever get answered."

Malcolm clearly found it difficult to accept that those in managerial positions in the Agency had no more discretion than did child support officers. As the officer we spoke to about this case observed:

> "There was never any question of defining Mr Bridley as the absent parent. It was covered at our basic training: if both parents share care, then the one who has the Child Benefit book is the PWC. There is no flexibility in this."

It was during this third phase that Malcolm wrote letters objecting to the CSA's "nauseating literature". He took exception to being labelled a 'client' (just as he objected to 'absent parent'). He resented too that his wish to pay child support direct was trumped by his ex-wife's request for payments to be made via the Agency. As he put it, "this jargon of me being their client, and customer services and all the rest of it, it's a joke, a very sick joke . . .". In keeping with this he also protested against the imposition of assessment and collection fees for the "service" he had received. The slow or non-response to his stream of letters and telephone calls was a further source of exasperation. Indeed it would appear that by this time the Agency had become a consuming preoccupation for Malcolm: "It's absorbing mental energy and emotional energy enormously. It's extremely stressful."

In mid-September 1994 Malcolm was finally notified of his child support assessment (£36 a week). It is worth summarising the strands that contributed to his sense of injustice at this time: that he had been assessed at all when he was already caring for the child to the same extent as the stipulated parent with care; that the amount demanded from him was too high and bore no relation to the true cost of child support; that the child support he paid would go straight to the government since his ex-wife was on benefits; that he was effectively being asked to maintain his ex-wife many years after the relationship between them was severed; that his child would be worse off since he could no longer afford to contribute directly to the joint fund for her upkeep; that the assessment process had taken so long; and that he was being forced to pay fees to the Agency for their incompetent bungling. Although many of these grievances do not relate directly to the Agency's handling of his case, they affected the way Malcolm responded to his maintenance assessment during a bellicose fourth period of contact with the Agency. He explained to us at this time that whilst he planned to pay the full amount due, he would be withholding the arrears as a way of fighting back, and would continue arguing his case in the meantime. In September 1994 he accordingly made an application for a review as a preliminary step to lodging an appeal. In the application he accepted that the calculation of his assessment was correct, but argued, first, that the formula itself was inherently unjust and, secondly, that procedural impropriety should prevent the Agency enforcing the assessment.

When we next spoke to Malcolm in mid-October 1994 he described himself as having had "a number of skirmishes" and one major argument with the customer services manager of the Agency. The argument had just been an emotional outpouring, however, with no practical consequences: "In a strategic sense, nothing has happened." He had received his bill for arrears which he was supposed to start paying off from November. He was waging what he described as "guerrilla warfare" on that front:

> "I'm trying to argue they shouldn't be looking at cases like mine because I am paying. But their answer is, I should pay because the law says I should pay. I'm also arguing that I can't afford to pay, but will offer to pay off at one pound a week. I have to hold my horses and make reasonable statements, like offering to pay a few pounds a week. But I think they simply can't keep up with the correspondence."

In fact one way to increase the likelihood that the Agency will look at a case is to raise objections or queries. It appears that Malcolm's constant flow of letters ensured that his case was processed more quickly than it would otherwise have been. One indication of this is that the Agency was quick to threaten a deductions of earnings order. By mid-November, Malcolm, now somewhat cowed, had settled into a pattern of paying his weekly assessment plus £30 monthly against his arrears. He explained to us at this time that he did not want the Agency to contact his employer as he worked for a small organisation and it could cause embarrassment. He also felt that he did not want to prejudice his pending tribunal appeal by "fighting on too many fronts at once".

The resulting ceasefire marked the fifth distinct period of Malcolm's contact with the Agency. There were few significant developments over the following six months. Malcolm's application for review was refused, as he had expected, and he duly lodged his appeal in mid-December 1994. By May 1995 it was clear that he was no longer pinning much hope on the tribunal, but saw it primarily as a procedural hoop through which he had to jump: "I confidently expect to lose. But I have to go through this stage before I take it further and can go to my MP and try and change it in other ways."

The appeal, which Malcolm duly lost, was held a couple of weeks later. Our attendance at the hearing enabled us to make contact with Selena Ericson for the first time. Her perception of events, and indeed of the justice of the child support legislation, was fundamentally different from Malcolm's. She told us that the shared care arrangement was a comparatively recent development, and that after she and Malcolm separated he had been awkward when it came to paying any child maintenance. She said that she resented being labelled as "unemployed" by Malcolm in the appeal papers, of being said to be incapable of keeping a job, and of having chosen a "benefit lifestyle". She had required major surgery in 1994 and had to give up work for a time in order to recuperate.

Selena Ericson had nothing against the Agency or the way it had handled her case. She had always co-operated with the Agency and regarded it as helping her in her struggle to make Malcolm pay a more realistic amount towards Sheree's maintenance: "He has always applied a distorted logic to financial matters." She depicted Malcolm as lacking compassion, as chauvinistic, and as needing to win. She also claimed he lied whilst nonetheless convincing himself that what he said was true. He was, she said, the kind of man who liked "to throw all the feathers in the air". The Agency had dealt with her in a straightforward manner, and she strongly supported its intervention. There was, in her view, no substance to Malcolm's allegations of injustice, nor to his claim of injured relationships.

Malcolm was, predictably, disappointed at the outcome of his appeal. However, his ire at this point was largely directed at his ex-wife. He objected to what she had said in the tribunal and to the contents of a letter she had written in response to Malcolm's grounds for appeal. He claimed this correspondence "was disgusting . . . it was factually untrue—a clear attempt on her part to smear me . . . to paint me in the worst possible light".

Malcolm was now faced with filling in an annual review form sent to him by the Agency. He believed (erroneously) that he faced an increase in his assessment because he now lived with a partner. He was planning to minimise the amount of any new assessment by moving out of the house for a few days so that he could say that at the date of completing the annual review form he did not live with her. He told us: "I don't particularly want to lie, but I have to balance up what I win or lose. I will try to get a calculation done and see what it will be."

In mid-September 1995 we conducted our final interview with Malcolm. The ceasefire with the Agency appeared to be over and Malcolm described himself as "moving into a phase of non-compliance". He acknowledged that his income had increased since the last time he had given an account of his finances to the Agency, and that he and his new partner had also realised a sum from the sale of her house. He was determined, however, not to pay any more than he currently paid and so had decided not to fill in the annual review forms he had recently received:

> "The fact that I'm paying money to someone who doesn't work and doesn't bother to work grates on me . . . the thought of transferring money for something I consider unjust causes serious emotional problems . . . They say that if I don't fill in the forms they will go on the existing information, which suits me fine, but they may add thirty per cent on top of that to make me jump."

Malcolm had abandoned any hope of redress from the Agency or from the child support appeal tribunal. He was due to see his MP in a few days' time and was considering an approach to the Equal Opportunities Commission and the European Court of Human Rights. Despite this, he felt that the issue of child support "doesn't dominate my life to the extent it did a year ago".

Almost by accident Malcolm had finally stumbled on a strategy that was likely to pay dividends. For unless his ex-wife raised the issue of Malcolm's change of circumstances it was very unlikely that the Agency would take any further steps in his case, at least for the foreseeable future. Under the post-driven regime of the Agency, Malcolm's failure to return his change of circumstances form would not even be noted, still less acted upon.

This case illustrates well how perceptions of the Agency can change over time and are shaped as much by personality and expectations as by justified grievances. It also illustrates the value of examining the perspectives of others involved in a child support case. Selena Ericson's views were at odds with those of her ex-husband on virtually every issue, including that of the standard of service provided by the Agency. And whereas Malcolm saw the handling of his case as Kafka-esque, to the child support officer whom we interviewed "this was a routine case . . . it was all done very promptly".

3. DELAY

The initial manifestation of the Agency is threatening and formidable. It announces itself with a resounding thud through the letterbox, and the sheer length of the initial forms, plus the speed with which they are required to be returned, creates in the minds of parents an expectation that the Agency will deal with their case in a thorough and speedy fashion. Parents eventually come to realise that these first appearances tend to mislead: the Agency is a tiger with vegetarian instincts.

The first cause for complaint by many parents was the long period of silence which followed the return of their forms to the Agency. In most of the cases which we studied many months elapsed before the Agency took action. Similarly, when queries were raised, answers were slow in coming if they came at all.

As Table 5.1 indicates, we noted twenty-six cases in which the assessment was notified within six months of issuing the maintenance application form, suggesting reasonably prompt action in a significant minority of cases; unfortunately however the majority saw a long period of apparent inactivity following the return of the maintenance application form. This contributed to massive disillusionment on the part of parents with care.

Table 5.1 Period from issuing maintenance application form to notifying parents of assessment[4]

Less than six months	26	31 %
Between six and twelve months	22	26 %
Between one and two years	12	14 %
Over two years	1	1 %
No assessment within the research period	23	27 %
TOTAL	84	

From the perspective of a parent with care who stands to gain financially from the operation of the child support legislation (a rare bird, as we have explained) the crucial step is the issuing of the maintenance enquiry form to the absent parent. In theory any delay after that point should not reduce the absent parent's financial liabilities since, unless a court order for maintenance is already in force, the assessment is back-dated to "the effective date", this being one working day after despatch of the mainte-

---

[4] We have excluded from this Table all cases in respect of which this information was unavailable.

nance enquiry form. It can therefore be particularly upsetting if it takes many months to get to that stage. Lynette Bass (case 108) first contacted the Agency in June 1993, but the maintenance enquiry form was not sent to her husband until January 1994. As she put it: "They lost me that whole eight months' maintenance because it can't be back-dated." This was by no means unusual, as was confirmed by the child support officer in case 64 who told us that the eleven months' delay in issuing a maintenance enquiry form in that case "was not unusual at that point".

Our final example on the theme of delay involves Anthea Wigley, the parent with care in case 59. She was contacted by the Agency immediately following her application for Family Credit. She returned the maintenance application form promptly but did not hear from the Agency for over a year. As she observed:

> "They rush this form to you within one or two weeks of the Family Credit form as if there's some huge emergency, and then not to hear anything for 12 months is absolutely extraordinary. If I was like that in my job, I'd be out."

4. TARGETING

There were a few cases within our sample in which the Agency had acted with commendable speed, as in case 61 where the total length of time from issuing the maintenance application to notifying the parents of the child support obligation was less than three months. In this case the carer was in receipt of Income Support and the absent parent was in employment, tempting one to conclude that the Treasury interest in having such cases pursued may have been a factor in the quick turnaround. Some parents with care whom we interviewed contrasted the treatment of their self-employed ex-husband with the approach adopted towards their new partner who was salaried. As it was put by Cheryl Gaines (parent with care, case 64): "They go for the easy ones, the naval people, the police." This was likewise the view of Alec Morley, absent parent in case 62:

> "I know that targets are being placed on the Agency to bring back money that has been paid out to unemployed people claiming benefit. Now one of the targets, and let's face it I am an easy target, is 'OK, this guy has got a regular income, he earns £1,200 a month, let's go for it'."

Our respondents were less aware of the fact that a significant proportion of all Agency assessments are made against the softest targets of all, those absent parents who are themselves in receipt of state benefit. These parents are required to pay the minimum child support contribution, thereby helping the Agency to meet its performance targets. Thus, of 46,000 assessments completed between April and August 1995, 20,700—45 per cent of the total—were for £2.35 per week or less.[5]

It is now widely accepted that by making benefit savings a key target for the Agency in its early days, the government created a sense of injustice amongst absent parents and their new families. As it was observed by the Social Security Committee in January 1996:

> "In order to fulfil the target set by the government it is in the Agency's interest to pick on the soft targets amongst those groups from whom it is charged to collect maintenance . . . it is not action against claimants, or parents who are already paying some maintenance, which is most demanded. It is, rather, action against those who are allowed to cock a snook at the Agency and thereby tax-payers by refusing to fill in and return the first communication sent to them by the Child Support Agency . . . a re-ordering of their goals . . . [would] strike a note with the electorate that the Agency was concerned about enforcing public perceptions of fairness."[6]

The Agency's business plan for 1995–6 indicated that the reduction of expenditure on social security benefits was no longer to be a target. It remains to be seen whether this shift in policy will increase public support for, and co-operation with, the Agency.

5. PRESSURE FROM PARENTS

The impression of parents which one might glean from some media and official accounts is that they are organised saboteurs, frustrating the Agency at every turn. But we found that some 'clients' did their best to move their cases through the system. This was not only true of parents with care: absent parents also spoke of their efforts to clarify their obligations.

Peter Farrow, the parent whom we quoted at the beginning of this chapter, had experience of the Agency both as an absent parent and as the new partner of a parent with care. He kept a diary of all his contacts with the Agency. He also made a point of noting the name and title of whoever he spoke to, and quickly learnt his way around the Agency's compartmentalised system. Six weeks after his partner, Lynn, sent in her maintenance application form he made his first telephone call to the business team dealing with the case and was told that the maintenance enquiry form would be sent to Lynn's ex-husband "shortly". In fact it took another six weeks and a further three phone calls from Peter (including one to the customer services manager) before the business team sent the maintenance enquiry form. A month later Peter rang to

---

[5] House of Commons Social Security Committee, (1996a) xi.
[6] *Ibid.*

check on progress. The maintenance enquiry form had by that stage been returned. It then took a further nine weeks, and a further six telephone calls from Peter, before the maintenance obligation was notified to both parents. The whole process took just over six months and it is probable that without the eleven phone calls from Peter it would have taken somewhat longer. Other parents whom we interviewed had found it difficult to make phone contact at all. One told us: "I tried for three hours yesterday and I tried again just before you came. It's engaged all the time."

Conventional bureaucratic wisdom holds that whereas queries made over the phone can be ignored and their existence later denied, putting something in writing produces results. This appears not to be true of the Child Support Agency. In many of the cases which we followed we were told that the Agency had failed to acknowledge letters and certainly had not responded in a constructive manner.

Equally, we came across cases in which the Agency had acted efficiently. An example is case 61 where Pam Aristides's Income Support was cut by the amount which she was supposed to be receiving as child support from her former husband. She was left short of money when the maintenance payments failed to arrive. She rang the Agency and a child support officer immediately arranged for her Income Support to be restored and for all future maintenance payments to be made to the Agency rather than to her. This was confirmed by letter. Pam thought that the child support officer concerned had been "really good, very pleasant, very helpful". Similarly her ex-husband had found the Agency to be "brilliant on the phone . . . I can't really fault them. A very well-balanced organisation." If the Agency could operate in this manner in the majority of its cases it would no doubt come to enjoy a strong measure of public support.

Some of our respondents had learned the value of enlisting the support of their Member of Parliament. We have already noted the value of an MP's involvement. When we approached the Plymouth office to arrange an interview concerning case 108 we were told that the file was being held at Lytham St. Anne's because "there is an MP involved . . . therefore it can't be released as it's very important that it be done quickly".

But we observed other cases in which neither parent made any effort to contact the Agency over a period of many months, the result of which seemed to be that if they did not trouble the Agency, it would not trouble them. There was no stimulus to prod this 'post-driven' organisation into action. Thus in case 64 there was a delay of eleven months between Cheryl Gaines returning her maintenance assessment form and her ex-husband receiving the maintenance enquiry form. When she eventually telephoned she found:

"Nothing has been done, absolutely nothing. The guy on the phone said to me 'Why doesn't your ex-husband send the forms in?' I said 'I've told you that he will not because he feels that if he doesn't, you're not going to bother—and he doesn't bother.' I'm going to pester them now. I think I've been pretty good but now I'm going to ring them all the time. I wasn't one of those women who kept on ringing every day or anything like that, but I'm going to now."

Within a month of Cheryl having adopted this strategy an interim maintenance assessment had been imposed, and this in turn had prompted the return of the maintenance enquiry form. A maintenance assessment was then calculated, but still no child support was forthcoming and arrears had mounted to £6,000 when we interviewed a child support officer about the case. She told us: "The debt management section are about to impose a DEO [deduction of earnings order]. We would have got round to it eventually, but probably not yet if she hadn't complained." Almost two years after Cheryl first applied to the Agency, she received her first payment of child support.

Because the Agency may take no action in a given case for a long period, and because it appears to respond to prompting from parents, its practice fails to reflect one of the supposed benefits of administrative authority—the so-called 'arm's length' principle. That is to say, the creation of the Agency should have enabled parents with care to obtain a fair level of maintenance without having to take any steps in person. It is the Agency that conducts the assessment and which is responsible for enforcement. But the arm's length principle does not seem to determine practice. For example, we discovered that the Agency might inform the absent parent that it was only acting because under pressure from the parent with care. Cheryl Gaines (case 64) alleged that such a breach of confidentiality had occurred in her case. It seemed almost as if the Agency was itself seeking to operate at 'arm's length', putting the responsibility for its actions on the parent with care. The breach of confidentiality may be treated as a separate—albeit no less serious—issue, but what we are seeking to highlight here is the Agency's failure to operate independently, in accordance with its own rules and procedures. Instead it responds to pressure from parents—a characteristic which should not in principle be associated with an administrative authority.

Of course this is not to say that because parents badger the Agency they always do so effectively. They face the fundamental difficulty that many of the issues which they raise are of no relevance as far as the Agency is concerned. The formula means that many justice-related points have no bearing on the assessment. As a consequence we commonly found that the occasional nugget of legitimate grievance would be lost amidst a mass of deeply-felt, floridly-expressed but sadly irrelevant verbiage. Alec Morley (absent parent, case 62) provides one example of this. He bombarded the Agency with complaints about his assessment, one of which was a legitimate and pertinent query about the effective date employed when calculating his arrears. This was missed within the Agency. The child support officer whom we interviewed told us: "He keeps writing to Customer Services, but we don't know why." It was not until the matter went to a tribunal (eighteen months after the maintenance assessment form was issued) that the issue concerning the effective date was finally resolved in Alex Morley's favour.

6. CONTACTING THE RIGHT PERSON

Even those parents who made a point of asking for the name of the child support officer dealing with their case often found it difficult to establish a productive relationship with a member of the Agency staff. In their experience staff turnover at the Agency was such that it was not possible to have meaningful contact with one person over a period of time. A helpful member of staff might be encountered, but then that person would move on and be replaced by someone who appeared to lack knowledge of the case. We have already noted that as a consequence of 'functionalisation' the Agency operates in compartmentalised fashion. The steps requiring to be taken in a particular case are undertaken by a series of child support officers, none of whom need talk to one another. Functionalisation was criticised by some staff, but this was as nothing compared with the views of parents on the same subject. When parents tried to telephone to discover what was happening in their cases, they might be passed from one department to another. As Peter Farrow (new partner, case 65) put it to us:

> "It's all over the place. I mean, you're speaking to one and they say 'I have to pass you to another department.' You might wait five minutes. You get through and they say 'I'm sorry I don't know anything about your case'."

This problem extends to interviews conducted by field officers. One might have thought that these would provide a way in which misunderstandings could be cleared up. But because field officers usually know nothing about a case for which an interview has been arranged, they can only act as an intermediary. As it was put to us by Brett Enderby (case 65):

> "The person I spoke to said she didn't do the assessments anyway, so she just took my points down and sent them off to Plymouth. It was a waste of time."

Child support officers whom we interviewed conceded that parents who telephoned might fail to secure an informed response. A natural response to these frustrations is to try to speak to someone more senior. As we saw in the Malcolm Bridley case-study, there is little to be gained in speaking to line managers if the object is to avoid strict application of the formula. But many parents simply want to see their cases processed more quickly, and here the tactic of asking to speak to someone more senior can pay dividends. Lynn Enderby (parent with care, case 65) claimed:

> "The only way of getting anything is by going higher all the time. If you can get hold of someone who knows what they are talking about, like a manager or a supervisor, you do get better results. Once you've got a name and you can keep getting in contact with them, it helps."

7. RESISTANCE

Whereas the Australian child support scheme assesses liability on the basis of information already supplied to the tax authorities, the Agency has to start from scratch.[7] It relies on the co-operation of parents in returning their maintenance application forms and maintenance enquiry forms, and in supplying details of income and expenditure. The refusal of many parents to do these things—or their failure to do them promptly—has contributed significantly to the Agency's workload and to its inability to meet its targets. Such tactics have been well chronicled in the media and in official reports. We too came across numerous examples of parental resistance. For example, in case 58 the absent parent, Phil Morris, took three weeks to return a partially completed mainte-nance enquiry form, a further nine weeks to respond to a request for details of his self-employment, and a further three months to return information about his mortgage. Even then he failed to provide verifica-tion of his endowment policy, thus causing further delay. Eventually, some eight months later, the Agency sent out the assessment. Phil's new partner told us: "I've really got no complaints about the Agency. A bit slow, I must admit, but then that's been in our favour really."

Thereafter Phil Morris resisted paying the assessment of £313 a month. He telephoned the Agency to say he could not afford that amount but that he would pay what he could. He also claimed to have suffered a sub-stantial drop in income since completing his maintenance enquiry form. The accounts department engineered an agreement with Phil whereby he would pay a reduced figure. At the same time a change of circum-stances review form was despatched to him. This was not returned for a further three months. Meanwhile Phil did not honour his agreement to pay a revised monthly amount. Since a deduction of earnings order was not an option in his case, the Agency was left with the possibility of County Court action.[8] This step had not been taken at the conclusion of

---

[7] Eekelaar (1991), 517.

[8] See now Child Support Act 1991, s. 33(5), inserted by Child Support Act 1995, Sched.3, para. 10.

our fieldwork. A child support officer commented: "What we've done, we've done correctly, but we've done it slowly. Maybe he has buried his head in the sand and hoped it will go away." This would appear to be one of those occasions, rare in life but not so uncommon with the Agency, when burying one's head in the sand does indeed result in the offending object "going away". Phil Morris meanwhile told us that he was paying £100 a month "just to keep them quiet . . . I'm going to carry on paying and hope for the best". This level of payment was slightly less than Phil had previously paid under a court order, and considerably less than he acknowledged would have been a fair amount. He had learned that the Agency lacked effective power when it came to enforcing payments against the self-employed, and he was prepared to take advantage of it.

8. THE TOOTHLESS DRAGON (OR VEGETARIAN TIGER)

The difficulties caused by the reluctance or inability of some parents to provide the information required by the Agency are compounded by problems in verifying whatever information is supplied. Often one parent will allege that the other has not given a complete account of his or her financial circumstances and will demand that the Agency launch an investigation. Section 15 of the Child Support Act 1991 confers a power on inspectors to enter places of work and obtain such information and documents as the inspector may reasonably require. Whilst there exists therefore the possibility that the Agency will authorise inspection of the absent parent's accounts, this seems to be regarded as an exceptional rather than a standard course of action. We encountered several instances of a failure to investigate what, in the view of the caring parent, were blatantly misleading statements.

A difficulty needing to be overcome by any mechanism designed to reallocate financial resources on relationship breakdown is the parties' capacity to manipulate or conceal those resources. The discretionary model operated by lawyers prior to the advent of the CSA did not overcome this problem.[9] Considerations both of cost and of the need to limit delay led courts (and opposing legal advisers) to tolerate some degree of concealment. In theory solicitors had the power to pursue full disclosure through interlocutory applications and, again in theory, the court had draconian powers to enforce its own procedural orders. So whilst either party might be able to get away with some measure of concealment, solicitors could claim that for the most part they succeeded in exposing (and remedying) any flagrant attempts to conceal significant assets.

[9] Davis, Cretney and Collins (1994); Davis (1994).

When the Child Support Agency was mooted many critics predicted that it would be unable to satisfy parents of the fairness of its operations because it lacked the resources to go behind whatever information was provided to it. Our research has confirmed this to be the case. What is more, it strongly suggests that the Agency is *more* vulnerable to these manipulations than are the courts, where one would normally expect the applicant to be legally advised.

Some parents, thanks to their previous experience of divorce, were able to compare the two systems. This was Virginia Preston's account (case 81):

> "I had a divorce that took a full year to have everything tied up. I had five or six different solicitors through them leaving the firm or changing offices. So solic-itor-wise I didn't have a good deal, but I was quite happy with the judge's deci-sion. You have to swear an affidavit, and as I'd seen his before, I could query anything and get it settled before the court. But with the CSA, I don't know the information that has been given, the CSA won't investigate it, so basically if you've got an employer who is quite happy to lie for you and fiddle wage slips it is quite possible to alter the outcome. . . . They basically say you have to prove it before they can act. Whereas when you have solicitors working for you, you've got them to and fro between the two, and you know what's going on."

This theme of the Agency's inability or reluctance to go behind the statement of income supplied to it by absent parents is fundamental to our assessment of its effectiveness.[10] When determining financial oblig-ation upon relationship breakdown there is an overriding need to obtain a full and accurate account of the parties' financial circumstances even where one (or both) is reluctant to provide this. There was a complete failure to grapple with this issue in the debate preceding the Child Support Act 1991 even though it had lain at the heart of the practice of private family law.

This lack of investigative capacity is consistent with the parallel failure to take effective action against parents who offer a more flagrant chal-lenge to the Agency by simply failing to supply the information requested of them. However threatening the Agency might appear in its initial pre-sentation to parents, our respondents found that if they held their nerve and their tongue these threats were seldom implemented. Thus, Gareth Milton (absent parent, case 63) was at first quite unnerved by the peri-odic review form which he received. As he put it to us:

> "It's always on my mind—when I got that form through last week, I got really panicky and I didn't know what to do. They are really scary forms they send you."

However Gareth was not scared for long. When we talked to him some months later he was in chipper mood:

[10] See further discussion in Ch. 8.

"To me, the CSA's got nothing to do with us at all. I don't bother with them at all but they keep sending me hassle letters and all this . . . I just get their letters, read it, chuck it . . . they've got no hold over me."

Since Gareth had been underpaying child support for some eighteen months by the time of this interview but had yet to receive anything other than a warning letter (notifying him of outstanding arrears of £4,600) it is not surprising that he had learned not to fear the Agency. It is doubtful whether the non-paying absent parents whom we encountered will ever be brought to book.

9. ARREARS

Because child support is payable from the day after the maintenance enquiry form is sent to the absent parent, substantial arrears may have built up by the time parents are notified of the assessment. Thereafter, arrears may accrue because payment is not made in the amount ordered. To parents with care it often appeared that the Agency was quite unconcerned about arrears. In case 63, referred to above, Gareth Milton opted to pay maintenance direct to the parent with care (not, as ordered, to the Agency direct) and at a much lower level than required. Anna Milton told us in September 1994 that she had complained repeatedly to the Agency about this. Eventually a supervisor told her that something would be done:

"She told me they would do him a letter, saying what was due, saying how much arrears, and he would get two weeks to reply to that and if he didn't reply they would send a final warning letter and then it would be taken out of his wages."

This sounded promising. However when we spoke to Anna some six months later disillusionment had set in: "I haven't heard anything, not anything, and I've just given up now to be honest." When we spoke to a child support officer about this case in July 1995 we learnt that the only action taken on the arrears had been a letter sent to Gareth in early May (that is to say, seven months after Anna had been promised swift action). The £4,600 arrears dated back to February 1994. Our last telephone call to Anna revealed that she had given up further contact with the Agency, preferring a regular but lower payment of child support to the stress involved in seeking to have a higher level of maintenance enforced by the Agency. This would suggest that the private bargaining model of determining child maintenance is as much a feature now as it ever was, with 'authority' still a distant spectre for many parents.[11]

[11] See further Ch. 9.

10. FROM FORMULAIC PRECISION TO DISCRETIONARY ROUGH JUSTICE

A feature of the way in which divorce courts handled child maintenance was their practice of consolidating the various claims made by the parents before them—that is to say, they were prepared, in the course of the one hearing, to reassess the maintenance obligation, to review arrears, and to make a new consolidating order. Typically, they sought to make an order which would achieve regular maintenance payments in the future, rather than trying to calculate how much was owed over various periods in the past. Under this rather rough and ready approach to the maintenance issue it was quite common for arrears to be written off. Arguably child maintenance was downplayed as an issue, and certainly the justice meted out was approximate, but courts' willingness to consolidate meant that everything was brought up to date. By contrast, the Agency operates in classic bureaucratic mode—each decision taken is regarded as separate from every other decision in that same case. Everything has to be done precisely within the terms of the formula, with each review being treated as entirely distinct: there is no attempt to consolidate. In theory the maintenance obligation should by this means be assessed accurately at each stage, with every significant 'change of circumstance' leading to a modified assessment. But such an outcome is only possible if the Agency is on top of its work and able to deal promptly with each separate application. This is not the way things have turned out.

The inability of the Agency to process its backlog of review applications and new claims has meant that it can be several reviews behind in any given case. This means that the same absent parent can be both owing arrears (from the first assessment) and yet have made an overpayment of child support because a change of circumstances review has been delayed or not yet effected. This in turn generates further work. There is now official recognition of the counter-productive effects of the Agency's fragmented decision-making processes. The 1995 White Paper *Improving Child Support* stated that where the Agency was responsible for delay in setting maintenance, consideration would be given to not enforcing more than six months' worth of arrears provided the absent parent gave a commitment to meet his or her ongoing liability.[12]

11. ACCOUNTABILITY

It has been argued by Mashaw[13] that the justice of an administrative system depends upon "those qualities of a decision process that provide

[12] Department of Social Security (1995) 8-9.
[13] Mashaw (1983),24–5.

arguments for the acceptability of its decision". In applying Mashaw's concept of administrative justice to the British social security system, Sainsbury[14] identifies accuracy of decision-making and a fair procedure as the primary such arguments. Fairness and accuracy, in turn, require that claimants be allowed to participate in the decision-making process. This assists the collection of information relevant to the decision and can also "serve to convince individuals that a decision is accurate in their particular circumstances". It is also important that claimants understand the reason for a decision.[15]

It is apparent that the Child Support Agency has not met these criteria. The experience of Fred Winsford (absent parent, case 40) provides one illustration of this. Fred received several letters from the Agency between August 1993 and March 1994, each citing different sums in respect of which he was said to be in arrears. He was not given an explanation of how these figures were arrived at, nor why they changed from month to month. This was despite several requests for clarification. This was his comment upon receiving one such letter:

> "This £600-odd quid, it was just a bombshell. I thought 'What the hell does that mean?' I tried to contact them and I finally spoke to a young woman who could offer no explanation. She promised to ring back but there was no response at all. I mean, if somebody says to you 'You owe £600', they've got to offer a reason. And this organisation couldn't."

It was a further ten weeks, during which time Fred received another unexplained demand for arrears, this time for £413.96, before he was finally given a written breakdown of payments he had made. This showed that there was a balance of just £51.10 outstanding. The value of explanation both to the client and to the Agency may be inferred from Fred's observations in response to this:

> "That breakdown was true because there were certain parts of my interpretation that were wrong. I admit that I sometimes make an error, but when I see it I accept it. So that breakdown, as far as I follow it I accept it. I followed it carefully, and they were correct."

These difficulties reflect in part the complexity of the Agency formula—a complexity which is not a feature of other jurisdictions. The fact that the calculations are impenetrable to most parents undermines any attempt which the Agency might make to render itself more accountable. The complexity of the system is designed to achieve fair outcomes, but in the end it has proved one of the main factors undermining both the effectiveness of the Agency and confidence in its operations.

---

[14] Sainsbury (1994b), 304.
[15] *Ibid.*, 305.

12. CONCLUSION

Redistributing income between parents, and between parents and the Treasury, to the extent envisaged under the child support legislation was bound to lead to friction between the Agency and some parents. There have been reports of death threats as well as routine day-to-day abuse of Agency staff. It should not be assumed that it is possible to devise a system that would deal with child support to the satisfaction of all or even most parents. Nor should it be forgotten that the people whom we interviewed often had very negative things to say about the former court-based system for dealing with financial issues on relationship breakdown. Nevertheless the gains that it was hoped might follow from the switch from a lawyer-led system to an administrative one have clearly not been realised. These aspirations might be summarised as greater efficiency and consistency of approach, combined with a raising of child support payments to a more realistic level. The reality has been a slow and complex process which may indeed produce assessments more in line with the true costs of child support but which does so in such a fragmented and error-prone fashion that it can take several years before a settled pattern of child support payments is achieved. And of course this is exacerbated by parental resistance which was always going to be a feature of any more thoroughgoing attempt to extract large amounts of maintenance from absent parents. Meanwhile the Agency has found itself caught in a vicious circle whereby its inability to process its workload in a timely manner has led many parents to lose patience and register further complaints and appeals, which in turn have led to more work and still longer delays in processing cases.

As previously discussed, the government has taken a number of steps which are designed to ease the workload of the Agency and to promote a more efficient service. It should however be borne in mind that there is a new factor in the equation which was not present at the inception of the Agency. This is that parents have become familiar with the ways of this organisation and have learned that in many cases they can thwart or delay its attempts to assess and enforce child support obligations. It will take time to convince these people that the Agency really has changed – that it can do business and that it means business.

6

Redressing Grievances through Second-Tier Reviews

1. INTRODUCTION

This chapter is concerned with the Child Support Agency's system of internal reviews, and with the relationship between these and the child support appeal tribunals. Nearly all state agencies operate such internal reviews and in many instances the resulting decisions carry a further right of appeal to an independent tribunal.[1] What is unusual about decisions taken under the child support scheme is that they may lead to one private citizen benefiting at the expense of another. Accordingly, at every stage in the process the interests of *both* parents must be taken into account. This naturally adds to the complexity of the procedures and creates the potential for the kinds of delay and administrative breakdown that we have previously documented in relation to assessment and enforcement.

It is necessary to begin by distinguishing the formal redress procedures within the child support scheme from the mechanisms for responding to complaints which we discussed in the last two chapters. The type of grievance procedure available depends on the subject of the complaint. Certain decisions made by Child Support Agency staff are taken "on behalf of the Secretary of State for Social Security", whereas others are taken by Agency staff "acting as child support officers". Generally, there are formal rights of appeal against the latter, but not against the former.

Secretary of State decisions typically concern the way in which a case is handled, especially in the areas of information gathering, collection, and enforcement. Somewhat confusingly, Secretary of State decisions can be taken by people who, wearing another hat, are child support officers.[2] The redress available to a client in respect of a Secretary of State's decision is to ask the Child Support Agency to reconsider, or alternatively

---

[1] For a general survey see Lewis and Birkinshaw (1993).

[2] Child Support Act 1991, s.13(1)(b). For critical discussion of this division of decision-making responsibility see Partington (1991) and Baldwin, Wikeley and Young (1992), 29–31. Under the Social Security Act 1998 all first tier decisions will be taken by the Secretary of State, which has raised concerns about the quality and independence of such adjudication: see Adler and Sainsbury (1998).

to make a complaint to the customer services manager of the office concerned. As we saw in the previous chapter, parents encountered difficulty in having their complaints dealt with effectively in this way. Short
of judicial review, however, no formal method of redress was available to
them as an alternative.

Child support officers may be thought of as representing the first stage
in the adjudicative machinery created by the Child Support Act 1991.[3]
These officers are charged with calculating assessments, carrying out
change of circumstances reviews, and deciding whether to cancel an
assessment. Once a child support officer has taken a decision, it cannot
be overturned by a superior within the Child Support Agency. Such decisions may only be changed on review by another child support officer, or
through an appeal to a child support appeal tribunal.[4] In this chapter our
focus is on the grievance procedures that apply where a decision of a
child support officer is challenged.

In preceding chapters we have noted various administrative failings of
the Child Support Agency. But of course efficiency and cost-effectiveness
were very much in the minds of policy-makers when they designed the
child support scheme. The former court system, with its attendant legal
aid costs, was seen as expensive, slow, and inconsistent in its results.
Partly as a reaction to that, and partly in keeping with a move away from
discretion within the field of social security more generally,[5] the child
support scheme was designed to minimise discretionary decision-
making. In its idealised form the job of child support officers is simply to
collect information and enter it into a computer which will then produce
an assessment according to a formula. So in comparison with what had
gone before the new system was intended to operate quickly, efficiently
and cheaply. These goals would be threatened, however, if parents were
afforded extensive rights of appeal. This explains why an appeal cannot
succeed on the ground that a child support assessment is causing exceptional hardship, and why, generally speaking, there is little scope within
the child support scheme for parents to avoid the rigours of the formula
employed.[6] It would, however, have appeared a denial of justice to provide *no* right of appeal (other than through the residual and expensive
remedy of judicial review).[7] The solution adopted was to create a two-

    [3] Child Support Act 1991, s.13(1) and (2).
    [4] *Ibid.*, s.13(3) and (4).
    [5] On this see Baldwin, Wikeley and Young (1992), 7–12.
    [6] Since the fieldwork for this research was completed, the Child Support Act 1995 has
allowed for "departures" to be made from the formula in a limited number of specified situations. See further Ch. 2.
    [7] As the White Paper which preceded the Child Support Act 1991 put it, "There must,
of course, be a right of appeal if one of the parties to the assessment made believes the
decision to be mistaken": Department of Social Security (1990), vol.1, 25.

step[8] system of internal review and external appeal within which challenges are permitted only on narrowly defined grounds.

There are in fact four main types of internal 'review'.[9] First, there is the s.16 periodic review which examines whether the financial circumstances of the parents have changed such that the assessment should be revised.[10] This review was originally supposed to take place on an annual basis, but now is scheduled biennially.[11] Secondly, there is the section 17 change of circumstances review which can be initiated by either parent.[12] If the change in circumstances leads to an assessment which differs by at least £10 per week from the original assessment, then the new figure will be implemented[13]; otherwise, the original assessment remains in force. Thirdly, there is the section 18 second-tier review, which is implemented following a challenge by one of the parents to a decision made by a child support officer. Finally, there is the section 19 review, which enables a child support officer to review a decision of his or her own motion.[14] Only the section 18 review should properly be regarded as part of the adjudicative machinery for redressing grievances (hence its tag within the Child Support Agency as a 'second-tier review'). The other types of review are better treated as part of the administrative process for arriving at correct assessments. So it is that within the regional Child Support Assessment Centres second-tier reviews are conducted by a specialist reviews section whereas all other reviews are conducted by the Business Teams responsible for the original assessment. Whether the Agency's clients appreciate the distinctions between the various forms of review is a matter considered further below.

The section 18 review is a creature of some complexity.[15] It is typically initiated by a request from either parent for the revision of a child support assessment.[16] The reviewing exercise must be carried out by a

[8] A child support officer's decision to issue a reduced benefit directive can, uniquely, be appealed direct to a child support appeal tribunal without need for a prior review : Child Support Act 1991, s.46(7).

[9] In addition to the four types of review listed here, a child support officer may "set aside" (or cancel) a decision in the interests of justice: Child Support (Maintenance Assessment Procedure) Regulations 1992, S.I. 1992 No. 1813, reg. 55. These arrangements are modified by the Social Security Act 1998.

[10] Child Support Act 1991, s.16.

[11] Child Support (Maintenance Assessment Procedure) Regulations 1992, S.I. 1992 No. 1813, reg. 17, as amended by Child Support and Income Support (Amendment) Regulations 1995, S.I. 1995 No. 1045, regs.34 and 37.

[12] Child Support Act 1991, s.17.

[13] In some situations the difference may be less than £10. See further Knights and Cox (1997), 343–4.

[14] Child Support Act 1991, s.19. This can be on the ground of a change of circumstances, or on the ground of a mistake of law or fact in the original assessment.

[15] See Jacobs and Douglas (1997) for an exhaustive analysis. Only a brief outline is attempted here.

[16] Some other types of decision taken by a child support officer, such as a refusal to carry out a change of circumstances review, or a refusal to cancel an interim maintenance

different child support officer from the one who made the original assessment.[17] A child support officer may conduct a review only if of the opinion that there are reasonable grounds for supposing that the decision in question was wrong in law, or made in ignorance of, or mistake as to, a material fact.[18] If this threshold is passed then both parents are given fourteen days' notice of the review, and of the applicant's reasons for applying, and are invited to submit oral or written comments.[19] If either parent wants to make oral representations the child support officer will arrange an interview. If both seek an interview it is standard practice to offer separate interviews. A fresh maintenance assessment will be undertaken if the reviewing officer is "satisfied" that such an assessment should be made.[20] There is a right of appeal against a refusal to conduct a section 18 review, or, where it has been conducted, against the outcome. This appeal will be to a child support appeal tribunal.[21] Whilst this chapter focuses on second-tier reviews and Chapter 7 considers tribunal appeals, other formal mechanisms for handling grievances are built into the child support scheme. For example, if an absent parent considers that a deduction of earnings order made against him or her is defective, or that payments received from an employer have wrongly been treated as earnings, then an appeal may be made to the magistrates' court.[22] Paternity disputes are likewise handled by the courts and not by the child support appeal tribunals.[23] We confine our attention to second-tier reviews and tribunal hearings on the basis that these procedures lie at the heart of the Child Support Agency's review and appeal mechanisms.

2. THE TWO-STEP SYSTEM FOR CHALLENGING AN ASSESSMENT

Internal administrative reviews and appeals to an external body are both mechanisms by which decisions of officials can be looked at again and overridden. Nonetheless they serve different purposes. There are good reasons why a bureaucracy such as the Child Support Agency should be empowered to correct its own mistakes. There are equally good reasons, to do with maintaining the legitimacy of the child support scheme, why

---

assessment, are also subject to review under s.18. For a full list of the decisions subject to a s.18 review, see Knights and Cox (1997), 346–7.

[17] Child Support Act 1991, s.18(7).

[18] *Ibid.*, s.18(6).

[19] *Ibid.*, s.18(8), and Child Support (Maintenance Assessment Procedure) Regulations 1992, S.I. 1992 No. 1813, reg. 25(2).

[20] Child Support Act 1991, s.18(9).

[21] *Ibid.*, s.20(1).

[22] See *Ibid.*, s.32(5), and Child Support (Collection and Enforcement) Regulations 1992, S.I. 1992, No. 1989, reg. 22.

[23] Child Support Act 1991, s.27.

parents should have a right to appeal to a body independent of the Agency. What is questionable is the two-step or sequential nature of the grievance procedure provided by the Child Support Act 1991. This effectively requires parents who are aggrieved at a decision to appeal *twice* before their case will be accepted by a child support appeal tribunal. In the first instance they must request a section 18 review. Only when that review has been completed (or their request has been refused) is there a right of appeal to a tribunal, the appeal being against the decision reached by the reviewing officer.

This two-step review and appeal system has become increasingly popular with government since the early 1980s. In different forms it has been introduced into housing benefit, the social fund, disability benefits, and now child support.[24] It may be contrasted with the system employed in mainstream social security adjudication in which the claimant has a right to bring a grievance directly before a tribunal (albeit lodging an appeal will result in an internal review being carried out as well).[25]

The White Paper which preceded the Child Support Act 1991 argued that one of the principles governing an appeals system for child support was that it "should be as easy as possible for the parents to use".[26] The government proposed that "in the first instance, the Agency should be required to review its decision and check that the decision has been made accurately"[27]; no right of appeal to a tribunal would arise until this review had taken place. Quoting this passage, Sainsbury has claimed that the government failed to argue a case for requiring parents to complete the internal review stage before allowing them to appeal to an independent tribunal.[28] It might be thought however that the White Paper's very next sentence does contain an argument of sorts: "If a mistake is detected then it will be corrected at once without the need for any other formal procedure."[29] Thus the implicit advantage claimed for the internal review procedure compared with appeal to a tribunal is the speed with which errors can be corrected. The speed argument also underpinned the introduction of a sequential two-tier review system for both the social fund and disability benefits, but, as Sainsbury (1994a) has pointed out, it is disingenuous. The system of appeals in mainstream social security adjudication allows officials to correct errors through an internal review just as quickly as can child support officers. The only difference is that whereas decisions affecting social security claimants are reviewed as an incident of an appeal lodged with a social security appeal

---

[24] For a review of this development see Sainsbury (1994a).
[25] See Baldwin, Wikeley and Young (1992), Ch. 3.
[26] Department of Social Security (1990), vol.1, 27, para. 3.46.
[27] *Ibid.*, 25, para. 3.40.
[28] Sainsbury (1994a), 296.
[29] Department of Social Security (1990), vol.1, 25, para.3.40.

tribunal, clients of the Child Support Agency must find their way through a two-tier review and appeal system. This places considerable obstacles in the path of those seeking redress. What presumably lies behind the sequential approach is a belief that requiring parents to jump through two appellate hoops will reduce overall expenditure on the appeals system, given that many parents who request a review will not go on to seek a tribunal hearing. This might be acceptable if reviews produced accurate outcomes, and were perceived by parents as fair.[30] But if reviews are handled badly and if parents typically abandon their appeals through exhaustion or a failure to grasp the need to appeal a second time, then the two-step system becomes very difficult to justify.[31]

3. THE STORY OF STUART AND DOREEN MULLINS

Stuart Mullins (absent parent, case 122) made extensive use of the formal grievance procedures open to him, 'succeeded' at both the second-tier review and a subsequent tribunal appeal, but in both instances found that his child support assessment was deemed to be higher, not lower. Since Stuart was an articulate man, used to legal proceedings (for recovery of business debts), his might be thought a best-case scenario. If the grievance procedures failed in his case this probably cannot be attributed to deficiencies on Stuart's part in collecting evidence or in stating the basis of appeal with sufficient clarity. In this chapter we examine Stuart's experience of the review process. In Chapter 7 we shall consider his subsequent appeal to a tribunal.

The child support assessment

In 1977 Stuart and Doreen had a brief relationship followed by an acrimonious separation, and the birth of Mark. A court order for maintenance was ordered, but lapsed when Mark was 16 years old. At that time the amount payable was about £20 a week. Mark continued in education and, because Doreen was a benefits claimant, the Child Support Agency became involved. It sent Stuart a maintenance enquiry form in September 1993, and this was completed and returned in early October 1993. Stuart explained in it that he was a director of a company that had suffered in the recession and that, on professional advice, a formal decision had been made at the beginning of 1993 to reduce his salary to

[30] For an elaboration of the criteria one might adopt in assessing internal reviews from the standpoint of administrative justice, see Sainsbury (1994b).

[31] The two-stage process appears to have been abandoned under the Social Security Act 1998.

£11,000 *per annum*. He enclosed copies of both the advice and the decision in order to show that the salary reduction preceded any Agency involvement and was not a tactic designed to minimise his child support obligations. Stuart used the space on the form left for "any other information which you think might be useful" to portray himself as a responsible father. He pointed out that he had paid for Mark for sixteen years even though his son had been born out of wedlock. He also asserted that Doreen was living with a man who was obviously contributing to household costs since they enjoyed a "comfortable way of life".

The Child Support Agency subsequently asked for detailed records of Stuart's earnings. It appears that the Agency lost the first set of accounts that Stuart sent in and, in the event, the assessment (for £32 a week) was not made until March 1994, five months after the maintenance enquiry form was returned. The key to determining the assessment lay in the calculation of Stuart's earnings. Under the law as it stood at the time, for those absent parents who were paid monthly, income was assessed by a child support officer on the basis of the two months ending with the "relevant week". The relevant week comprised the seven days prior to the day on which the maintenance enquiry form was sent to the absent parent (which day would usually constitute the effective date for the maintenance assessment).[32] The law further provided that where the assessment did not, in the opinion of the child support officer, produce a figure which accurately represented the parent's normal earnings, a different period could be used to achieve this, even taking into account earnings *due* to be received if that seemed appropriate.[33]

Because Stuart's salary had been reduced during the course of the 1993–4 tax year, his monthly earnings varied a good deal. The child support officer who calculated the original assessment decided to use three months in early 1993 (when Stuart's monthly income was £2,500 gross) and three months in late 1993 (£400 per month gross). Unfortunately this was not explained to Stuart when he was notified of his assessment.[34] He was thus at a loss to understand the outcome since the income figures used to calculate the assessment related neither to his salary for the tax year 1993–4, nor to a continuous period prior to the effective date, but to

[32] Child Support (Maintenance Assessments and Special Cases) Regulations 1992, S.I. 1992 No. 1815, reg. 1(2) and Sch.1, para.2(1)(b). For a more detailed discussion of the formula, see Ch. 2.

[33] See Child Support (Maintenance Assessment and Special Cases) Regulations 1992, S.I. 1815, Sch.1, para.2(4). On 18 Apr. 1995 the rules for calculating earnings became more flexible: Child Support and Income Support (Amendment) Regulations 1995, S.I. 1995 No. 1045, reg. 54(4).

[34] Notification of an assessment must set out various matters, including the absent parent's assessable income, but the basis for calculating this income does not have to be explained: Child Support (Maintenance Assessment Procedure) Regulations 1992, S.I. 1992 No.1813, reg. 10(2) as amended by Child Support and Income Support (Amendment) Regulations 1995, S.I. 1995 No. 1045, reg. 39(5).

six unidentified months, three before the effective date and three after. In other words the Agency was trying to be fair, but was not explaining itself in a way that the absent parent could understand. From Stuart's perspective, to paraphrase his letter of March 1994 in which he sought a review, the child support officer had based the assessment on figures that apparently bore no relation to actual income earned. Stuart's letter initiated the section 18 second-tier review process.

The section 18 review

Stuart argued in his letter that the Child Support Agency should calculate his wages on the basis of what was now known about his earnings, rather than on his earnings prior to the effective date in September 1993. He enclosed evidence of his earnings for the whole of the tax year 1993–4 and suggested that it would be reasonable to divide the total figure by twelve in order to arrive at a figure representing his monthly salary. This suggestion illustrates the problems that the Child Support Agency creates for itself by taking so long to complete assessments. Whilst Stuart could see why the Agency would usually work back from the effective date in order to calculate child support liability for the future, it seemed to him inappropriate for this method to be adopted in his case, given that the exact salary earned in the period of child support liability was now known. Thus Stuart asked for a "re-assessment" rather than a "review".

One might argue that the Child Support Agency should have treated Stuart's request as a trigger for a section 17 change of circumstances review, or it could at least have discussed this possibility with Stuart.[35] But Stuart had written in his letter that he wanted to exercise his right to have the decision looked at again through the procedure notified in the assessment, namely the section 18 review. Accordingly his request was passed to a second-tier review team. The reviewing officer then sought to establish whether the original decision had been correct, not whether the situation had now changed.

In June 1994 a child support officer put the review process into operation by accepting that there were reasonable grounds for believing that the original assessment had been based on an error of law or a mistake of fact. As part of this process, the Agency communicated Stuart's claims about Doreen's cohabitation arrangements to the appropriate Benefits Agency office, this being standard practice when such allegations are made. The Benefits Agency subsequently decided that there was nothing irregular about Doreen's benefit position.

[35] In this particular case a change of circumstances review would not have resulted in a revised assessment because the difference between the old and new assessment would have been less than £10 per week.

The review proper was not carried out until September 1994, almost six months after Stuart had initiated the review process. Minor miscalculations in the original assessment were uncovered, and this led the reviewing officer to make a fresh assessment.[36] The reviewing officer decided, however, to take the same period for calculating Stuart's earnings as had been used by the child support officer who had made the original assessment. In the event, the result of the review was a slightly higher assessment of £34 per week, backdated to the effective date of mid-September 1993, and an assessment of £32.50 from 7 February 1994 (due to a change in child support law effective from that date). In other words, the assessment resulted in a slight worsening of Stuart's position to the tune of £2 a week. Moreover, when notifying Stuart of the outcome of the review the Child Support Agency did not explain in what regard the first decision had been incorrect. So Stuart had no idea why his maintenance assessment had gone up.

The Agency's failure to give reasons for its assessment contributed to Stuart's sense that the outcome was unacceptable. It was scant compensation to him that the review process had at last furnished him with an explanation of how the first child support officer had calculated his income.[37] Indeed, Stuart assumed that the reviewing officer must have taken a different period since that was the point he had raised in applying for a review. As Stuart was later to comment in interview with us: "I appealed against the first assessment so they re-assessed it and they took another period of time and made it worse, which I just don't understand."

Stuart sought to discuss his revised assessment with the Child Support Agency but his letters went unanswered. Accordingly, in early October 1994 he lodged an appeal with the Independent Tribunal Service.

4. ANALYSIS OF KEY THEMES

We shall now explore a number of themes illustrated by the above case-study, and by other cases which we monitored. From the perspective of parents, much of what happens in the course of a review is indistinguishable from the earlier assessment stage. Indeed, many of the problems encountered by the Child Support Agency in processing reviews mirror those experienced in processing assessments. Accordingly we

---

[36] Using her power under the Child Support Act 1991, s.18(9).

[37] In law, the notification of a fresh assessment following a s.18 review need only set out the same information as must be notified on the making of the original maintenance assessment (except that the right to appeal to a tribunal must also be explained): Child Support (Maintenance Assessment Procedure) Regulations 1992, S.I. 1992 No. 1813, reg. 10 (as amended).

shall find ourselves revisiting some themes explored in the previous two chapters, themes which we believe illuminate the central problems of the child support scheme as it currently stands.

(i) Lack of evidence upon which to base decisions

A lack of good evidence on which to take decisions is a problem at all stages of decision-making within the Child Support Agency. It is a potent factor in the generation of errors and, as a corollary, in generating requests for review. We were told by a review officer that most such requests are based on claims by absent parents that either their income or their housing costs have been miscalculated. For example, the 'wrong' wage slips may have been sent in with the maintenance enquiry form or, if the absent parent had stated that he was paying an endowment mortgage and supplied evidence in support of that, he would not necessarily have stated what kind of endowment it was or what the premium was. Getting this type of information could be difficult and, we were told, sometimes the business teams did not bother—they just made a rough guess.

Review officers also found it difficult to obtain the required information. Sometimes parents were unco-operative and sometimes the Agency's requests for information were unclear. It also appears that on occasion, as in the Mullins case-study, information sent in to the Agency went astray. As we saw in Chapters 4 and 5, the potential for letters to be lost within the compartmentalised and overburdened Child Support Agency is great indeed. All these factors help to explain why the Chief Child Support Officer[38] found that decisions within the reviews process were often taken on the basis of inadequate and incomplete evidence.[39] Such monitoring involves the raising of an "adjudication comment" if the process of adjudication has been inadequate in some way—as, for example, if a decision is made on insufficient evidence, is based on an incorrect finding of fact or error of law, or is not recorded accurately. In 1994–5, of eighty-five review cases examined, adjudication comments were raised on sixty-six (78 per cent).[40] The two main deficiencies were the same as those identified in respect of first-tier determinations of maintenance, namely insufficient evidence and faulty application of the law.

---

[38] The role of the Chief Child Support Officer is to advise child support officers on the interpretation of the law, to advise on the discharge of their duties when carrying out assessments, and to keep operations under review. See, in particular, Child Support Act 1991, s.14.

[39] *Annual Report of the Chief Child Support Officer 1994–5*, (1995), London: HMSO.

[40] *Ibid*, 13, para. 30.

Another area of reviews work concerns "shared-care" cases, where the absent parent claims that he has care of the child for at least two days per week. The way in which Agency staff cope with the evidential difficulties in these cases is illuminating. One reviews officer told us that her strategy was to look at the file and see what had been said about care originally, and to see whether there had been any further relevant correspondence. Where there was insufficient information on the file she would write to the parents seeking more information, often using pre-printed letters. Where the parents' versions did not tally, then her decision would be "on the balance of probabilities". In other words she would decide which parent was more likely to be telling the truth. This attempt at truth-finding in the absence of oral evidence or any opportunity for cross-examination seems somewhat inadequate in light of the opposing interests which can be at stake on review, especially if one takes into account parents' differing abilities to communicate effectively in writing.

(ii) Failures of communication

In order to render a decision acceptable, it helps to give reasons.[41] Where reasons are not given, and the basis for a decision is opaque, it is likely to be regarded as arbitrary or unfair. This point is clearly illustrated by our case-study. Stuart Mullins was not provided with sufficient information to grasp the basis for either the original assessment or the outcome of the second-tier review, thus prompting a further challenge on each occasion. Time and again we saw these failures of communication on the part of the Child Support Agency: it failed to communicate the basis for its calculations; it failed to communicate why some matters could not be taken into account; and it failed to provide an account of the rules or principles upon which its case-management (and so its timetable) were based. These problems were as evident in the context of second-tier reviews as in conducting the original assessment.

Having made these general observations, it is important to analyse more closely the organisational and legal structure governing internal reviews.[42] This has a number of distinct elements. First, a parent has to request a section 18 review in a way which an officer acting on behalf of the Secretary of State will recognise as valid. Only then will the request be passed to a review section to be considered by a child support officer. Secondly, a parent has to provide grounds for seeking a review which the reviewing child support officer considers legitimate within the terms of the legislation. Only if this requirement is satisfied will the review process

---

[41] Sainsbury (1994b), 305.
[42] Jacobs and Douglas (1997), 68, note that the legal structure is "complex and not entirely clear".

be initiated. The third element comprises the review itself, when a child support officer decides if there is a case within the terms of the legislation for revising the original assessment.

Thus the first hurdle that those seeking a review need to overcome is to have their request passed to the specialist section 18 review team. Applications for a review will only be passed on if they are "duly made".[43] The main requirement is that the request must "give the applicant's reasons (in writing) for making it".[44] It appears that a significant (but unknown) number of requests for section 18 review are not passed to a child support officer. This is sometimes because the letter seeking the review does not satisfy what are considered to be the criteria for proceeding further. That is to say, if the letter does not contain evidence that the original decision was based on a mistake of law or fact, the request may be ignored.[45] Another reason for not passing cases to the review section is that where parents challenge their assessment without specifying reasons it may not be clear that it is a section 18 review they are seeking. For example, the person reading the letter may think that the grievance concerns a change of circumstances and may conclude that the change identified would make no difference to the assessment.

As communications from the Child Support Agency concerning its decisions are typically imprecise and unsupported by reasons, it is worthy of note that the Agency requires such full and carefully worded communications from those who seek to have its decisions reviewed. Indeed, the processing and eventual outcome of a request for a second-tier review seem largely to depend on the applicant stating precisely what is wrong with the assessment, in terms that are covered by the legislation. A child support officer explained to us how this worked in practice:

> "Basically we have to check the case to see if there's grounds for review, and if he's given sufficient grounds for review they'll accept the case and they'll reassess the whole case from scratch to see if it's been correctly calculated . . . to see if anything has been missed out or things that should have been taken into account which weren't taken into account." (Child support officer, Dudley)

If the applicant simply states that he or she cannot afford the assessment, the request will be refused—though the assessment may indeed be wrong. As another child support officer explained:

---

[43] Child Support Act 1991, s.18(6).

[44] *Ibid.*, s.18(5).

[45] If a parent then seeks to appeal against what may be perceived by them as a refusal to carry out a review, the new letter will be treated as a further request for a second-tier review (since no right of appeal to a tribunal can arise until a child support officer has either reviewed the original decision or formally refused to carry out such a review): Knights and Cox (1997), 347.

"If it's just 'I can't afford it', then we'd have to say, 'No grounds.' If they say, 'I can't afford it because you've assessed my wages incorrectly' then we could say, 'Oh, a material fact was wrong', but otherwise there's no grounds. If you can put your ideas down on paper, you've got more chance of getting a review than if you can't express yourself properly, and I don't think that's fair. . . ." (Child support officer, Plymouth)

The more articulate and well-informed the parent, the better equipped he or she is to negotiate the procedural minefield of the section 18 second-tier review. Of course, many absent parents *do* challenge an assessment simply because they cannot afford to pay it. This contributes to a feeling amongst Agency staff that many requests for review are a waste of time. Thus one officer told us that section 18 reviews were typically sought when "there is nothing wrong with the case, but the caring parent or the absent parent thinks there is something wrong".

If a child support officer decides to carry out a review, he or she will seek representations from both parents. This creates yet another opportunity for confusion, particularly given that the parent seeking the review may have outlined his or her complaints at length in the initial letter. It is asking a lot of parents for them to understand and comply with everything that is asked of them at each stage in this convoluted process, particularly given that the Agency does not express itself clearly.

The final stage in the review process is the notification of the child support officer's decision to both parents. One might suppose that those who successfully challenge their assessment would be happy to pay the revised amount, whilst those whose challenges fail would at least be provided with an explanation of why the original assessment was deemed correct. Unfortunately, as illustrated by the Mullins case, explanations are not always provided. Moreover, many requests for review are not pursued; in the jargon of the Agency they are "no grounded". A statement that no review is to be undertaken because the aggrieved parent has provided insufficient information is not designed to induce that parent to reach for his wallet.

Even those who are 'successful' in challenging an assessment may be dissatisfied. Contrary to parents' expectations, a review is as likely to result in a higher maintenance assessment as a lower one. One of the child support officers we interviewed about the Mullins case explained how second-tier reviews that produced higher assessments made it even harder to collect arrears:

"It's one of the things that is very difficult because as many reviews go up as go down. They are convinced it's going to go down. Because they've asked for a review, they wrongly believe it can only go down. It's very difficult to chase the debt then." (Child support officer, Dudley)

Our evidence suggests that there is a pressing need for fuller and clearer explanations to be given to people whose second-tier reviews result in higher assessments. More fundamentally, however, the Child Support Agency needs to improve all aspects of its communications with parents.

(iii) Deflection

It can be seen from the above that there is ample scope for requests for review to be deflected and defeated. Whilst some of this can be attributed to a failure of communication, it also reflects an administrative system overburdened with cases. As one Birmingham presenting officer explained:

> "What they [the Agency] are doing, more often than not, is looking at the letter requesting a review, and if that letter itself does not contain anything that should be looked at, then that request is turned down: they are not looking necessarily at how that calculation was made. I can understand it because of the pure volume of work coming through."

This policy of requiring any challenge to an assessment to spell out the legal grounds on which it is based (such as a mistake of fact or law) meant that at the time of our fieldwork refusals to conduct reviews were commonplace.[46] This in turn reduced the workload of the review sections since further stages of the review process were not then undertaken. The application of this policy is a discretionary matter for each officer. One review officer told us that she would *sometimes* seek more information about grounds where the original letter was deficient in this respect, but if she did not receive a reply within a specified period she would turn down the request for a review. She estimated that only about half of the requests for review led to a review actually taking place. The rest were "no grounded". We can only speculate on the extent to which review officers seek clarification of requests for review before "no-grounding" them. One might expect some variation in the stringency with which "the requirement to state grounds" is applied. The monitoring teams of the Chief Child Support Officer found numerous instances of officers refusing to conduct reviews where there were in fact grounds for proceeding.[47]

The widespread refusal of requests for review has obvious implications for the child support appeal tribunals since parents are entitled to appeal

[46] Between Aug. 1994 and Dec. 1996 43,973 requests for second tier reviews were either refused or withdrawn, while only 29,735 were completed: Hansard, HC Debs., Vol. 290, col. 707 (20 Feb. 1997).

[47] *Annual Report of the Chief Child Support Officer 1994–5*, (1995), London: HMSO, 13, para. 30.

against a refusal to carry out a review. One experienced full-time tribunal chair was sharply critical of the way in which the Agency was processing requests for reviews. He told us that the failure to initiate a section 18 review reflected "a misinterpretation of the Act". The legislation states that "reasons" have to be given, not "grounds". Thus if a person writes saying they cannot afford the assessment, their request for a review is duly made as they have provided a reason for making it. This interpretation is supported by the leading text on the child support legislation,[48] and appears to us to be correct, at least in the sense that the official acting on behalf of the Secretary of State should always pass any letter which gives reasons for seeking a review to the review section for further consideration.

However, the argument that the reviewing child support officer should then check the case as a whole to see if any grounds for a review can be detected is somewhat dubious. To carry out such a check would amount to carrying out a review, and the legislation does not mandate automatic reviews on receipt of a written request from a parent. Rather, the child support officer need only act if there are reasonable grounds for supposing that the original decision was wrong in law or based in ignorance of or mistake as to a material fact. If the letter does not supply such reasonable grounds it is understandable that an officer might conclude that no such grounds exist.

On the other hand, in light of the high error rate in the determination of maintenance assessments[49] one might argue that it would be sensible for child support officers to presume that reasonable grounds existed for proceeding with a review in each and every case that was passed to them by the Secretary of State. This was certainly the view of the presenting officers whom we interviewed when we attended hearings of child support appeal tribunals. This was one example:

> "When the review section gets a letter, if that letter just says, 'I can't afford to pay it', or something like that, then they won't review it. . . . So a lot of appeals are based on a refusal to do a second-tier review. When they do the appeal submissions at Lytham they have to check the assessment, and they always find some arithmetical error, or something done wrong, and then it's mentioned in the appeal submission. . . . I'd prefer to see the review stage changed so that if someone asked for a review the assessment was looked through and if anything was found it could be put right. If they still weren't happy with that they could appeal, and at least the assessment would be written up in the submission and I would know it was right." (Presenting officer, Birmingham)

---

[48] Jacobs and Douglas (1997), 68, 426 and 435.
[49] In the CSA's second year of operation the Chief Child Support Officer found that less than half of the maintenance assessment examined were definitely correct in cash terms: *Annual Report of the Chief Child Support Officer 1994–5*, (1995), London: HMSO, 4.

Whilst refusals to conduct a review doubtless reduce the workload of the review sections, this practice must transfer some work (and cost) to the appeal stage. In addition, a successful appeal against a refusal to review will result in the case being remitted back to the Child Support Agency for a review to be carried out (since the tribunal itself has no power to determine the correct level of child support).[50] If the outcome of this review is not to the appellant's liking then a further appeal may follow. If this is successful then the case will once more be remitted to the Agency. As Jacobs and Douglas note, "the two-tier adjudication procedure in child support can send parties around in circles before an issue can be finalised".[51] Nonetheless, earlier research suggests that sequential review and appeal systems do indeed filter out many appeals at the internal review stage. Sainsbury, in summarising these findings (relating to the social fund and housing benefit reviews), concludes that "some 90% of the losers at internal review actually give up".[52] As he notes, it does not follow that this would be replicated under the child support scheme.[53] Our research was not designed to provide quantifiable evidence on this issue, and we must await research into this aspect of internal reviews before reaching any definite conclusions.[54] But Sainsbury is surely right in judging that this filtering effect (and the consequent cash saving) is the feature of internal reviews which most attracted government, notwithstanding the legitimising rhetoric that reviews provide a quicker means of redress than do tribunals. It is also reasonable to suppose that the child support review and appeal process, because it is two-stage, and circular, will have an especially pronounced filtering effect.

[50] Note, though, that in identifying the error in the original assessment which should have been taken as a ground for review the tribunal may in practice be perceived by the reviewing child support officer as directing a particular decision to be reached: Jacobs and Douglas (1997), 72.

[51] Jacobs and Douglas (1995), p.x.

[52] Sainsbury (1994c), 16–17. The original studies were by Dalley and Berthoud (1992) and Sainsbury and Eardley (1992).

[53] In later research into the review and appeal system for disability living allowance and attendance allowance it was found that 37 per cent of claimants who were dissatisfied with the outcome of an internal review nonetheless decided not to appeal (or were unaware that they could appeal): Sainsbury, Hirst and Lawton (1995), 205.

[54] The available statistics are unhelpful. For example, the CSA reports that in 1994–5 27,295 requests for second tier reviews were received, 28,272 requests were cleared, and 6,654 appeals were received from the Independent Tribunal Service: Child Support Agency, *1994–5 Annual Report and Accounts*, (1995), London: HMSO, 16. No information is provided on how many requests for reviews were refused, how many reviews carried out did not give the applicant what was sought (reviews can make the applicant's position either worse or better), and how many of the appeals received related to these categories of review decision. In the absence of such information it is impossible to judge how many of those who "lose" at the review stage press on to an appeal.

(iv) Delays in decision-making

It is evident that the processing of reviews has not been conducted in the efficient manner promised by the White Paper which preceded the Child Support Act. The Social Security Committee has received evidence that substantial delays in dealing with reviews and appeals are seriously undermining the effectiveness of the child support scheme.[55] The modest targets which the Agency set itself for 1995–6 (50 per cent of second-tier reviews to be cleared in thirteen weeks; 80 per cent in twenty-six weeks) is another indicator of the scale of the problem.[56] To some extent this reflects government failure to recognise the workload that the child support scheme would produce. But in any event the complex structure of the review process, combined with the fragmented nature of child support procedures, was almost guaranteed to generate long delays.

As with other areas of work within the Agency, progress on a case is dependent on its repeatedly "surfacing" along an administrative conveyor belt. Thus we saw that it was three months before Stuart Mullins' request for a review was accepted by a child support officer as containing valid grounds, whilst it took a further three months for another officer to process representations made by the parties and actually carry out the review.

Equally we must not overlook the fact that parents themselves contribute to delay, in particular by not providing information when asked to do so by a review officer. It was clear from our conversations with review officers that it was almost always necessary to seek further information from parents during the review process. From the review officer's perspective, the time taken to process a review depended largely on the level of cooperation received from parents—and some parents were so unco-operative that reviews took a year or more to complete. Officers were particularly sceptical about requests for review based on claims of shared-care, many of which were thought to have been inspired by pressure groups. In these cases there was unlikely to be any documentary proof of the claims made (unlike with mortgage costs and wages), so making progress on the review was difficult and time-consuming.

(v) The failure to keep assessments up to date

The fact that the Child Support Agency is so far behind with its workload means that many of its decisions have an air of unreality, relating as they do to periods many months, if not years, in the past. At the time of our

---

[55] House of Commons Social Security Committee (1996a), p. xix.
[56] *Ibid.*

fieldwork section 18 reviews were taking at least six months. By the time a review is complete there may well have been changes in circumstances that render the new assessment out of date. Indeed, many reviews are conducted using figures which are *known* (by the parents) to have been superseded. In case 108, for example, a nil assessment of the absent parent, Perry Bass, had been based on the first six weeks' earnings from his new business. As his start-up costs were high, he had earned little over that period. But by the time the nil assessment was made (five months later) Lynette Bass, the parent with care, believed that Perry was now making a good living. She therefore "appealed" against the assessment and collected information that she thought would assist the Child Support Agency in launching an investigation. The review was carried out by a child support officer some eleven months later, but the nil assessment was left unchanged. Lynette observed:

> "What I was annoyed at was that they did not do any further investigation of his finances when I asked for the review. . . . They could have done an awful lot. Because I was certain he was ripping the books off . . . a lot of information came back to me from people in the village about where he was working and who for . . . so I sent that off to the CSA and said, 'Look, I know he has worked for these people . . . this gives you a starting point.' They didn't request any further paperwork from me at all, or any further paperwork from Perry. All they did was look back on what both of us had already provided; which wasn't my point of dispute."

The problem here is that the Child Support Agency dealt with Lynette's 'appeal' as a request for a section 18 review. The reviewing officer therefore looked to see if the initial assessment was in error. From his point of view any information relating to Perry's income later in his first year of business was irrelevant.

It is arguable that the Agency should have treated Lynette's application as falling under section 17 rather than section 18, as the obvious inference to draw from the information she provided was that she was alleging a change of circumstances rather than an error in the initial calculation. Even Perry Bass thought the handling of the case was odd. When asked by the Agency for his comments following Lynette's application for review he had rung and asked if he should send in another statement of earnings. The response bemused him:

> "They said 'No, we work on the figures we've got.' It struck me as slightly ridiculous. They were working on my first ten weeks. Now I knew that they would not be typical for the year, but they didn't want any other information so when the letter came through to say she was going to a second review [i.e. a tribunal appeal] I just ignored it, because I knew it would be the same."

This case illustrates how difficult parents find it to make sense of a process in which every decision is taken in isolation from every other one, and which focuses on distant time-periods. The root of the problem is that the Child Support Agency lacks a discretionary power to consolidate assessment decisions. From the perspective of child support officers, the redress procedures merely increase the administrative difficulties inherent in a process that insists on continual and precise revisions to assessments on the basis of a complex formula.

We asked officers whether it would ever be possible to deal satisfactorily with cases where people's circumstances change as often as they do, particularly when a significant proportion of clients are exercising their right to challenge assessments. The general feeling among staff at the Child Support Assessment Centres seemed to be that, if they had more time and if the computer system were adequate, then it might be possible; but currently it was not.

The complications resulting from the need for continual reassessments—when there are formula changes, changes in circumstances, and errors, all combined—are illustrated by the Radcliffe/Banks case (114) in which an appeal tribunal directed that the maintenance assessment should be reduced by almost £20. The resulting recalculations would, we were told by a child support officer, take place in several stages:

"The first one was the maintenance requirement and it was reassessed the same day. It was done again one or two times, I've no idea why. Then we've got to the letter we had, asking for the change of circumstances to be looked at. . . . It shows that it breached compliance with protected income, so that's why it went down by £9, but it was still not enough to breach tolerance. So when we were actually putting the information into the system, it had actually gone up by another £2. Then, April 95, the formula changes came in, and the system automatically reassesses that one. So it just went down by that £1.30, so that would automatically have been deducted. Then from then to 11th August the assessment team completed the appeal, and so it went down to £32.19—it's £14 a week difference. The final thing was, when we've done the appeal we have to look at the April changes. I would say that as it is now it's probably about 30 per cent of his net income, so his protected income has increased with the formula changes. His exempt income will also increase because he's had a partner and a child . . . he would have had between 75 per cent and 85 per cent of his housing costs allowed. After 17th April we wouldn't have apportioned it. That would have increased his exempt income and lowered his assessable income. So those two would have gone together and decreased the assessment . . . and this is going to have to be reassessed again when the periodic review is completed. . . ." (Child support officer, Dudley)

This procedure understandably takes time—and the potential for error and further delay is present at every stage. Fortunately, not all cases are as complicated as this one; but nor is it completely atypical. Small wonder then that nearly every assessment produced by the Child Support Agency appears out-of-date.

(vi) Incoherence, rigidity and fragmentation

A major difficulty within the child support scheme concerns the boundary between a second-tier review and a change of circumstances review. One child support officer, working on a section 18 review section, said:

> "One major thing at the moment is, what is a review? It's a stupid question but there are four types of review, and . . . we've got six months backlog and they're going to contain lots of change of circumstances. Do we have a point where we say we've addressed the initial query and everything else is change of circumstances? And so it's passed to the business team. . . . Different CSACs are doing different things. It's because we're new all these things need working through and establishing." (Child support officer, Plymouth)

Requests for section 18 reviews are first examined by business teams, then passed to second-tier review teams, then passed back if a change of circumstances review is called for. It goes without saying that, just as with the assessment procedure itself, this kind of fragmentation increases the chances of error and delay.

The fact that the Child Support Agency reviews particular decisions rather than considering each case as a whole increases the likelihood of outcomes which parents view as incomprehensible or absurd. Thus we saw above how the 'appeal' by Lynette Bass (case 108) was treated as a request for a section 18 review when it seemed clear to both parents that the challenge was based on the fact that the absent parent's circumstances had changed. The same pattern was observed in the Stuart and Doreen Mullins case-study, where again the need for a change of circumstances review was overlooked.

The contrast with the former lawyer-led system for determining child maintenance is striking. There, the focus was on achieving settlement, which might mean compromise on both sides (although more usually on the side of the caring parent).[57] But the Child Support Agency is not empowered to do deals with parents, however beneficial these might be for all concerned (including of course the Treasury). It is concerned only with the accuracy of the assessment and with applying the law as it finds it.

This institutional inability or unwillingness to strike deals is well illustrated by our case-study. On Stuart Mullins' own calculations the correct level of maintenance in his case was just £2 less than the figure arrived at by the Agency. He claimed that he was prepared to pay all his arrears as soon as his assessment was calculated in the way that he thought correct. Since that would have been within the discretion of the child support officer who made the initial assessment, it is perhaps unfortunate that

---

[57] See Ch. 8.

Stuart's suggestion was not adopted. At that initial stage, however, the child support officer was unaware of Stuart's view of the correct period on which to base the assessment since this had not been stated on his maintenance enquiry form. He had simply given his annual salary and his erratic monthly earnings.

The possibility of reaching common ground with Stuart did arise, however, within the context of the section 18 review. Once a child support officer had concluded that there were reasonable grounds to suppose that the original assessment had been based on an error of law or fact and had accepted the case for review, she had the power to conduct a fresh assessment. It was therefore open to the officer who carried out the section 18 review to change the basis for calculating Stuart's earnings. That she did not exercise this power may have been because "in practice, as a matter of comity or courtesy, one child support officer's view would not readily be substituted for that of a fellow officer . . .".[58] By contrast, the officer who wrote the tribunal submission at the appeal stage had no power to change the assessment since the official advice at that time was that a section 19 review should not be carried out in the appeal context.[59] In practice, the only way Stuart could achieve what he claimed he wanted was to pursue his grievance to appeal and hope that the tribunal would have less compunction about departing from the view of the original child support officer.

5. CONCLUSION

The government's avowed aim of making the child support review and appeals mechanism as easy as possible for parents to use has not been achieved in practice. Internal reviews typically do not provide a speedy means of redress, do not provide accurate re-assessments, and are not perceived by parents as fair. It would be quite wrong to lay the blame for this on individual child support officers, or even on the Agency as a whole. Rather, the fault lies with the structure of the review and appeals system as laid down in legislation. The Thatcher government's wish to deflect and stifle challenges to maintenance assessments in the interests of cost-saving determined the nature of the reviews and appeals process on offer. In essence this was designed to place the Child Support Agency in firm control of the business of determining the correct level of child maintenance. It was not designed for the convenience of parents. On the

[58] Jacobs and Douglas (1997), 73.

[59] *Child Support Adjudication Guide*, para. 9530, Central Adjudication Services, London: HMSO. The Child Support Act 1995, s.16 (inserting s.20A into the Child Support Act 1991) now allows a review to be carried out at this stage. Appeals will lapse, however, only if the result of such a review is the same as that which would have been obtained if the appeal had succeeded.

contrary, it is a bureaucratic obstacle course. This in turn is exacerbated by a total inability to consolidate child support liabilities. The review process then comes to represent a further stage of drift and irresolution, in keeping with many parents' earlier experience of the Agency.

7

The Child Support Appeal Tribunals

In chapter 6 we examined second-tier reviews operated by the Child Support Agency. If either parent is aggrieved at a reviewing officer's decision he or she can appeal to a child support appeal tribunal.[1] We now turn our attention to the justice on offer at this tribunal.

Child support appeals are heard by a paid chair (part-time or full-time) and two volunteer lay wing members.[2] The tribunals are currently under the ægis of the Independent Tribunal Service (ITS), a government funded organisation presided over by a judge appointed by the Lord Chancellor. The Lord Chancellor also appoints the tribunal chairs (lawyers of at least five years' standing), while the ITS President appoints lay members and has responsibility for training and for the general administration of the system. The Independent Tribunal Service was established in 1984 to guarantee the independence of the newly created social security appeal tribunals.[3] In addition to child support appeal tribunals it is responsible for medical appeal tribunals, disability appeal tribunals and vaccine damage tribunals.

Whilst child support appeal tribunals are formally independent of the Child Support Agency, they draw on Agency resources in two important ways. First, on receiving an appeal from a parent, the Independent Tribunal Service asks the Agency's Central Appeals Unit at Lytham St Anne's to produce an appeals submission. This sets out the basis for the contested decision and provides a response to the appeal. It is made available to all interested parties in advance of the hearing. Secondly, a presenting officer from the Child Support Agency attends the tribunal in order to explain the original decision. This officer is trained to perform

---

[1] Child Support Act 1991, s. 20(1).

[2] The Child Support Act 1995 makes provision for a tribunal chair to sit alone, although at present this is confined to certain "departures" issues: Child Support Appeal Tribunal (Procedure) Regulations, S.I. 1992 No. 2641, reg. 11A.

[3] Then known as the Office of the President of Social Security Appeal Tribunals (OPSSAT). The future of the Independent Tribunal Service is now uncertain in the light of changes included in the Social Security Act 1998: see Adler and Sainsbury (1998).

the role of *amicus curiae* (friend of the court) rather than advocate for the Agency.[4]

One significant difference between a section 18 internal review and a tribunal hearing is that both parties may attend the tribunal to argue their case. Another is that the appeals submission provides parents with a much fuller explanation of the original assessment than they will have received in earlier dealings with the Agency. At the hearing they will have an opportunity to discuss the assessment with an officer from the Agency as well as with the lawyer chair and two lay members. There is thus far greater scope than at internal review for explanations to be provided, points of view to be aired, and the issues thoroughly discussed from different perspectives. Consistent with the policy of seeking a *cheaper* alternative to court hearings for determining child support, legal aid is not available to cover the cost of representation at tribunals. Parents are almost invariably unrepresented.

Following the hearing, if an appeal against the decision of a reviewing officer is allowed the tribunal must remit the case to the Child Support Agency, giving such directions as it considers appropriate.[5] In practice tribunal decisions are sent to both parents and to the Agency's Central Appeals Unit within a few weeks of the hearing. A child support officer at the Unit determines how the tribunal directions should be implemented by the relevant Child Support Assessment Centre and also decides whether to appeal the tribunal decision. It is open to either parent and to the child support officer to challenge a tribunal decision by appealing to a Child Support Commissioner (and from there to the courts), but only on a point of law.[6]

We attended twenty-three tribunal appeals, eighteen of which were lodged by absent parents and five by parents with care. The absent parent attended in fifteen cases and the parent with care in nine. In five appeals both parents attended, and in four neither did so. Stuart and Doreen Mullins were both present for Stuart's appeal, and we now resume our account of their case, focusing upon the tribunal hearing.

2. THE STORY OF STUART AND DOREEN MULLINS (CONCLUDED)

(i) The pre-hearing stage

In his appeal letter Stuart presented himself as a concerned father whilst accusing Doreen, the parent with care, of living with another man with-

---

[4] See Jacobs and Douglas, (1997), 449. For critical discussion of this function see Wikeley and Young (1991).

[5] Child Support Act 1991, s. 20(3) and (4).

[6] Child Support Act 1991, s. 24, as amended by Child Support Act 1995, Sch.3, para.7(2) and (3); see also Child Support Commissioners (Procedure) Regulations 1992, SI 1992 No. 2640. Leave must be obtained for such an appeal.

out declaring this to the Benefits Agency. He also railed against the incompetence of the Child Support Agency. He did however set out the legal basis for the appeal in a relatively straightforward manner. Explaining that his earnings over the tax year 1993–4 had been erratic, he asked for his weekly salary to be determined by dividing total earnings for that year by fifty-two.

It was eight months from Stuart's appeal letter to the tribunal hearing. Most of this delay was attributable to the time it took the Child Support Agency to produce its appeals submission. Whilst the submission contained an acknowledgement that minor mathematical errors had been made at the review stage (and that therefore the appeal should "succeed"), it rejected Stuart's argument that the child support assessment was based on atypical earnings. The submission did not address Stuart's proposal that his earnings should be calculated by taking his salary over the whole tax year.

In the months leading up to the tribunal hearing a deduction of earnings order was issued to Stuart's employer. No deductions were in fact made and no enforcement action was taken against the employer.

(ii) At the tribunal

The appeal was eventually heard in May 1995. Doreen arrived first and we spoke to her in the waiting room. She claimed that she was only attending because Stuart had alleged in his correspondence with the Agency and the Independent Tribunal Service that she was cohabiting with her lodger. She was here to refute Stuart's "ridiculous claims" which were "just being used by him to get out of paying for his son".

As we talked further with Doreen it became clear that she had come armed to challenge Stuart's version of the facts across a broad front and, in particular, to argue that he had far greater financial resources than he had disclosed. Thus she told us that Stuart was a "very wealthy businessman" who despite his "opulent lifestyle" was claiming that he could not afford the assessment. She showed us estate agent's details of a house Stuart had just sold and of one he had just bought. She had brought these "to prove he's lying—he's got money". When asked if Stuart was likely to attend she replied: "No, he's swanned off to London with his son to see a football match, Chelsea or Arsenal, but of course he's no money." At this point the clerk to the tribunal approached Doreen and told her that, contrary to her expectations, Stuart would be attending. Clearly shaken, she was shown into a separate waiting room.

As soon as Stuart arrived the couple were ushered in to the tribunal room by the clerk (with scarcely a nod of acknowledgement between them). The chair explained the procedure to be followed, addressing his remarks primarily to Stuart as the appellant:

> "I start by seeing if the presenting officer wants to add anything to the submission. Then you can add anything you want to. It's informal, but we are bound by law."[7]

In fact the presenting officer had nothing to add. The chair asked Stuart and Doreen whether they wished to add anything to the submission. Both declined. The chair continued by stressing the tribunal's independence from the Child Support Agency but added that it was "bound by the same rules".

Stuart was then asked to give his reasons for appealing. In his oral presentation, as in the appeal papers, Stuart portrayed himself as a responsible father with a legitimate grievance. As in the appeal papers, he referred to the alleged incompetence of the Child Support Agency in handling his case. Most of his presentation, however, was concerned with demonstrating that the Agency had used atypical months in calculating his income. He concluded:

> "All I want is my annual salary divided by 52 . . . that's the only point I want decided. They do that with your savings—they look at the whole year, so why not your earnings?"

At this stage in the appeal it must have seemed to Stuart that his argument was accepted as the chair agreed that the period following the effective date could be relevant if taking an earlier period would be atypical and unfair.

The chair then asked for comment on the other ground for the appeal, saying to Stuart that he had "also raised the issue of Mrs Mullins' income". Stuart seemed reluctant to pursue this, saying: "She has a lodger. I've pointed that out to the Social . . . it's up to them". The chair responded by observing that it could make a difference to the amount he would have to pay in child support. Stuart however, made it clear that he did not want to pursue the matter further, remarking that he and Doreen "were never engaged, let alone married". Doreen winced at this but said nothing. The panel made no response.

The chair then asked Doreen if she had any questions for Stuart. He added that she would have the chance to say anything she wanted to later on. This appeared to be quite a formal way of proceeding, requiring Doreen virtually to engage in the art of cross-examination. In the event she immediately started to make fresh points of her own. She began by

---

[7] Although we did not tape-record tribunal hearings, we observed tribunals in pairs, and the two sets of field notes enable us to report what was said with a reasonable degree of confidence.

passing the estate agent's details of Stuart's houses to the panel. As they looked at these she stated in a matter-of-fact way:

> "When the assessment was made, he put down his mortgage costs. He has since sold that house and bought another. He sold the house for a quarter of a million pounds and bought a smaller one. Presumably that equals a mortgage reduction. That's all I've got to say."

Doreen's aim here seemed to be to convey to the panel that Stuart had a lavish lifestyle and, secondly, that his housing costs had nonetheless gone down (so that a higher child support assessment would be appropriate). The chair asked the presenting officer: "Does it make any difference to the calculation?" The presenting officer replied that it could do, depending on when the first property was sold. Stuart said it had been sold in the late summer of 1994 (almost a year after the effective date of the original assessment). The presenting officer observed: "It won't affect this, but it will affect later claims." Neither the presenting officer nor the panel seemed willing to explore the implicit point made by Doreen that Stuart may not have fallen on such hard times as he had claimed. Stuart, however, understood the import of Doreen's observation and responded with vigour. He stated that his new housing situation was "an indication of my reduced income". He had been forced, he claimed, to sell his first house due to the financial difficulties he was experiencing. He had not received "anything like" the asking price for the property.

Neither the panel nor the presenting officer made any attempt to delve further into the issue of Stuart's housing costs. The chair continued by asking Doreen if she had any other points that she would like to make. Doreen responded: "Not in relation to that. Presumably you want to ask me questions about the man that lives with me?" The chair replied: "Well, Mr Mullins has raised it. . . . ." At this point Doreen asked that she be allowed to speak to the panel in private. The chair replied that this was not possible: the tribunal could only hear evidence with both parties present. Doreen accepted this without demur. She explained that she had originally lived with her lodger not as a couple but "on a sharing basis. We shared the costs of various expenses such as electricity, and I tried to be independent and manage without benefit. But I couldn't manage. I had to claim benefit." She said that the relationship between her and her lodger had been thoroughly investigated by the Benefits Agency and that it had been accepted that they were not living together as a couple. She concluded: "He pays a nominal rent to me, that's all."

Thus, in rejecting Stuart's claims about her alleged cohabitation, Doreen was keen to assert that she was morally deserving and had claimed benefits through need rather than choice. The chair, however, responded only to Doreen's observation that she now received nominal rent, asking the presenting officer if this had been taken into account. He replied that as Doreen was on Income Support the rent would have been taken into account in that calculation. The chair then pronounced that if the Benefits Agency was satisfied with Doreen's account of her circumstances then the tribunal would also accept it.

The hearing, which had lasted for fifteen minutes, was then adjourned. During the fifteen-minute adjournment Stuart and Doreen waited in separate rooms. Doreen spoke of her shock at seeing Stuart again after so long and then burst into tears. Stuart made further allegations concerning Doreen's allegedly intimate relationship with her lodger, but then added: "I'm not bothered really. It makes little difference as she's on benefits. Mark's eighteen in two months' time and then I'm free of all this aggro. It only comes to an extra two pounds a week. . . ."

(iii) The tribunal decision

Stuart and Doreen were called back to hear the tribunal's decision. The chair announced that the panel had accepted that the period used to calculate Stuart's earnings was unrepresentative and that it would be fair to take an entire twelve-month period as Stuart had suggested. Accordingly, the child support officer would be instructed to consider the twelve-month period commencing October 1992. No-one made any comment. Everyone trooped out of the tribunal room under the impression that Stuart had been given what he wanted. In the corridor Stuart asked the presenting officer: "What happens now?" The presenting officer explained at length. Doreen hurried from the building.

Stuart then went to the waiting room and started going through documents with a calculator. He quickly realised that the tribunal had taken the "wrong period" in working out his wages. Whereas he had asked them to employ the tax year April 1993 to March 1994, the tribunal had actually directed that the twelve months prior to the effective date (September 1993) should be used to calculate his earnings. Since this twelve months would include several months in which he had been receiving his former high salary, the tribunal-directed assessment would be considerably higher than both the original assessment and the assessment following the section 18 review. Stuart muttered angrily: "I'm going back in again. This will make the assessment worse, not better." He hurried down the corridor in the direction of the tribunal room, but was blocked at the door by the clerk and told firmly that the hearing was concluded. He left shortly afterwards in a state of high dudgeon.

In our subsequent interviews with the panel members we pursued the question of why the tribunal had used this particular period for calculating earnings. The chair observed: "The appellant should have been satisfied, because he got what he asked for. I don't know about the lady, I don't know whether she was happy about it." Similarly, one of the wing members commented: "We sort of thought the whole twelve month period was fair, and it was the twelve month period that was requested, so he got what he wanted." This wing member clearly regarded Doreen's interest in the case as marginal. When we asked if she thought the outcome was fair to the parent with care, she replied: "Yes, she's quite happy. He gives the son pocket money and she gets her income from benefits". Only the second wing member seemed aware that the decision did not in fact favour Stuart. It emerged that it was her view of the law on calculating earnings that had determined the outcome:

> "I was quite decisive as to what period I thought it should be. They [the Agency] hadn't put it in the papers at all. If you read the regulations it actually says that unless it's almost impossible to, you should always work it backwards from the relevant date. But his hadn't been worked that way at all, it was some of it forwards and some of it backwards. He was asking for twelve months' wages to be taken in, so we took it twelve months backwards from the relevant date. Now, apparently, he's not satisfied with that . . . that was the wrong twelve months according to him. But then he didn't make it clear. We asked him and he said he wanted to go back the whole twelve months, sort of thing, from the relevant date. Whether he didn't understand what the relevant date was, I don't know."

No doubt an experienced representative would have done a better job than Stuart in clarifying that he wanted the tax year from April 1993 to be used in calculating his earnings. But Stuart at no point said that he wanted the tribunal to "go back" twelve months from the effective date of September 1993. Moreover, the chair had himself acknowledged that if working backwards from the effective date would produce an atypical earnings figure then another period could be used.[8] The thrust of Stuart's case was clear, and it was similarly clear that the legally qualified chair understood it. Yet he allowed a non-legally qualified wing member's view of the law to form the basis of the tribunal decision.

This was not made explicit at the conclusion of the hearing, thus creating the impression that Stuart had been successful. When we interviewed Doreen a few weeks later she still thought that Stuart had 'won':

> "I know from the papers the reason for his appeal was that he said the months that they have assessed him over weren't the correct months. They were good months and he wanted to be assessed over the year. Which in the end he got . . . He got what he wanted, didn't he?"

Doreen was not inclined to challenge the tribunal decision or to pursue her allegations about Stuart's lifestyle. It seemed that she had found her dealings with the Agency too frustrating and time-consuming to contemplate any further action:

[8] The relevant law is discussed in Ch. 6.

> "I suppose I could push them and say: 'Look, get it reassessed', but it's all too much hassle to be honest with you. I'd have all those forms to fill in."

Stuart for his part concluded that he had, as he put it:

> "...won the battle and lost the war. It nearly got sorted out. It was so near. This kindly old gentleman [chair] sitting in the tribunal said 'oh yes, we'll do what you want, we'll take your wages over the full year.' The doors had shut on me by the time I'd registered what dates he'd used. I even wrote them down, but it didn't sink in till just after. I said to the clerk 'well I'll wait till he comes out' and he said 'you can wait all night if you want to, he won't discuss the case' ... I have now appealed so that the appeal can be set aside or be reviewed."

(iv) Challenging the tribunal decision

Stuart's 'appeal' took the form of a letter stating that the tribunal had obviously made a mistake and could the chair please change the decision. While accidental errors in a tribunal decision can be corrected,[9] the decision in Stuart's case had been deliberate and so Stuart's request was refused. We talked to him again some two months after the hearing:

> "They just won't accept they've made a mistake. That's just typical of a solicitor, isn't it? He's not going to say, 'sorry, I got it wrong.' He's saying 'no, sod you, that's what I've decided and I'm sticking to it.' You can't run a tribunal like that can you? Because he said that he approached the other two people [wing members] and they've both agreed with him. Well those two little old ladies, they don't even know what bloody day it is, let alone how to work out someone's income. Two Sunday school teachers, they're just there to make the numbers up."

We asked Stuart what he planned to do next. He told us that he had written a letter asking the chair to set aside the decision "so that we can start again on the basis that it's just to do so because they've obviously based the calculations on the wrong year...." If this request were refused he would contemplate an appeal to a Child Support Commissioner. Even though Stuart was not actually *paying* the maintenance ordered, he seemed exasperated:

> "So the whole thing is going to drag on and on and on and on again. It's worse than [going back to] square one because if they work it out on the year that he's said, I shall end up paying about twice as much as I was paying before the bloody appeal."

Stuart added that the Child Support Agency had not been in touch with him since the appeal two months earlier. As he put it, "they probably

---

[9] See Child Support Appeal Tribunals (Procedure) Regulations 1992, S.I. 1992 No.2641, reg. 14.

don't know what to do . . . they don't know what I earned the year before, because I haven't told them." He clearly had no intention of supplying the details of his earnings that the Agency would need in order to implement the tribunal decision.

Our final interview with Stuart was in September 1995, four months after the tribunal hearing. He told us that his request to have the decision set aside had been refused . . . "because apparently they can only set it aside on a point of law." He had given up the idea of appealing to the Child Support Commissioner.[10] He was considering beginning the appeal process again but spoke of this in a rather vague and dispirited way.

By this time the Child Support Agency had issued a second deduction of earnings order but Stuart's salary was apparently too low for it to take effect. As a company director he could ensure that this remained the case: "The only way I would have to pay now is if I get a substantial increase in salary. Well I won't be doing that. I can leave the money in the company and draw it out when I retire." Nonetheless Stuart seemed weary of battle. He told us:

"I got fed up with it all and phoned [the CSA] and said could I have a meeting, discuss it with them, and get it all sorted out. All I have got to do is say that my circumstances have changed, which they have, and the tribunal result all becomes totally irrelevant. The girl said, 'yes, we can arrange that.' That was two months ago, and since then I've heard nothing. . . . If they base the payments on the salary that I was drawing in the period for which the payments are due, I will give them a cheque there and then. I've saved the money up. I've always thought that I would have to pay the money eventually."

Two years after the effective date of the assessment, Stuart had still not paid a penny in child support. He had finally realised that the administrative remedy in his case was a change of circumstances review. But even this need not benefit him in practice. When and if the Child Support Agency finally organised a field interview with Stuart it would have to be pointed out to him that the assessment would not be altered unless the difference was at least £10 per week (which would not be true in Stuart's case). Moreover, there would be difficulties in backdating the change of circumstances in the way that Stuart would presumably want.[11] The formal grievance procedures had not availed Stuart, and his planned attempt to sort things out through negotiation with the Agency seemed destined to fail also. On the other hand he had still not paid any

[10] As the tribunal decision did not reveal the questionable interpretation of the law on which it was based, the possible error of law in this case remained undetected.
[11] A change of circumstances review takes effect from the first day of the maintenance period in which the application for review is received. There is no provision for backdating the request: Child Support (Maintenance Assessment Procedure) Regulations 1992, S.I. 1992 No. 1813, reg. 31(3).

maintenance. Since the Agency had proved itself completely ineffective in enforcing Stuart's arrears (totalling over £3,000 by the time our research monitoring ended), and since it did not have the information to implement the tribunal's decision, it appeared that a complete stalemate had been reached.

3. ANALYSIS OF KEY THEMES

(i) Reasons for appealing and patterns of attendance

Parents had a variety of reasons for appealing. Some were aware that they had no legally valid grounds, but felt that the tribunal offered an opportunity to present their complaints of bureaucratic inefficiency. Others believed that the Child Support Agency had made an error in their assessment and viewed the appeal as a final attempt to have this rectified. Others simply wanted to delay the enforcement process. These different motivations for appealing were reflected in rates of attendance at tribunal hearings.

The high rate of non-attendance by appellants at social security appeal tribunals is well documented.[12] The picture in respect of child support appeal tribunals is less clear. For example, even where an appellant does not turn up, the other parent might still attend. Complete non-attendance is thus less likely (occurring in just four of the twenty-three cases which we observed).

We were able to speak to five parents who had not attended their tribunal (two absent parents and three parents with care). Reasons given included illness and the desire to avoid confrontation with their former partner. Others, such as Miles Saltford (case 66), were aware that they had no grounds:

"Because of the way the law is written I couldn't win no matter what I said. I wasn't expecting to win".

Miles admitted that he had only appealed as a delaying tactic and had never meant to attend the hearing. Conversely, Mary Fletcher, the parent with care in case 111, did not attend because she accepted that her former partner had a valid ground for challenging the assessment.

The appellant attended the hearing in seventeen of the twenty-three tribunals which we observed, whereas the respondent was only present in seven. Although many appellants expressed apprehension beforehand, the hearing was generally viewed as an opportunity to have an injustice remedied. Typically, *both* parents were anxious to paint them-

---

[12] See Baldwin, Wikeley and Young (1992), Ch. 6.

selves as responsible and reasonable. As far as respondents were concerned, this was usually the reason they chose to attend. For example, Selina Ericson, parent with care in case 45, felt throughout that the real argument was between the absent parent, Malcolm Bridley, and the Child Support Agency, but in making his case Malcolm had blackened her name. She attended in order to challenge what she asserted were his lies about her.

(ii) Child Support Agency influence on the process of appeal

Although child support appeals are handled by an independent organisation, the process is heavily influenced by Child Support Agency procedures. A major feature, as illustrated by our case-study, is the delay in generating submissions. By September 1994 the average time taken for the Agency to produce a submission was 17.7 weeks. That this largely determines the scheduling is clear from the fact that over the same period it took an average 26.1 weeks from lodging an appeal to securing a tribunal decision.[13]

In 1994 the Agency decided to centralise appeals work at its Lytham St Anne's office. As a consequence twice as many appeals were dealt with in the second half of 1994–5 year as in the first.[14] Nevertheless the Council on Tribunals has continued to express concern about the still substantial delays encountered in the production of submissions,[15] and the Social Security Committee has endorsed this concern.[16]

The delays in the appeal process cause major difficulties for some appellants, especially where incorrect maintenance assessments have resulted in overpayments. For example, in the case of Nathan Banks (case 114) it took seven months to reach a hearing and a further three and a half months for the maintenance assessment to be recalculated, in which time Nathan had overpaid more than £1,000. This additional financial burden left Nathan's second family impoverished and affected his health to such an extent that he threatened suicide. Partly as a result of these threats and partly because of his MP's involvement Nathan's case was 'fast-tracked' by the Child Support Agency and the Independent Tribunal Service. Even so, the appeal process took nearly a year.

[13] Council on Tribunals, *Annual Report 1993–4* (1994), London: HMSO, 2, para. 1.4. This suggests that the Independent Tribunal Service is not primarily responsible for delays in appeals being heard, contrary to the thinking underlying the Social Security Act 1998: see Adler and Sainsbury (1998).

[14] Child Support Agency, 1994–5 *Annual Report and Accounts* (1995), London: HMSO, 13.

[15] Council on Tribunals, *Annual Report 1994–5* (1995), p.10, para. 1.35, London: HMSO.

[16] House of Commons Social Security Committee (1996a), p.xix, para. 39.

Other appellants welcomed the long delays. Once an appeal has been lodged the Child Support Agency is reluctant to initiate periodic reviews, to carry out change of circumstances reviews, or to take any further steps towards enforcing an assessment. Thus in the Mullins case a child support officer explained to us that a debt management team would "sift through cases to see whether they need any action on them, and obviously because we're waiting for the appeal they won't actually look at this case until after". In fact enforcement action *was* taken in Stuart Mullins' case in that a deductions of earnings order was issued to Stuart's employer. But by the end of our research monitoring, seven months later, the employer had not deducted any money from Stuart's wages and the Child Support Agency had taken no action against the employer for failing to do so. We suspect that this was because the tribunal decision had still to be implemented.

Attempts to speed up the delivery of submissions are likely to have a detrimental effect on their quality, and they are already subject to severe criticism. Critical comments were made about eighty-four of the eighty-six submissions examined by the monitoring teams of the Chief Child Support Officer in 1994–5.[17] The most common weakness was that points raised by the appellant were either inadequately covered or not covered at all. The submission in the Mullins case exemplifies this. Following the standard format, it provided a detailed explanation of the assessment but paid little attention to points raised by the appellant. Other criticisms made by the monitoring teams in 1994–5 referred to inadequate summaries of facts, inadequate reference to legislation, and the supporting of incorrect section 18 decisions. Whilst the scrutiny concentrated on the way the submission was written, the content was of a similar standard to that found in first-tier adjudications and section 18 reviews. In other words, it was poor.

Nonetheless, submissions do serve to correct earlier mistakes. Errors in the assessment and/or at the review stage were highlighted in over half the cases we observed. Such flaws were usually fairly minor. Typically they were unrelated to the appellant's grounds of appeal.

At the time of our research the Chief Child Support Officer's advice was that the Central Appeals Unit had no power to correct errors at this stage in the process.[18] Presumably it was believed by the architects of the child support scheme that any errors would be detected at the internal review stage and that the appeals process would not expose a need for any fur-

[17] See *Annual Report of the Chief Child Support Officer 1994-95*, (1995), p. 14, paras. 32-33, London: HMSO.

[18] See now the Child Support Act 1991, s. 20(A), (inserted by the Child Support Act 1995, s. 16) which allows an appeal to lapse if the decision reached by a child support officer following a review of the decision under appeal is the same as that which would have been reached if the appeal had succeeded.

ther corrective action prior to the hearing itself. The inability to take such corrective action was criticised by some panel members and by every presenting officer. A comparison was often made with mainstream social security adjudication where the case is reviewed as an incident to the appeal and the earlier decision may be superseded. A Bristol presenting officer summed up the problem:

> "The way the Social Security legislation is framed, a case wouldn't go to appeal unless the Benefits Agency thought they had a watertight case. Whereas cases come to a child support appeal tribunal all the time where the CSA has clearly got it wrong."

In the event, submissions often conclude with an invitation to the tribunal to remit the case back to the Agency so that the assessment can be corrected.

(iii) Child Support Agency influence at tribunal hearings—presenting the submission

Child Support Agency influence continues at the hearing. First, the tribunal agenda tends to be set, at least initially, by the submission prepared by the Agency's Central Appeals Unit. Secondly, a presenting officer from the Agency appears at the tribunal in the role of *amicus curiae*. Most chairs, after a brief explanation of the tribunal's function, ask the presenting officer either to summarise the appeals submission or to indicate whether they have anything to add.

As noted above, the first task of the presenting officer is commonly one of acknowledging that the child support assessment is flawed. One presenting officer told us that having to explain all the mistakes found when the case was being prepared for appeal, left her "feeling like an idiot". On the other hand, by highlighting the errors in the assessment the presenting officer establishes his or her *amicus curiae* credentials. As one Bristol appellant, Lynette Bass (case 108) put it:

> "The chappie from the CSA actually took some of the pressure off with his statement; in fact, he proved my point with his opening statement that he acknowledged that enquiries hadn't been made that should have been. So when I heard him say that, I thought: 'Thank you very much', and it made points that I wanted to raise a lot easier because he had already laid the ground."

We saw no cases in which a presenting officer took an adversarial stance or sought doggedly to defend the original decision. Indeed, to the non-appellant parent, where present, the presenting officer might appear insufficiently partisan. Doreen Mullins was one parent who thought he should have taken up cudgels on her behalf:

"The guy that was at the tribunal wasn't any match for Stuart at all . . . They needed someone who was a bit more au fait with the workings of the CSA there. I think the guy backed down too quickly."

Our own criticism of the presenting officer in this case is rather different. In the hearing he did not defend the original child support officer decision, nor did he question it. Yet after the hearing, in discussion with us, he effectively supported Stuart's argument :

"I couldn't see any reason why they couldn't have taken a longer period in the first place. That way, everybody would be happy really. But they decided to look at a six month period, three months high and three months low. There isn't really any reason for it."

If the presenting officer had performed the role of the *amicus curiae* in full the tribunal would have been nudged in the direction of a decision acceptable to Stuart. One might also criticise the presenting officer for not drawing attention to the possibility of a change of circumstances review.

In general, once presenting officers had highlighted any errors detected in the appeals submission they were largely passive. This may be because the potential to act as an *amicus curiae* was undermined by lack of specific knowledge of the case. The presenting officer is in the same position as the other panel members in only having the information contained in the submission papers and is therefore not well placed to answer specific queries. Appellants were often critical of presenting officers for this reason, and disappointed that they were unable to explain how their assessment had been calculated or why certain procedural problems had arisen. Jeremy Hebden, the appellant in case 117, observed of the presenting officer:

"He didn't seem to know a great deal about the case. . . . I don't know if he was just given a folder with this in and that's it, or whether he has the case papers. . . . It just seems to be a let down on the CSA side."

It is possible that the procedure would be more effective if cases were presented by the officer responsible for preparing the submission. This is usually what happens with Income Support appeals.[19]

Most presenting officers with whom we raised this issue thought there was value in being able to distance themselves from the initial decision. As one Birmingham presenting officer put it:

"I don't find that I am in a defensive situation, which I think the other officer might find themselves in if they were presenting the case; so there might be a slight conflict of interest."

[19] Wikeley and Young (1992b).

This is consistent with earlier research which found that social security adjudication officers responsible for reconsidering their own decisions were more reluctant to concede that a mistake might have been made than were specialist appeals' officers reviewing decisions taken by others.[20] This is presumably what lies behind the decision to require internal reviews to be carried out by someone other than the officer who took the original decision.[21]

On the other hand it is worth bearing in mind what is lost through divorcing the presentation function from appeals work within the Agency. Wikeley and Young's analysis suggests that tribunals can play an important part in raising the standards of adjudication within administrative agencies where adjudicating officers have to appear in person to explain the basis for a decision.[22] In other words, working practices are likely to be improved where officers experience this form of accountability.[23] As things stand the presenting officer's role at the tribunal is another manifestation of the tendency for a case to pass through so many hands that no one person (or even team) has a full understanding of what has gone on.

(iv) The handling of appeal hearings—justice or rule-based?

We now turn to consider the kind of justice on offer at tribunals. Since the essence of the child support scheme is its reliance on a formula it would appear at first sight that the tribunal's powers must be limited to reviewing the accuracy of a child support officer's decision. As we shall demonstrate, this is not in fact the case. Even the most rule-bound of decision-making tasks involves the exercise of discretion.[24] That is true of child support officers, and it is true also of tribunals.

Maclean and Eekelaar have argued of the child support scheme that "where discretion remains, it is unappealable".[25] This is an overstatement. For example, it is possible for a tribunal to characterise a child support officer's choice of time period as so unreasonable as to amount to an error in law, thus giving the tribunal power to overturn any refusal to review.[26] The tribunal may also require the Agency to carry out further investigations into a matter which is not, strictly speaking, the subject of

---

[20] Baldwin , Wikeley and Young (1992), 71–83.
[21] See Child Support Act, s. 18(7), and, governing disability living allowance, Social Security Administration Act 1992, s. 30(10).
[22] Wikeley and Young (1992b).
[23] Another possibility is for the regional child support assessment centres to make use of specialist appeals officers to write submissions and to liaise with child support officers.
[24] See Hawkins (1992); Davis (1969), 4.
[25] MacLean and Eekelaar (1993), 222.
[26] See Jacobs and Douglas (1997), 72–3.

an appeal.[27] And thirdly, the Child Support Act 1991 places no technical restrictions on the basis upon which a tribunal can uphold an appeal.[28] Thus, for example, the panel may substitute its judgement for that of the reviewing officer, as occurred in the Mullins case. This inevitably means that tribunals are in the business of reviewing earlier exercises of discretion and deciding for themselves how such discretion should be exercised. In short, their role extends well beyond merely checking whether the decision made on review was technically correct on the evidence before the reviewing officer.

On the other hand it is true that tribunals lack broad discretionary powers to do justice as they see fit. In many cases the appellant has appealed on the ground of his not being able to afford the assessment, or because the assessment has failed to take into account specific circumstances. The tribunal is bound to reject such appeals unless errors are found in the original calculations. Panel members regarded child support law as exceptionally rigid:

> "It's more frustrating [than social security appeal tribunals] because there's so little room for manœuvre; there's so few you can substantially alter. It gets to the point where you look through and it's some minor triumph if you can find something that you think you can get your teeth into and perhaps allow." (Birmingham chair)

When we completed our fieldwork there was still some uncertainty whether a tribunal's jurisdiction ran to the date of the appeal hearing or was confined to events prior to the section 18 review.[29] Most chairs confined the appeal to issues relating to the assessment in force at the time the appeal was lodged.[30] In the Mullins case a subsequent change in housing costs came to light during the hearing. Whilst this had no bearing on whether the assessment under appeal was correct, one might have expected the tribunal to at least explain the possibility of a change of circumstances section 17 review. Both Stuart and Doreen Mullins had regarded the section 18 review and associated appeal as a means of achieving a proper level of child support for the future, not simply as a way of correcting mistakes in the original assessment. This was an opportunity missed.

Notwithstanding their narrow conception of the issues raised, panels were often keen to exercise their discretion. Six of the hearings observed

---

[27] For a discussion of the use of the power to give directions under the Child Support Act 1991, s. 20(4) see Jacobs and Douglas (1997), 81–2.

[28] For discussion of the legislative history see Bird (1993), 127.

[29] For analysis of the complex legal position at the time, see Jacobs and Douglas (1997), 73–5. Tribunals can now deal with maintenance assessments subsequent to the date of the review decision appealed against, as well as changes of circumstances since that date: Child Support Act 1995, Sch. 3, para. 5, amending Child Support Act 1991, s. 20.

[30] One chair we observed was exceptional in that she sought to examine each and every matter that might affect the amount of child support payable, regardless of whether this related to before or after the date of assessment

at Birmingham raised the issue of whether the Agency had used a representative period in assessing earnings. Of these, four were resolved in the appellant's favour. In these cases the panel seemed responsive to the appellant's arguments although it was not always clear to us that the Agency had based the assessment on an atypical period of earnings. Even in the other two cases, where the period remained unchanged, the tribunal clearly wished to help the appellant but had realised that to allow the appeal would make the his position worse, not better.

Many tribunal chairs and wing members serve on other social security appeal tribunals or industrial tribunals. They tend to regard sitting on child support appeals as a natural extension of their other tribunal work, an involvement which had enabled them to help vulnerable appellants. A key difference, of course, is that the issues that arise in child support appeal tribunals concern not just the relationship between the State and the citizen but also that between two parents. The panel found it easier to deal with those cases in which ruling in favour of one parent did not have adverse consequences for the other. This attitude was apparent in the Mullins case where one of the members thought that Doreen would be "quite happy" to see Stuart win his case since she derived her income from benefits. The panel hearing Jocelyn Cannon's appeal (case 107), faced with her non-attendance, responded sympathetically to the absent parent's denial of paternity even though they were told of this just five minutes before the start of the hearing. The fact that the father, Roy McLellan, attended the tribunal whereas Jocelyn (on benefits) was absent enabled the panel to respond as if it were Roy who had appealed. In general therefore it was easier for tribunals to exercise discretion when faced with just one parent (whether or not this was the appellant). Where the hearing was genuinely tri-partite (Agency–parent–parent) they were more constrained.

(v) Tribunals as an arena to resolve disputes between parents

Many commentators had regarded the potential for a conflict of interest between parents as presenting child support appeal tribunals with a particularly demanding and distinctive task.[31] Most tribunals under the Independent Tribunal Service umbrella, including the closely allied social security appeal tribunals, pit an individual appellant against the State. But in child support appeal tribunals any decision in favour of one parent may well have adverse consequences for the other. This makes it harder for the tribunal to enter the arena in order to help one or both

[31] See, for example, the views of the President of the Independent Tribunal Service as reported in Council on Tribunals, *Annual Report 1992–3*, HC 78 (1993), London: HMSO, 50, para. 2.111.

parents state their case. The Mullins case-study provides a good example. The chair in this case avoided delving too deeply into the underlying arguments. He mostly left it to Stuart and Doreen to develop these in whatever way they liked. This worked to Stuart's advantage. He had the air of someone used to commanding respect, and he presented his case in a quiet, confident manner. By contrast, Doreen was reluctant to say much at all during the hearing. She seemed to be looking to the tribunal to query Stuart's financial position on her behalf. The chair, however, was reluctant to act on her cues.

An adversarial procedure tends to favour whichever side presents their case more effectively, and in the Mullins case that was clearly Stuart. As Doreen was to observe later in interview:

> "With someone like Stuart, who is on his guard, who is clever and tells lies, it is difficult to catch them out. I don't think they went into it enough, not to draw it out of him. I mean he's got a new boat . . . they only needed to look more into his lifestyle to find that he's got money. . . . I suppose the only disappointment was that they didn't go more for him and sort him out. He's just far too clever. They just accepted everything he said."

In fact, as we have seen, the tribunal did not give Stuart what he wanted, although two at least of the panel members thought they had ruled in his favour. We took this to be a further consequence of tribunals' reluctance to engage with the arguments of the parties. So a further cost of seeking to remain aloof, when faced with unrepresented parents not used to presenting a case, is that the tribunal may end up missing the point.

(vi) Relevance and order

Tribunal chairs have a responsibility to confine discussion to issues relevant to the appeal. This is a particular problem in child support appeal tribunals where the parties commonly feel that they have suffered months or even years of poor service from the Child Support Agency. The tribunal may represent their first chance to express their frustrations directly to someone in authority. Also, some parents remain bitterly at odds. Unless these situations are handled skilfully by the chair, he or she may lose control.

There were marked differences in the way tribunal chairs approached this problem. Some allowed parents to let off a certain amount of steam, whilst others acted quickly, often too quickly in our view, to stifle any contributions deemed not legally relevant. But what is 'legally relevant' in the context of child support appeal tribunals? The legislative framework is complex, and we observed differing interpretations. As noted earlier, most tribunal chairs were not prepared to deal with matters which had arisen subsequently to the decision appealed against. In view of the long delays involved in bringing a case to hearing such a limitation could make the discussion seem artificial, not to say absurd, thereby considerably adding to parents' frustrations. As Tim Wilcox, appellant in case 109, observed of the chairman who heard his case:

> "He wasn't going to listen to anything I had to say about what was happening in the present. All he was concerned about was when I put this appeal in, Christ knows how long ago, must have been a year and a half or two years ago. He wouldn't listen to what was happening right now, and that's what concerns me, what is happening now, not two years ago."

Some tribunal chairs adopted a particularly legalistic approach, refusing to entertain the slightest deviation from what they perceived to be the issues in the case. In one Birmingham tribunal appellants were repeatedly chided and told that the tribunal was not a complaints' bureau. A dismissive attitude towards an appellant's presentation of grievances against the Agency could exacerbate feelings of powerlessness, as with Rodney Eltoff (case 116):

> "It was upsetting me because I kept losing my thread. He [the chair] was saying 'It's not a complaints bureau', but I wanted to put my point forward about all the telephone calls and all the letters I've written [to the CSA]. . . . I thought it was everything to do with it because I wrote twenty letters in ten months, plus the phone calls I tried to make. I've really tried my hardest to sort this out. I've really tried my damnedest."

In another case heard by the same tribunal, the appellant, Patrick Beamon (case 118), was aware that his maintenance assessment was correct and therefore that he had no grounds for appeal. However, he viewed the hearing as an opportunity to air his grievances about the way in which the Child Support Agency had handled his case. This he was not allowed to do. In a subsequent interview Patrick observed caustically that the chair had done his job "brilliantly. . . . He wouldn't let me talk about anything. He didn't want to discuss it. So he did his job". Likewise in case 109, before a Bristol tribunal, the chair rejected every point raised by the appellant, Tim Wilcox. Tim was rebuked for his failure to bring his copy of the submission papers to the hearing. His solicitor's advice was dismissed as offering no grounds for an appeal. When Tim sought an explanation of why he had received three differing assessments from the Child Support Agency, the chair refused to explore this, declaring "this is not a CAB". Thereafter the hearing degenerated, with hostile remarks flying between the chair and the appellant, culminating in Tim storming out of the room.

While the breakdown of this appeal hearing reflected the chair's inability or reluctance to fulfil an enabling role, it also highlights the difficulty facing panels when they have to deal with appellants who have no valid ground for appeal. Arguably, cases such as those of Beamon and Wilcox could better be dealt with by the Child Support Agency if only it were more efficient in handling clients' complaints. An apology or explanation from the Agency would no doubt deter some legally hopeless appeals[32] from being pursued. Apart from being a more cost-effective way of dealing with grievances, it might spare the appellant from embarking on a course of action which, with hindsight, many viewed as a complete waste of time. Another possibility is for tribunal chairs to review cases in advance of the hearing and, where necessary, to raise with the appellant the question whether there are valid grounds for the appeal. At present, as we discuss further below, chairs do not seek to manage cases at the pre-tribunal stage, and this can lead to frustration at the hearing. As Tim Wilcox (case 109) complained to the chair when constantly rebuked for having nothing relevant to say: "Why didn't you write to tell me that I had no ground for appeal?"

Parents' frustration at the tribunal's apparent inability to respond to their grievances could create a problem for the chair. The potential for some loss of control was greatest where both parties attended, especially when accompanied by new partners. Our earlier description of the Mullins hearing illustrates some of the problems of control that can arise where both parents attend. In fact both Stuart and Doreen acted with restraint. There were nonetheless clear differences of view and these occasionally led to sharp exchanges. For example at one point Stuart declared: "I would like to point out that I was never even engaged to this woman. . . ." It might be argued that the chair should have softened the impact of this statement by declaring it legally irrelevant. On the other hand the strategy of most tribunal chairs is to make no response to statements that have no legal bearing on the appeal. In this way, we suspect, they hope not to encourage the kind of legal irrelevancies which prolong hearings, whilst at the same time not closing off discussion in a way which might unsettle the parties and create a perception of unfairness.[33]

Doreen's discomfort at references to her living arrangements led her to ask to be allowed to discuss this without Stuart present. In fact there is no option for parents to present their cases separately. Each has a right to question the other directly.[34] Thus Doreen was obliged to talk about her personal life in Stuart's presence. Even so, the proceedings remained orderly. Both parents kept roughly within the procedural bounds set by a

[32] The intention of the government under the Social Security Act 1998 is that social security and child support decision-making procedures should include an explanatory stage as a means of limiting the number of appeals.

[33] See further Baldwin, Wikeley and Young (1992), 118–21.

[34] Child Support Appeal Tribunals (Procedure) Regulations S.I. 1992, No. 2641, reg. 11(4). The House of Commons Social Security Committee (1996), p. xxiv, para. 52, recommended that all parties be warned from the start of the assessment process that confidentiality might be broken in the event of a case going to appeal.

rather formalistic chair and both largely pulled their punches, neither wanting to be seen as vindictive. As the presenting officer put it to us after the hearing: "Parents tend to be on their best behaviour in front of a tribunal." In consequence, and somewhat to our surprise, there were few outbursts, despite these being somewhat tense occasions.

(vii) Advice and representation

At child support appeal tribunals both appellant and respondent may be represented.[35] As with most other tribunals, however, the legal aid scheme does not cover this. This is despite evidence from several major studies that advice on appeals and representation at tribunals should, in the interests of justice, be more freely available.[36] In the absence of such representation, parents struggle to present their case effectively. The inquisitorial stance adopted in hearings where only one parent was present rarely compensated for the lack of written evidence, evidence which one would expect an expert advisor to have gathered in advance.

Professional representatives figured in only two of the cases which we observed. In each instance this was an advice agency worker who specialised in child support; in both cases she skilfully achieved a successful outcome for her client. Family members acted as representatives in a further three cases. Several parents told us that they did not know where to get advice about their appeals, let alone obtain representation. Solicitors were often discounted, either because of expense or because they seemed to know little about the Child Support Agency. The following accounts were typical:

"The only advice I could get was probably a solicitor, because they are the people who would probably know more regarding a tribunal. If I could afford £90 an hour I wouldn't be complaining about this [maintenance assessment]." (Patrick Beamon, appellant, case 118)

"We phoned solicitors in Kidderminster and they said, 'No, we can't help you; we don't know anything about [the CSA]'." (Bryoni Banks, appellant's wife, case 114)

"Well, talking to [solicitor] about this in general, he can't really help you with it. He says because the CSA is sort of a government thing, there's not a lot he can do about it that's going to make any difference. He's not really offered to represent me. But if he had represented me with this, it's going to be even more money to fork out. But he doesn't seem that interested." (Jeremy Hebden, appellant, case 117)

[35] The Child Support Appeal Tribunals (Procedure) Regulations S.I. 1992 No. 2641, reg. 9.
[36] Bell (1975); Genn and Genn (1989); Baldwin, Wikeley and Young (1992).

The lack of available advice was also noted by the advice agency worker referred to above:

> "We seem to be the only Bureau in the area that's dealing with it in depth. We have referrals from solicitors, who I have to say have given some very poor advice in the past and now don't seem to want to handle it at all."

A few appellants had obtained legal advice prior to the hearing. This included help with completing tribunal papers and advice on how to present their case. Where the client is claiming Income Support the cost of this advice is covered by the green form scheme. This, however, is no substitute for representation. We have already noted, for example, how the chair in case 109 peremptorily dismissed a solicitor's letter as disclosing no grounds for appeal.

In the Mullins case-study the solicitor who had acted for Doreen at the time of her separation from Stuart had also advised her how to handle the appeal. His advice that she should try to give the tribunal as much information as possible about Stuart's financial circumstances was no doubt sound, but it did not enable Doreen to rectify the power imbalance. A professional representative would have raised this issue in advance, would have organised the collection of more solid evidence of Stuart's lifestyle, and would have presented that evidence much more forcefully than did Doreen. This supports the conclusion of other commentators that an inquisitorial and relatively informal mode of procedure, even when pre-hearing legal advice has been obtained, cannot make up for the lack of publicly funded expert representation at the hearing.[37]

(viii) The role of wing members

Tribunal chairs are supposed to enable all those present to participate fully, and this includes their wing members. We could only observe the hearings themselves, and it is worth bearing in mind that members discuss cases both before and after the hearing. Indeed it is a requirement that chairs preview each case with their wing members at the start of each session. We were told by the chairs and members we interviewed that this discussion was generally brief, but helped focus on the critical issues.

During the hearing most chairs invited contributions from wing members, for example asking if they had any questions to put to the appellant or the presenting officer. Such questions were few and far between, although on occasion wing members' interventions did help to clarify

---

[37] See, in particular, Genn and Genn (1989); Young (1993).

the issues. The relatively passive role of wing members was not unexpected given that this is how they have been observed to behave in social security appeal tribunals.[38]

On bringing the hearing to a close the chair usually asks the parties, the presenting officer and any observers to leave the room to allow the panel to deliberate in private. Decisions are usually unanimous but there is provision for majority decisions, in which case both the majority decision and the minority dissent must be given in writing.[39] Whilst one wing member argued that the chair's role was "to cleverly manipulate the lay people into getting the decision that he wants", other wing members and all the chairs whom we interviewed stressed the importance of wing members' contributions. As we saw in the Mullins case it is possible for a wing member effectively to determine the outcome of an appeal. Wing members' contribution appears generally to be modest, however, as is indicated by the fact that post-hearing deliberations are typically brief. Most panels which we observed took between five and ten minutes before inviting everyone back into the tribunal room. In about a third of the hearings the chair announced the panel's decision without adjournment.

The relative passivity of wing members during the hearing means that it is easy for appellants to misunderstand their role. In interview, Tim Wilcox (appellant in case 109) complained of them "sitting there like dummies", whilst Stuart Mullins characterised the wing members at his appeal as "two little old ladies who didn't know what day it was". In fact the wing members in the Mullins case were both intelligent people who possessed relevant experience. One was an ex care-worker who had sat on tribunals for some ten years. At the time of Stuart's appeal she had attended over thirty child support appeal sessions and was sitting once or twice a week on child support appeals alone. The other member had previously been a deputy manager of an advice agency and had sat on half-a-dozen child support appeals. Stuart's strictures were understandable, however, given the way the chair dealt with the hearing. In common with all the tribunals we observed, the function of wing members was not explained and nothing was said about their experience and background. The only comment made by the members during the hearing was to agree with the chair that they had sufficient information to retire and make a decision. In the circumstances it was predictable that Stuart would see their role as marginal.

[38] Wikeley and Young (1992a).
[39] Child Support Appeal Tribunals (Procedure) Regulations 1992, S.I. 1992 No. 2641, reg. 13.

(ix) Tribunals' investigative powers

In accordance with what is meant to be the inquisitorial character of child support appeal tribunals, the chair has power to require either parent to provide further information.[40] Our case-study illustrates what we found to be a general disinclination to do this. Thus, when Doreen queried Stuart's finances, the chair could have adjourned and directed that Stuart produce details of his bank and building society accounts. He did not do this and so could not test Doreen's contention that Stuart had not given a true account to the Child Support Agency. It is likely that the tribunal was reluctant to act upon Doreen's allegations partly because these were not made until the hearing and partly because the case was seen as 'owned' by Stuart rather than Doreen. As a benefit claimant, she may not have been regarded as having an interest to protect.

By contrast, in the five cases in which the parent with care was the appellant the appeal was explicitly based on the ground that the absent parent had not made a full disclosure of his income and that therefore the maintenance assessment was too low. These cases raised more directly the question of the tribunal's ability to discover the truth. In theory the tribunal has considerable investigative powers, certainly when compared with social security appeal tribunals.[41] Thus it can summon witnesses, order the production of documents and take evidence on oath.[42] However it cannot enforce a summons, has no power to require an affidavit and has no direct powers of discovery. Its powers are thus weaker than a court's.[43] In practice there is considerable reluctance to exercise even those powers which the tribunal does possess. In order to understand this it may be helpful to go back one stage.

Prior to the hearing, either a full-time chair based at Salford or the chair appointed to a case can issue directions. It appears that the Independent Tribunal Service envisages that the full time chair will do this only exceptionally, it being thought that directions are best issued by the appointed chair on receiving the appeal papers.[44] The chairs are warned, however, that directing the disclosure of fresh evidence in advance of a hearing might "require the hearing of an appeal to be postponed or even the whole session to be aborted".[45] This discouraging message is developed as follows:

[40] Child Support Appeal Tribunals (Procedure) Regulations 1992, S.I. 1992 No.2641, reg. 5.

[41] See Jacobs and Douglas (1997), 442.

[42] Child Support Appeal Tribunals (Procedure) Regulations 1992, S.I. 1992 No. 2641, reg. 10(1).

[43] See further Priest (1997), 69–70.

[44] Jacobs and Douglas (1997), 429.

[45] *Ibid.*

"Chairmen will wish to exercise their powers . . . sensibly and with caution in order to balance their desire to ensure that the proceedings are conducted in a just, effective and efficient manner with the undesirability of bringing disruption to the listing of appeals with resulting delay to the parties to other appeals, including child support officers. . . . Chairmen will need to be mindful that the resources available to provide the administrative and budgetary support that may be required by, or as a result of, their directions are limited, as are the means by which compliance with a direction can be encouraged or secured. They should not exercise this power in a manner that will undermine confidence in the tribunal system."[46]

It is unsurprising in the circumstances that tribunal chairs appear seldom to issue pre-hearing directions.

An illustration of the Independent Tribunal Service's wish to avoid further delay was provided by one of our Bristol cases (case 106) which was listed for hearing despite the fact that no appeal submission had been sent to the panel members or to the parties. The presenting officer allocated to the case had sought a postponement. The parent with care also sought a postponement on the ground that she could not easily get time off work on the day of the hearing. A full-time chair refused both requests although no reasons were given. At the hearing itself the presenting officer made it clear that he did not think the case could go ahead without the submission. Despite this the chair allowed a preliminary discussion in order to see if the appellant could be persuaded to withdraw his appeal. He was reluctant to do this so the hearing was adjourned to a later date when, it was hoped, the papers would be available.

Another possibility is for the hearing to be adjourned and directions given for fresh evidence to be produced at a reconvened hearing. This is rarely done, for the same reasons as pre-hearing directions are discouraged.[47] The chair in case 107 (who decided not to adjourn despite the non-attendance of the appellant and a last minute denial of paternity by the respondent) explained to us that "we are urged not to adjourn unless there are very good reasons". The Independent Tribunal Service is acutely conscious of the costs incurred when hearings have to be rescheduled and places great emphasis in its training programmes on adjourning only where there is good reason to do so.[48]

When a case is adjourned the question arises as to who should be directed to produce the new evidence. In only one case (case 110) did we see a chair address the possibility of using the tribunal's powers to secure the co-operation of a parent. His uncertainty about attempting this was all too evident. Although the hearing was adjourned so that witness summonses could be issued to the absent parent and his employer, it was

[46] Jacobs and Douglas (1997), 429–30.
[47] *Ibid.*, 456–7.
[48] See generally Harris (1996).

suggested to the appellant, Anna Birch, that she should herself collect evidence to support her claim that her ex-partner's earnings were higher than he had declared. This was daunting for Anna, who would have preferred any investigation to be undertaken by Child Support Agency inspectors:

> "... because it would mean that I didn't have to. Because my relationship with him has been a very painful thing; a lot of things have happened, so it's very hard for me. I feel I am in a position where I have to go and be a private investigator, and apart from having to care for the children, the emotional things that this is going to bring up for me are not going to be comfortable. And I might well get in some sort of trouble if I go round his house photographing his grounds and things like that. I might be in some kind of dangerous situation, but I can't see any other way of gathering the information".

Rather than issue a summons that is likely to prove unenforceable, most tribunal chairs ask the Child Support Agency to carry out any further investigation, either adjourning the case or, more usually, remitting it to the Agency for implementation of its decision.

In all four cases where the Agency was asked to investigate, the appeal had been lodged by the parent with care on the ground that the absent parent had not made a full and honest declaration of his earnings. In each case both the Agency and the tribunal were ineffective in enforcing compliance. In case 123, for example, the tribunal chair promised to expedite matters so that the parent with care, Ravinder Jivraj, was not prejudiced by an adjournment. By the time of our last contact with Ravinder, four and a half months after the adjourned hearing, she had still not been given a date for the new tribunal. As it had taken seven months from lodging her appeal to the first tribunal she now felt that matters had dragged on too long and she told us that she had lost her will to fight. Likewise in case 67 the Agency failed to investigate Gerald Varley's income. The papers submitted by the Agency for the second hearing were completely unaltered. The presenting officer suggested to us that no-one had carried out the further investigation because it was unclear whose responsibility this was. She added:

> "We [the CSA] have not come to grips with self employment at all. . . . We don't have the powers of the Inland Revenue . . . and we don't have the knowledge either".

It is doubtful whether the reconvened tribunal would have got anywhere in this case had not the parent with care, Dawn Varley, herself devoted considerable time to collecting further evidence.

Another form of investigation, asking the Child Support Agency to make further inquiries on the remission of the case for implementation of the tribunal decision, is also problematic. Not only does this require the tribunal to take its decision in ignorance of what may be material evidence, it relies on the Agency to carry out the investigative task in the way intended. In light of the administrative paralysis besetting the Agency this is more fond hope than realistic aspiration. We can illustrate this by reference to case 108. We saw in the previous chapter that Lynette Bass was frustrated by the Agency's apparent refusal to collect information on her ex-partner's new business beyond its first few weeks. This was because the Agency had treated her complaint as a request for a section 18 review rather than for an section 17 change of circumstances review. When she appealed, the tribunal took a broader view of the case. Its decision contained a finding of fact that Perry Bass' income had been inadequately investigated, and that as he had now been self-employed for over a year the Child Support Agency should require the production of accounts. This appeared to mandate a change of circumstances review. Unfortunately the tribunal did not spell out the steps it now required to be taken, stating only that the Agency should conduct a full investigation of Perry Bass' income since January 1994.

The Agency interpreted this as requiring it to conduct a fuller investigation of Perry's income, but limited to the period used in calculating the original assessment. In other words it continued to address the grievance raised by the parent with care within the bureaucratic straitjacket of section 18. Predictably, the assessment was unchanged following this further investigation. As Lynette sadly concluded when she read the tribunal decision again in the light of the final outcome as notified to her by the Child Support Agency:

> "They did a field investigation as the tribunal instructed, but they only looked into the finances up to February 1994, which left me still 18 months behind. Although the tribunal put no date or time limit on it, the inspectors chose to interpret it like that. . . . The last 18 months to get to the tribunal was a total waste of time. But the tribunal did not set a time period. They did mention he'd been in business for a year, but they gave no time period."

It did not help matters that tribunal chairs appeared uncertain of their powers in giving directions to the Child Support Agency. In case 107, for example, the tribunal directed the Agency to determine the issue of disputed paternity when this is actually a matter for the magistrates' courts. The absent parent, Roy McLellan, left the tribunal a happy man, only to have his hopes dashed several months later when the Agency informed him that it could not resolve a paternity dispute in the way directed by the tribunal.

What the preceding discussion shows is that the investigative powers of tribunals are limited and that they find it difficult to require the Child Support Agency to extend its investigation beyond the original decision giving rise to the appeal. As guidance notes put it: "In most cases the CSAT will have to accept the fact that the burden of proof is on the appellant . . . and that it can only act on evidence before it."[49] This places the onus on parents with care to investigate their partner's finances, which is seldom a realistic option.

(x) Doing the sums

We have seen that tribunals are faced with much the same problem as child support officers in that they have to take decisions based on incomplete information. The potential for poor decisions is even greater at the tribunal stage since tribunals do not generally re-calculate a maintenance assessment. Whereas a social security appeal tribunal often concludes with a decision on benefit entitlement, a child support appeal tribunal can only issue directions which a child support officer at one of the regional Child Support Agency centres is then supposed to implement.

To the panel in the Mullins case, this was the least satisfactory aspect of child support appeal tribunals. As the chair explained to us:

> "We talked about it this afternoon before we sat. We all felt it was an unsatisfactory way of resolving an issue, or attempting to resolve an issue. We don't seem to be making full decisions. We are tending to look at a very specific area, like wages, how wages are calculated for instance, rather than deal with the whole thing. We're not really finalising the thing. We're sending it back and the CSA looks at that aspect of it and re-calculates it, or whatever, and then what happens after that I don't know. We never really know what the outcome is. I don't know why we can't make calculations ourselves—perhaps our mathematics are so poor? But if we did, then I suppose we would be in a position where a final decision could be made, and as long as we did it properly, I think that might be better."

The outcome of the Mullins case was in part shaped by the non-conclusive nature of tribunal proceedings. If the tribunal had been empowered to calculate the child support assessment the panel would have realised that taking the twelve-month period prior to the effective date as the basis for calculating earnings would result in a much higher assessment for Stuart. That would have given them pause for thought. It would certainly have made two of its members less confident in assuming that Stuart had been given what he wanted, and less willing to accept the questionable view of the law advanced by one wing member. As it was, the tribunal's decision was so divorced from the overall calculation of child support that its import was not immediately evident to the panel, nor to the presenting officer, nor to Stuart and Doreen.

---

[49] Jacobs and Douglas (1997), 430.

Tribunals can do *some* calculations of course, even if ultimately the task of recalculating the assessment has to be remitted to the Child Support Agency. A whiteboard was provided in the tribunal room at Bristol for just this purpose, but we never saw it used. Except in the case of one particularly thorough tribunal chair, we did not see any panel attempt to work out the figures. In our interviews with panel members it was apparent that they did not see this as their responsibility. One might argue, therefore, that decision-making by tribunals is hampered both by a lack of information about each case and by ignorance as to the implications of their decisions.

(xi) Implementing the tribunal's decision

While the tribunal's decision is implemented by a regional Child Support Assessment Centre, the Agency's Central Appeals Unit at Lytham St Anne's plays an intermediary role, translating the tribunal decision into terms that a child support officer is expected to understand. It follows that, as with most Agency procedures, implementing a tribunal decision is a multi-step process involving different people based in different places. Not surprisingly, if a tribunal finds errors in the way an assessment has been calculated it is generally many months before it is recalculated and the practical outcome of the appeal becomes clear.

The absent parent is expected to continue paying the incorrect maintenance assessment until the tribunal decision is implemented. The delay in implementing a decision can severely prejudice those appellants who, as a result of their appeal, stand to gain a substantial reduction in their maintenance assessment. Conversely, parents with care can lose out where the tribunal's directions are likely to result in an increased assessment. The following comment by Bryoni Banks (case 114) conveys the frustration felt by parents caught up in this convoluted process:

> "And this is what the tribunal [Independent Tribunal Service] told me from Salford as well. They said, 'Once you've been on the tribunal, the man who is there will decide on how much you've got to pay and that will be it'. Well he didn't come up with nothing. It was no benefit to us at all, not really, because we've still got to pay the same amount until it's been sorted out. I may as well have just sorted it out with the CSA anyway: it's been like a triangle."

We saw in the case-study presented in Chapter 5 how Malcolm Bridley came to regard his appeal as merely a further step in his bid to challenge the fundamental injustice of the child support legislation. He felt that he needed to exhaust the grievance procedures before he could take his case to a higher forum, such as the European Court of Human Rights. The last thing he wanted was for his appeal to be treated as a means of correcting mathematical errors in the assessment. But that is exactly what happened, much to Malcolm's disgust. All of his justice-related arguments were dismissed as legally irrelevant and the case was remitted to the Agency for it to correct minor errors in the assessment. As Malcolm later told us:

> "I am not concerned about the details, I am concerned with the grand picture. . . . I get really tired of them [the CSA] looking at it and getting it wrong and all that rubbish."

The impression that lingers from our case-monitoring is that child support appeal tribunals are not in the business of dispute resolution. Instead they offer a further stage in dispute processing. It was rare indeed to come away from a tribunal with a sense that the issue of child support had been finally resolved. Of course, Agency decisions are themselves never final—they are always open to review. This makes parents feel that they are trapped within a never-ending cycle. The divorce courts can also leave parents feeling like this (especially in disputes over children, where orders are never final), but our impression is that courts generate more real endings than does the Agency and its associated reviews and appeals. All too often these conspired to produce a stately administrative gavotte from which parents anticipated no conclusion other than that brought about through their children's majority.

4. CONCLUSION

Child support appeal tribunals are clearly flawed. This is not primarily the fault of those who hear cases, nor of the Independent Tribunal Service. The fundamental problem lies in the child support scheme itself. Investigation and decision-making are separate from one another and there is a lack of finality about the whole process. Neither the Child Support Agency nor the tribunals appear willing to use what powers they have to ensure that all relevant information is disclosed by the parties. As a result the onus is on the appellant to deliver this.

This might be viewed as an abdication of responsibility, but such an abdication is understandable within a system that, at all levels, is inadequately equipped for the tasks and targets it has been set. As in other judicial spheres, the independence of the child support appeal tribunals is not threatened by political interference in particular cases, but rather by a lack of adequate financial, institutional and legal resources. Against this background the regime under which lawyers and courts formerly determined child maintenance in their rough-and-ready way takes on a rather more attractive hue. That is the subject to which we now turn.

8

Lawyers and Courts

1. INTRODUCTION

Throughout the 1970s and 1980s a consensus emerged amongst divorce lawyers and district judges[1] that the principal objectives of ancillary relief negotiation were, first, to provide a home for the children of the marriage, and, secondly, to utilise state benefits to the fullest possible extent with a view to enabling the absent parent to preserve as much of his income as possible.[2] The interest of the Exchequer in making divorce settlements *less* benefit-efficient was not acknowledged by the courts, for reasons which the Association of Registrars made plain in their response to *Children Come First*:

"It is correct to say that many settlements approved by the courts have taken account of the fact that one or other party would be entitled to Income Support and a range of other benefits if income were below a certain level; this has been the case particularly where continued occupation of a matrimonial home by a wife and children has been at stake. The statement that 'avoidable dependence on Income Support is in nobody's best interests' is a statement of belief rather than fact; quite clearly in many of the cases falling into this category it has been in the best interests of the wife and children to make such an order and the courts will have been mindful of the statutory requirement to put the welfare of the minor children of the family as the first consideration. Courts have been criticised for ignoring the interest of 'the taxpayer' in property adjustment packages, but the simple reason for this is that the court is permitted to have regard only to the factors set out in the Matrimonial Causes Act 1973, s.25 and the interest of the public purse does not appear there. . . . Bearing in mind the statutory requirement to keep the interests of the children as the first consideration, the courts have striven and used considerable ingenuity to preserve a home for the children and the custodial parent. This has inevitably involved taking into account the state benefits to which the parents are or might be legitimately entitled and leaving a father, who may have been deprived of all his capital, with sufficient income to start a new life."[3]

---

[1] The judicial officers, formerly styled 'registrars', who adjudicate all financial and property issues in divorce proceedings in the County Courts.

[2] See discussion in Ch. 3.

[3] Submission of the Association of County Court and District Registrars in Response to *Children Come First* (1990), paras. 4.5 to 4.7.

The Registrars' Association was of course right to assert that the Treasury interest was not one of the factors which courts were required to take into account. This reflected the lack of any effective integration of public and private financial support for lone parents. There was no 'policy' as such, although clearly the respective financial obligations of the State on the one hand and absent parents on the other *ought* to have been a matter of public interest and debate long before the Thatcher administration was alerted to the fact that policy was being made by default by divorce lawyers and the courts.

Some solicitors and district judges with whom we discussed these matters in the course of our research confessed to having felt some unease at the way in which the private maintenance obligation had become so attenuated. They accordingly expressed support for what they took to be the key *principle* of the Child Support Act, conceding that court orders for maintenance had indeed been too low:

> "They tended to be pretty nominal maintenance orders, I am bound to say, in the past. You tried to spread around what little there was, and there's no doubt that you were relying on the State helping the couple through, and the wife would benefit by probably getting all the equity in the house. One can see the arguments both ways." (Solicitor for Joe Nixon, case 48)

Whilst some solicitors thought that child maintenance payments ought to have been given higher priority, their practice as family lawyers had made them aware that many separating couples simply could not support two homes—and perhaps maintain two sets of children—out of their own resources. Thus the question tended to be put in terms, first, of how great a priority should be given to preserving the privately owned matrimonial home for the parent with care and her children and, secondly, of the extent to which separated fathers should be required to support the children of their marriage rather than to devote their resources to new partners, new children, or even—as might be suspected—to their own pleasure.

It became apparent in the course of our interviews with absent fathers whose divorces had been concluded under the old regime that many had come to regard maintenance payments as optional—an act of generosity on their part. Alternatively they might be prepared to make some contribution just so long, in their eyes, as they could afford it. When they took on another major financial commitment, they would stop paying. This could hardly be considered irrational or unreasonable in the circumstances pertaining at the time. To illustrate this from one of our interviews, Alan Thompson (case 47) was asked to confirm that he was not in fact paying any maintenance for his children at the time of interview. He replied:

> "No. I've seen the children and they are doing OK financially. The situation was that every time I picked them up for quite some months they had new

clothes on every time, sort of to say, 'well, I'm alright, I can still manage with-out you here'. So I knew they were doing OK and I talked to them and they still seemed to be doing alright. So I don't think financially there is a problem. I think I would feel bad if financially they were struggling. But I mean I don't want to jeopardise this family by paying maintenance for the children when I know they are OK. If I wasn't paying these loans, which are quite substantial, I would probably continue to pay maintenance. It's just that I can't cover every-thing."

So for some men it was a matter of balancing one set of demands against another. But other fathers got away with paying little or nothing. Many men had enjoyed a far higher standard of living than their ex-wives and children and they had also been content to let the State carry the burden of supporting their families while they themselves lived well above Income Support level. This is why many lawyers agreed with the principle of imposing a more realistic maintenance obligation upon sep-arated fathers. As one solicitor put it:

"The CSA has revised people's ideas of what is reasonable maintenance. Before, the court just used to make a standard maintenance order for £15, which bore no relationship to the actual cost of looking after a child. The amounts were pathetic really."[4]

These pre-Child Support Act financial settlements were expensive to the State not only in being 'benefit efficient' from the point of view of the parties but also in the cost of lawyer time that went into them. In the twenty years prior to the advent of the Child Support Agency there was a dramatic rise in the cost of matrimonial legal aid, most of it devoted to the resolution of ancillary relief.[5] Private, lawyer-led negotiation of financial and property issues was made available through the Legal Aid scheme to a burgeoning divorcing population for whom home owner-ship had become the norm. We had a system of publicly funded, pri-vately negotiated divorce settlements which in turn determined the allocation of public resources through the benefit system and through the allocation of public housing. Even as the Thatcher administration prepared for the introduction of the Child Support Agency, the Lord Chancellor was signalling that the legal aid fund could no longer provide a demand-led service. Thus the financial backing essential to a system of lawyer-led negotiation was coming under severe threat.

[4] Occasionally in this chapter we do not supply a case reference when quoting a solicitor. This is because the interview in question was conducted at the outset of the research, for the purpose of improving our general understanding rather than to discuss a specific case.

[5] The gross cost of legal aid for family and matrimonial work (including green form advice and assistance) was £453 million in 1996–7. Net payments have risen from £272 mil-lion in 1992–3 to £393 million in 1996–7. If prices are held constant at 1986–7 levels (based on the retail price index) the average cost of "family" cases in the County Court has risen from £828 to £1,360 per person over the past ten years. Source: Legal Aid Board Annual Report 1996–7, (1997), HC 52, London: Stationery Office.

2. THE CHILD SUPPORT ACT 1991[6]

As we know, the Thatcher government had resolved that the low level of child maintenance payments by absent parents, coupled with the high level of state support for separated families, could not be allowed to continue. Following the Child Support Act the divorce court is no longer able to exercise the power conferred on it by statute to make, vary or revive periodical payment orders in respect of a child whose parents have separated.[7] Legal advisers can no longer negotiate outcomes which are benefit-efficient. They can no longer, in modest or low income families, preserve the family home and offset the woman's concession of maintenance against the man's concession of property.

Even if lawyers endorsed what they took to be the key principles underpinning the Child Support Act, they were concerned about the way in which an already fragmented system was to be rendered even more fractured and yet, at the same time, more rigid. Practitioners and the courts had exercised considerable ingenuity in overcoming the lack of any formal relationship between private and public contributions, but now they were going to have to come to terms with having one element of this complex jigsaw removed from their domain, while the level of payment imposed was bound to impact upon those elements of the financial package which remained under their control. The "three systems" identified by Finer had become four, and the lack of coherence between the various elements had been compounded. In particular there was concern lest the strategies which lawyers and courts had developed for ensuring that children were provided with secure housing would be undermined: it was anticipated that few men would be prepared to give up their share in a possibly appreciating equity if they were also to be faced with an onerous maintenance obligation.

These concerns, expressed by many practitioners in their conversations with us, reflected the fact that the Child Support Act operates in parallel, but on different principles, to the determination of spousal maintenance and property adjustment. The court system rests upon the considerations listed in section 25 of the Matrimonial Causes Act 1973,[8] the majority of which are not relevant to the Child Support Agency's assessment.

[6] All references to 'the Child Support Act' in this ch. are to the Child Support Act 1991.
[7] The courts retain jurisdiction to vary orders made prior to the creation of the Child Support Agency.
[8] These include, in summary: the financial resources of either party, including such resources as it would be reasonable for them to acquire; their needs, obligations and responsibilities; the standard of living enjoyed before the relationship broke down; the parties' ages and the duration of the marriage; their respective contributions to the welfare of the family, including looking after the home; the conduct of the parties, if it would be inequitable to disregard it; and loss of pension rights.

3. THE RESEARCH AGENDA

Our research focused primarily upon the Child Support Agency from the perspective of parents and the Agency's own staff. But we also wanted to discover how the Child Support Act affected the deals struck by lawyers in respect of the various other elements of finance and property. On the face of it there appeared a rather unwieldy relationship between the provisions of the Act and the court's residual role. To take one obvious example, the Child Support Act does not apply to step-children, and any application in respect of those children must still be made to a court.[9]

Another objective was to discover the impact of the Child Support Act upon solicitors' priorities. The legal profession had not previously played a significant role in processing welfare benefit claims, but solicitors might be seen as a natural source of advice concerning child support obligations. Furthermore, there were certain fairly obvious defences available under the Child Support Act—for example, denial of parentage—and we wanted to discover whether solicitors found themselves involved in disputes concerning these matters.

More generally we wanted to know whether the creation of the Agency had led to more or fewer disputes being referred to solicitors. Were solicitors becoming increasingly involved in the financial affairs of *unmarried* parents? In relation to divorce, did solicitors find that quarrels around the remaining elements of ancillary relief had become more or less intractable? How did the Agency influence the time-scale of ancillary relief proceedings? Did solicitors regard the Agency as a threat to their territory and, if so, how did they respond?

4. THE CHILD SUPPORT AGENCY AND ANCILLARY RELIEF

Prior to the introduction of the Child Support Agency solicitors and barristers had negotiated the various elements of ancillary relief, trading off one element against another and viewing the whole as a single "package" (and this term was, indeed, commonly employed by practitioners). As we have noted, child maintenance had not usually been a very significant component within this bargaining process, but its removal from lawyers' control and its prioritising could be expected to influence the tenor of the residual ancillary relief negotiation, if not always its outcome. The

[9] The Child Support Agency is concerned solely with the obligation to maintain 'natural' children. This is out of line with the established principles of English family law relating to obligations to 'children of the family' who need not be the 'natural' children of both parties to a marriage. So the concept of 'child of the family' is retained within divorce proceedings but is foreign to the Child Support Agency.

Agency had introduced a fixed element within what had previously been a fluid negotiation. One solicitor referred to it as a "rigid immovable block . . . that effectively clouds and colours the ability of the couple to negotiate". Whereas previously it had been possible to advance on all fronts, the imposition of a formula had closed off some options: "It provides a cuckoo in the middle of the negotiations which can't be got round. All negotiations now have to be in the shadow of the Agency . . . you are left with a *quid* for which there is no *pro quo*."

As an example, it was suggested that there was now a greater degree of intransigence in respect of marital debts. Whereas formerly absent fathers might have been prepared to accept responsibility for these, they were now less prepared to do so. The Agency assessment does not take indebtedness into account,[10] and since many marriages end not with assets but with debts, some fathers are inclined to adopt a tougher approach to this aspect of the negotiation than was typically the case before the introduction of the Agency.

Some solicitors also claimed that the introduction of the Agency was bound to have an impact upon negotiations in respect of the former family home. In 117 out of 123 cases in our research sample the parents had lived together, either married or unmarried. In eighty-one cases, six of which involved unmarried cohabitants, the home had been privately owned. This pattern of private ownership persisted to a degree post separation, although it was less pronounced. Excluding those cases in which the parents had not yet separated (n = 4) and cases in which the necessary information was not available to us (n = 8), at the conclusion of our research the parent with care was known to be living in privately owned accommodation in fifty-eight cases out of 111 (52 per cent), while the absent parent was known to be living in privately owned accommodation in sixty-four cases out 111 (58 per cent).

As has been well documented, the retrospective nature of the Child Support Act gave rise to a strong sense of injustice on the part of those fathers who had, as they thought, discharged their financial obligations to their former wives and children through a generous capital/property settlement.[11] As an indication of the scale of this particular problem, there had been, at the outset of our research, a settlement in respect of the privately owned former matrimonial home in sixty-six out of eighty-one cases (81 per cent). Further, in forty-three out of our total sample of 123 cases (35 per cent) there was a pre-existing court order for child maintenance. These therefore were cases in which the subsequent involvement of the Agency was almost bound to be resisted (at least by the absent parent) since any maintenance assessment would have to be

[10] Limited provision for such debts is now included in the departures scheme under the Child Support Act 1995.
[11] See also discussion in Ch. 2.

superimposed upon a lawyer-negotiated settlement and court order. As it was put to us by the solicitor acting for Phil Morris (case 58):

> "There's an awful lot of disgruntled fathers. A lot of them feel most unfairly treated because they have often paid solidly and reliably for years, and they believed the system was set up for the genuinely 'absent' fathers . . . not for those who have been dutifully paying."

This same solicitor observed that, in general, newly separated fathers were much less incensed: "As a proportion of their income, they're paying a very high amount, but there's not that sense of unfairness."

It is worth emphasising at this point that there never has been any attempt to secure an equitable financial settlement for separating parents on modest incomes who own the family home. This is because the child welfare principle has taken precedence over a fair division of capital assets. Where the home is privately owned, courts have worked on the assumption that unless there is enough money to enable it to be sold and the parent with care re-housed, she will have to remain there. There would need to be the prospect of a substantial equity before a sale would become a realistic possibility. So for these families there never has been 'justice' in divorce if by that we mean an equitable division between parents. As far as the home was concerned, the man tended to lose out.

Alan Loreto (case 70) was typical of the relatively high-earning man who found himself subject to Agency assessment some years after he had conceded what he believed to be a generous lump sum to his wife, thereby enabling her to purchase a new home for herself and the couple's children. In fact Jane Loreto had received £50,000 from the proceeds of sale of the matrimonial home, Alan retaining just £5,000 for himself. There was also a court order for £28.50 per week in respect of each of the two children. Alan asserted that the generous lump sum settlement was understood by both parties to be in lieu of maintenance:

> "Absolutely. This is why I went for it at the time. It was an option that was open to me and that indeed was the option that my ex-wife asked for. She wanted a clean break—in fact she wanted a house. I look back and think: 'Fine, so can I have £30,000 back please?' £30,000 in 1986 could be an awful lot of money now. If you invested £30,000 in the housing market in 1986 you'd probably have a house now worth £70,000 or £80,000 and none of that is taken into consideration. . . . Surely we should take into consideration the fact that at that time the State encouraged this type of settlement? What is already arranged they should have left alone. By all means change the law now and start warning people from now on that there won't be such a thing as a clean break divorce any more. . . . If that had been the case I would not have made the settlement that I made with her. . . . The thing that really gets to me is how they can justify overruling court orders. To me, the way I understand this is that at the moment the speed limit on motorways is seventy mph. If in three years' time they reduce the speed limit to fifty mph and the penalty for doing seventy mph is a £100

fine, I feel that it's like they can come back to me in three years time and say: 'At the time it was seventy mph, but we know that you travelled at seventy mph a hundred times and therefore it will cost you £10,000 because we are back-dating our fines to when it was no fault to do so.'"

So much for the Child Support Agency's *retrospective* impact. What has been the effect of the legislation upon *current* negotiations in respect of the home? Some matrimonial practitioners anticipated that the 'clean break', with the man transferring all his interest in the property to his former spouse, would become a thing of the past. This in turn would mean that negotiations over the house—or over capital derived from its sale—would be much more difficult to conduct. At the very least fathers would wish to retain an interest in the property which they could realise when the children became independent. The checklist of factors to be considered under section 25 of the Matrimonial Causes Act 1973 would still apply, but absent fathers would become much less willing to concede their entire interest in the property. This point had been made by the Association of Registrars in their response to *Children Come First*:

> "We have no doubt that the way the courts deal with property matters will change. At the very least a smaller proportion of such cases will be settled since husbands will be less inclined to 'give away' their capital if they know that they are to be liable for the full formula award."[12]

Even where the Agency assessment was not known, some solicitors maintained that the fact that the father was *likely* to face a substantial demand would influence negotiations over the property:

> "When advising a father you have to be a lot more cautious about getting them to accept anything less than their half-share [in the home]. There could always come a time in the future, whatever agreement they come to, when the CSA could come along if she's on State benefit and rip up whatever deal you've made. I know there is no one true answer anyway, but now it's less so because you have another imponderable to chuck at them."

Some of the fathers whom we interviewed confirmed this change in their thinking:

> "I've got a lot of equity in the house. Now from my point of view and from my wife's point of view the ideal situation is to say: 'You have all the equity'. That gives her a chance to move away from the area, which would probably have been a good idea. She could have moved away and started again, and I think financially we'd be ahead. I wouldn't have had the expense of paying maintenance. Obviously you've got an obligation, but financially they would be OK because I would have transferred all the equity. That would probably be more than what I will be paying in maintenance over the next few years until the

---

[12] *Submission of the Association of County Court and District Registrars in Response to Children Come First* (1990), 3.

children are of age, so financially they would have been better off and it would have helped me with my new family. That option has been taken away completely now. I've got to pay maintenance, so there is no advantage to me in transferring the equity. I might just as well sit it out and wait for my share. . . ." (Alan Thompson, case 47)

This development—or prospective development—was viewed with trepidation by those solicitors and district judges who had witnessed the popularity of the *Mesher* order[13] decline as it came to be recognised that many resident parents were in no position to buy out their former spouse when the children reached eighteen or ceased full-time education. Now, it appeared, these parents were once again to be required to accept a form of settlement which stored up problems for them in the longer term. As one solicitor explained:

"Two years ago the deferred charge with the husband retaining an interest in the property was gone. We just didn't do them anymore. Because they were hopeless. But my male clients are saying 'No, I will not. I paid once to get the house and bring the family up thus far, and I have now been booted out. I have got to live, I have got to rehouse myself, and the wife is saying she wants the whole of the equity in the property as well! What is fair about that?' And they won't do it. Opponent solicitors are encouraging their male clients to resist, and there is not much I can do about it. . . . If there is £20,000 worth of equity in the property, why should they give it all up, and keep paying at that kind of rate, and have to rehouse themselves and pay their own support as well? So husbands are saying: 'Well, yes, I'll transfer the house to you, but I want to retain an interest in it . . .' But that's no good to the wife at the end of the day, because she's aged, say, thirty now, got young children—say the youngest is two. It might be nineteen years before that youngest child is off her hands, which is when the husband's interest would then have to be repaid out of the profit. She is then fifty. What's she going to do about rehousing herself at age 50? She's not going to get a long-term mortgage, she won't get a 25-year mortgage; best she'll be able to do is probably get a 10-year mortgage, and the cost of that would be astronomical. So all you're doing is putting off a housing problem from today until 15–20 years' time. So it doesn't solve anything. All right, it's another way of keeping a roof over the heads of the children, but it is unsatisfactory all round and one would rather have a complete clean break and get all the bits sorted now."

The creation of the Child Support Agency is not the only factor bearing on these negotiations. Revised DSS regulations under which the Department will no longer meet interest payments on an *increased* mortgage have also had a significant impact.[14] Prior to this change being introduced it had been common practice deliberately to create an

[13] [1980] 1 All ER 126. The principle is that the absent parent retains a financial interest in the family home, but this interest will be realised (generally requiring the home to be sold) only when the children are independent.

[14] See Ch. 3.

increased mortgage liability for a parent with care who was claiming Income Support, thereby releasing additional capital for the husband. This had been a routine tactic, greatly facilitating the 'clean break' in respect of the home. One might argue that it was an attempt to introduce a "justice for parents" (specifically "justice for absent fathers") element into what were otherwise child-welfare dominated negotiations.

Despite the gloomy prognostications of some solicitors, most practitioners whom we interviewed in the later stages of our research reported that the pattern of capital settlements had not been significantly altered. It was conceded that there might be borderline cases in which a sale would now be ordered (and the parent with care required to move to a less expensive property) whereas in the past the man might have conceded his interest, but there was no evidence that courts were prepared to consign mother and children to local authority accommodation. It appeared that the key principle, as courts interpreted the legislation, was that children should either remain in the family home or be rehoused to a not significantly inferior standard.

A critical case in the evolution of the relationship between the Agency and clean-break settlements negotiated by lawyers was *Crozier* v. *Crozier*.[15] This involved an application for leave to appeal out of time against a consent order transferring the husband's interest in the matrimonial home to the wife. The application was made on the basis that a consent order may be set aside where there are new events which invalidate the basis upon which the order was made. In her judgment Booth J observed that the clean break doctrine had never applied in respect of on-going parental responsibilities. The position had not fundamentally altered despite the introduction of a new administrative authority. So the clean-break order was not undermined and the husband's application failed. Ruth Deech is one commentator who has supported the logic of the *Crozier* decision. She has argued that clean breaks can only be between adults, not between a parent and his children, and that it would in any event be difficult to calculate the value of the property transfer. Furthermore, absent fathers' increased housing costs are included in the formula, while the parent with care who keeps the home may be saddled with a mortgage—the home should not be seen as a free gift.[16]

The *Crozier* decision was probably essential to protect the courts from a deluge of retrospective appeals against clean-break transfers. As we have seen,[17] the 1995 Act introduced the possibility of some allowance for pre-1993 clean-break settlements through the departures system. As to property settlements made in full knowledge of the Agency's operations, there is no sign that courts are prepared to threaten the security of

[15] [1994] 1 FLR 126; [1994] Fam.114.
[16] Deech (1996), 95–6.
[17] Ch. 2.

the resident parent. Judges understand the weakness of *Mesher* orders, namely the risk that the children's carer will be rendered homeless when the postponed charge comes to be realised, and so are not prepared to increase the man's stake in the property as compensation for his being required to pay more maintenance. This means that in most cases there is little scope for the absent parent to retain a stake in the home, however aggrieved he may be at the child maintenance assessment which he also faces. The following solicitor's comment was typical:

> "Very often, in the kinds of cases I handle, the amount of equity in the house is fairly small. And it's such a rough and ready thing, thinking how much the charge back should be. [The CSA] has had an influence, but not the big dramatic difference that was expected. People were saying: 'This is the end of the clean break, we will never have that situation again . . . charge backs will be much higher'. But if you actually look at the orders that are coming through, they are much nearer to how they used to be. . . . "

Alan and Pam Aristides (case 61) provide a dramatic illustration of the Agency's limited impact upon property settlements. In this instance all aspects of ancillary relief were resolved after the advent of the Child Support Agency, so the lawyers would have known what they were doing. Despite the fact that Alan was assessed as having to pay £317 per month maintenance, he still conceded his entire interest in the family home, which at that point had an equity of some £30,000. This couple had three young children so it was inevitable given Alan's relatively modest earnings (£12,000 p.a.) and Pam's dependence on Income Support that she and the children would need to remain in the home. But it might be thought surprising that Alan (or his solicitor) did not seek a postponed charge. The suggestion that he might have conceded too much was put to Alan's solicitor. She argued that Alan had a reasonable income, and furthermore that his main concern had been that he should be able to buy a place of his own. He had started by wanting something out of the house, but she had advised him that this was not a practical proposition in the short or even medium term, given that his youngest child was aged only two. He would have had to wait a long while and in all that time he would have had to contribute to the mortgage on the former matrimonial home. So she advised Alan that he should relinquish his share of the equity in order to make a fresh start. The only significant difference following the introduction of the Child Support Agency is that Alan has had to pay much higher child maintenance. Pam's solicitor estimated that, prior to the introduction of the Agency, she would have been prepared to accept as little as £10 per week in child maintenance. Alan was now having to pay several times that sum and yet had not managed, in compensation, to secure any part of the former matrimonial home. The fact that her former husband was required to pay more maintenance did not immediately benefit Pam (or her children) since she remained dependent on Income Support. However it might be argued that the way is now open to her, when the children are a little older, to secure part-time work and so come off Income Support. Unfortunately this outcome would only be feasible if Pam were able to earn sufficient to meet her mortgage costs. This important reservation aside, the Aristides case might be regarded as a good example of the policy of the Act brought to successful fruition.

In considering the resolution of ancillary relief in cases such as that of Aristides one must also bear in mind the fact that the slump in house prices in the early 1990s left courts with far less room for manœuvre than they would have enjoyed in a period of house price boom. As it was put to us by one district judge:

> "At the moment, if there is a dispute, it's more likely to be over who's going to pay the debts. . . . If we ever get back to rising property prices and lots of people in full employment, then I am sure that by then the Child Support Agency will have worked its way through and it will be necessary for the calculations which we thought we were going to need at the outset."

As we write, there has been a modest recovery in house prices. Whenever there is equity in the family home the attempt to do justice between parents will come into conflict with the (generally overriding) principle that the 'roof' must be preserved for the children.

5. THE IMPACT OF THE CHILD SUPPORT AGENCY UPON THE NEGOTIATION TIMETABLE

Another question for our research was whether the introduction of the Agency affected the overall time-scale of ancillary relief. One or two solicitors told us that it had not, but the consensus appeared to be that there was significant delay created through having to wait for the Agency to deliver its assessment. Many solicitors took the view that they had no option other than to do this, thereby greatly adding to the delays which are endemic in these negotiations.[18] Given that so many Agency assessments take over a year to complete—even with the full co-operation of both parties—solicitors' case-handling was bound to be compromised. A typical scenario was one in which the resident parent was a borderline Income Support claimant. Were the assessment to result in her being floated off Income Support this would lead her solicitor to adopt a very different approach to negotiating the other elements of ancillary relief: most solicitors felt unable to conclude their negotiation until they knew whether or not this was going to happen. The resulting delays were worse

[18] Davis, Cretney and Collins (1994).

than under the old system, when all the finances would be placed in the hands of lawyers—or so it was claimed:

> "We have got many more cases now which should have ended simply, long ago, but haven't done so and are still remaining in the court. We have got numerous cases where either no assessment has been made, or we are waiting for a review. We can't proceed any further with the court case because the judge said he's not prepared to make a final order until he knows what the final assessment figure is . . . therefore he adjourns and there we are sitting for months and months and months. Meanwhile the case still goes on, your client's in touch with you, so it is increasing costs if the client has to repay their legal aid costs at the end of the day. It is just incurring a greater burden on the Legal Aid Fund because the case is not dealt with promptly and swiftly."

> "I have a client who separated in November, and it is now August and no assessment has been made. My client is now on Income Support, and her husband is a manager at the Co-op—so it's not as if it's a difficult case where he's self-employed—he gets a wage slip each month. We have been poised for a settlement for months now, but it is difficult to finalise without knowing what the CSA demand will be. Of course, I can do a calculation, but I wouldn't like to finalise on that."

Other solicitors pointed to the circularity involved in their attempting to anticipate an Agency assessment which would take into account the parties' housing costs while at the same time seeking to resolve the property issues—and so determine those very same housing costs. One way around this might be to proceed on the basis of undertakings, but this is obviously less satisfactory than having all the elements of the financial settlement weighed in the balance together. Instead we have a two-tier system which has done nothing to remedy the defects of publicly funded private negotiation, but which has added a separate bureaucratic layer which the lawyers struggle to assimilate as best they can.

In order to help us explore this question of the relationship between the Agency assessment and the rest of ancillary relief negotiations we now present a single case in rather more depth.

6. THE STORY OF ANNE AND PHILIP HUGHES

This was a second marriage for both parties, each having children of their previous relationship. There was also a daughter born of this second marriage. Anne left Philip in late 1993. Their relationship had become strained after he suffered a serious accident which left him permanently disabled. Thereafter Anne claimed Income Support and this led to the involvement of the Child Support Agency. She did not receive any maintenance for the children of her first marriage and nor did she look to Philip for maintenance for their daughter. But she had to comply with the demands of the Agency and therefore she completed the forms when these were sent to her. The former matrimonial home was council-owned and Philip continued to live there.

Shortly before we interviewed Philip in October 1994 he was awarded £120,000 in compensation for the injuries which he had sustained in the accident. Anne sought a relatively modest part of this award for herself in the divorce settlement—sufficient to enable her to buy a property of her own. Philip did not resist this in principle, although the amount was not agreed. Nor, he said, did he resist paying maintenance for his daughter. However he did object to paying when Anne's first husband did not con-tribute at all to the children of that marriage. Philip was also intent upon paying any money into a trust fund rather than to Anne direct as he feared she would not spend it on their child.

When we first spoke to Philip he was waiting for the Agency assess-ment to arrive, for the lump sum payment to his wife to be determined, and then for his divorce to be finalised. At the same time he was trying to complete the purchase of a house. His solicitor had advised him, he said, to spend as much as he could of his compensation award in order to limit his wife's claim against this. Philip made no reference to the compensa-tion award when he completed the maintenance enquiry form. He simply informed the Agency that he was in receipt of Invalidity Benefit. He understood that the approach from the Child Support Agency was not something initiated by his wife. His attitude was: "I'm willing to pay anything for Jane [daughter] but I'm not willing to pay for her other children."

When we spoke to Anne, also in October 1994, she appeared quite relaxed about the maintenance question. As she put it:

> "I never had any maintenance off my first husband. I managed without money from him, so why should I have money off Jane's father? He was always out of work anyway, so I thought 'What's the point in going for it, if he's out of work?' So I didn't bother."

Anne had calculated, in consultation with her solicitor, that she would require some £30,000 to enable her to buy a house for herself and the children. The court hearing to determine this issue was set for March 1995.

We can tell the remainder of this story through the eyes of the Child Support Agency. On 21 August 1995 we were granted a full interview with a child support officer, based at Dudley, concerning the Hughes case. He had access to the computer record as he spoke. He started by telling us that he felt fortunate that it was the Hughes case we wanted to discuss with him: it was about the simplest case that he had seen—a straightfor-ward nil assessment. Nonetheless it had taken eight months from Philip's return of his maintenance enquiry form for the Agency to arrive at this. Furthermore, periodic review forms returned in January 1995 had not been actioned at the time we conducted the interview (seven months later). Following the return of the maintenance enquiry form the Agency had asked Philip for "confirmation of your weekly rent". He had replied in March 1994, repeating the rent figure and observing: "I've confirmed it." In fact the Agency had wanted *verification* of the rent but the word used was "confirmation". As a consequence of this, Philip was sent forms 59 and 60, warning him that he would be subject to an interim assessment.

As far as could be discerned from the computer record, this interim assessment was never carried out. There was no notification on the file as to the reason for this. The Hughes case was not assessed until October 1994—nearly eight months after Philip had returned his maintenance enquiry form. He in fact was given a nil assessment, but this did not mean that the case was a dead file as far as the Child Support Agency was concerned; there was still an obligation to conduct periodic reviews. Indeed, the officer whom we interviewed told us that in due course he would expect to complete a revised assessment for a sum in the region of £80 per week.

In February 1995 Philip's solicitor wrote to the Child Support Agency, asking how it proposed to take account of Philip's compensation payment. The opening sentence said that the matter was "extremely urgent so that it is imperative we have a constructive reply by 12 March". The substance of the letter was as follows.

> "Our client encloses CSA form 5, the review form. We need a constructive reply so that this can be made available to lawyers representing the applicant, Anne Hughes, in Birmingham County Court in respect of a hearing on 20 March 1995, this being the final hearing on financial and property matters. In September 1994 Mr. Hughes received £120,000 in compensation for his injuries. Our question is: Does the fact that this money is for his long-term care affect the CSA assessment? With effect from 1 November 1994 Mr. Hughes completed the purchase of a house which required a net outlay of £60,000. Mr. Hughes's capital is necessarily fluid because he will shortly be completing the purchase of a fitted kitchen and bathroom. Further expenditure is required, such as for a ramp. . . . [Figures were provided for the remaining capital, and for the weekly interest].
>
> After the court case on 20 March 1995, and once it is apparent what sum has to be paid by Mr. Hughes pursuant to a child maintenance assessment, and what sum remains after the settlement with Mrs. Hughes, then it will be possible to take long-term decisions with regard to the investment capital remaining in the possession of Mr. Hughes. You will appreciate that at that stage reassessment may well be appropriate by your Agency. The point about which we are earnestly asking for your help is to carry out an assessment of Mr. Hughes based on the information currently available. . . . Please do not delay in replying with a constructive assessment."

So Philip's solicitor provided the Child Support Agency, admittedly only five weeks before the final ancillary relief hearing, with a full account of Philip's financial position and asked, in return, if the Agency could determine his child maintenance liability in order that this might then be taken into account in calculating other elements of ancillary relief, notably the lump sum to be awarded to Anne. We asked the child support officer what had happened in response to this letter. He replied: "We haven't delayed. We haven't replied at all", and laughed apologetically.

In fact, under the Child Support Act regulations the lump sum award would not affect Philip's initial assessment because it had not been available to him at the time the assessment was conducted. However, the income generated from the capital would be taken into consideration when his case came to be reviewed. In other words it was a significant—and relevant—change of circumstance. We asked why the solicitor had had no reply to his letter. The officer replied:

> "Basically this was before we went to the system whereby we action all post as it comes in. At the time we were using a BF (brought forward) system. This would probably have been BF'd. Put in a folder to look at as and when possible, and then the system changed and it has just stayed in there and never been answered."

Philip's solicitor had assumed, quite correctly, that the interest generated by the large capital sum would render Philip liable to a significant maintenance assessment. This in turn would be taken into account in any ancillary relief hearing. But the lawyers were given no assistance by the Agency in calculating what that liability might be. There was no response to the solicitor's letter in time for the court hearing—indeed, no response ever. Anne's ancillary relief application was made the subject of a court order on 20 March 1995 in the absence of any indication from the Agency as to Philip's long-term maintenance liability.

When we spoke to Philip again in April 1995 he had spent a considerable sum in renovating his new home. He had no inkling that the Child Support Agency might yet demand a significant sum from him in child maintenance. Anne Hughes was likewise content with her lump sum settlement and was not concerned about ongoing maintenance payments. She was happy to remain dependent upon Income Support.

Our final conversation with Philip was on 29 September 1995. He had been contacted by the Agency (this was immediately following our interview with the child support officer, suggesting that this had become a research-driven case).[19] Somewhat to his bemusement, Philip had been asked how much Council Tax he was paying. He was of the view that the

[19] The so-called 'Hawthorne effect' under which researchers influence the practices they seek to observe is a feature of socio-legal as of many other kinds of research. It does raise difficult ethical issues and, naturally, is something we strove to keep to a minimum.

deal struck by the lawyers protected him against liability for maintenance imposed by the Agency. This is not our understanding, but we did
not follow the Hughes case beyond September 1995 and so cannot report
whether a further periodic review was conducted, or whether this
resulted in a significant maintenance assessment against Philip. Were it
to have done so, we have no doubt that he would fiercely resist making
any such payment.

7. ANTICIPATING AN ASSESSMENT

The Hughes case was unusual in that it involved a large compensation
award, but the difficulty created by having two sets of financial calculations running in parallel was common to many of the cases which we followed. A few solicitors tried to anticipate the assessment, employing the
Child Support Agency formula; others would only do this when specifically asked to do so by their client; and others appeared to ignore the
whole thing. The following was one typical comment:

> "I generally don't, unless clients want me to, sit down and complete an assess-
> ment for them. This is because it takes so long to do it and the other thing is, to
> do the assessment properly you also need the other party's details . . . it
> becomes quite complicated. I can give them a rough idea, based on the adult
> allowance and what is allowed under Social Security regulations, of the sort of
> figure they would be after, but I normally don't go any further unless I am
> specifically asked to." (Solicitor for Laura Chapman, case 43)

But the lack of clear advice could be disconcerting for the client. This
was the reaction of one absent parent, Alan Thompson (case 47), whose
solicitor had conveyed a pessimistic view of his potential liability but
who had not actually undertaken the maintenance calculations himself:

> "My biggest concern at the moment is not knowing how much I'll have to pay.
> If I could go to my solicitor and he could say within a few pounds, 'this is what
> you're going to be paying', it would put my mind at rest. It doesn't matter what
> the figure is, at least I'd know and I'd be prepared. I'm just waiting for that let-
> ter to drop through the door and I'll have a heart attack. . . . At the moment I'm
> fearing the worst."

Other solicitors told us that it was routine for them to attempt the calculation—it made little difference which parent they were acting for,
although there were significant differences between benefit and non-
benefit cases. Where the carer was not on benefit, and unlikely to apply,
there was greater freedom of manœuvre since he or she could choose
whether to invoke the Agency. But even if it was decided to attempt a
private settlement, the solicitor would still need to know what the
Agency figure might be. So some solicitors told us that they would do the

calculation in every case. If it was a benefit case they would do the calculation with a view to letting their client know what the assessment would eventually be. In a non-benefit case they would do the calculation to discover what *might* happen should the caring parent make a claim (or be forced to make a claim) and, secondly, to provide one possible basis upon which the immediate 'private' negotiations might be conducted.

Some of these solicitors had embraced the technology which enabled them to anticipate the assessment:

> "We have a computer programme so that we are able to work out CSA assessments—Child's Pay. We have a Legal Executive here who has the task of working out these assessments and she usually deals with queries. It's just more work for us to have to do a CSA assessment at the start of the case to advise the client what they can expect to receive, and we keep having to do changes as it goes along, as their income changes, or the husband goes off and rents a property or something. We end up doing the CSA assessment three or four times during the case. But having the computer programme, you just have to alter the one figure and that's it."

Other solicitors adopted a much more rough and ready approach, not untypical of ancillary relief negotiations in general. The fact that the solicitor advising the parent with care could not predict the assessment was of a piece with her inability to get to the bottom of many other aspects of the husband's financial circumstances. It was just one more element which remained shrouded in a certain amount of mystery, but this was not necessarily deemed to be a fatal impediment to a successful negotiation:

> "I don't think that the CSA in itself has vastly interfered with the operation of a case from the solicitor's point of view. I personally take into consideration a CSA calculation, as far as I'm able to do so. I don't think it's a science particularly, I think there's a bit of an art to it. And I have observed other solicitors likewise who will make a CSA calculation when agreements are considered. I do it manually. I don't have any of these computer things, and I think you start developing a bit of a gut reaction, so we're readily able to advise on the calculation that they are likely to get." (Solicitor for Paul Tranter, case 7)

One might imagine, in non-benefit cases, that a hypothetical Agency assessment would be a powerful weapon in the hands of the solicitor acting for the parent with care, but it was seldom used in this way. That may be because solicitors (and more importantly, courts) are wedded to their old ways of thinking, believing that the more important goal from the perspective of the carer and her children is to secure a roof—and to secure a roof it may be necessary to make substantial concessions on the maintenance front. It may be true, as one solicitor put it, that "the richer the client, the more frightened they are of the Agency", but that did not necessarily mean that solicitors would conduct a hypothetical Agency assessment in order to negotiate a higher maintenance figure: it would very much depend on the needs of the parties in that particular case. But if there were some prospect of the caring parent claiming Income Support that was something that would be borne in mind in negotiating other elements of the income/property package. This made for considerable difficulty for the absent parent (and his legal adviser) because in negotiating a private settlement he had to bear in mind the possibility that he might be faced with a much more onerous maintenance obligation at some point in the future.

8. SOLICITOR KNOWLEDGE OF AND DIRECT INVOLVEMENT
WITH THE CHILD SUPPORT AGENCY

For the most part, as they themselves acknowledge, matrimonial practitioners have not striven to make themselves expert in the operation of the Child Support Agency. This was noted with dismay by some clients , this being the reaction of Lynn Enderby and her new partner (case 65):

> "He should be able to say: 'Well yes, this is the course of action to take.' But he doesn't advise you. Certainly on the CSA they haven't a clue. It is something they seem to back away from. . . . I came out of there, I told him what was going on, and he just agreed with me basically. So I didn't come out of there any the wiser, did I?" (Lynn Enderby)

> "I do believe that lawyers should have somebody set up in their own department to sort this out, because they seem totally oblivious to all this. When you go to a solicitor, when you look at the fact that we pay £215 an hour, and you ask a question about the CSA and they say they can't help you, it's a bit off-putting to be honest with you. You need someone who can say: 'Oh yes, we have someone in the department who can assist you and knows some legal loopholes'." (Peter Enderby)

We had direct evidence of solicitors' inability to advise their clients about the Agency. For example, when we attended the child support appeal tribunal in the case of Paul Roberts (109) the appeal papers included a letter from Paul's solicitor in which, as the main plank of the solicitor's argument, he asserted that his client was "financially incapable of meeting the payments". The solicitor also referred to the fact that the assessment had not taken into account his client's travel and household expenses. The chair's dismay in the face of these legally irrelevant observations was a sight to behold. He observed that "many solicitors appear not to understand the basis upon which the Agency operates and so give very bad advice".

Clearly it is desirable that solicitors understand the formula and the procedures adopted by the Agency, but it has to be remembered that the

Legal Aid fund does not pay them to advise in this area, and furthermore that separating parents are now increasingly selective in the help which they seek from solicitors. This did not stop some parents being highly critical of their solicitor's lack of expertise, but others were more understanding. This was how Tim Wade (case 56) viewed the matter:

> "I tend to be a bit independent in that I will use a solicitor in respect of what needs to be done, but I prefer to back it up with my own research. So I expect to be able to get that information from the CSA direct and not to have to rely on my solicitor to get it. I was informing her of what the situation was with the CSA. I wasn't looking to her for support—not with the CSA anyway. I actually prefer to deal with them direct, and all I was really doing was copying correspondence to her, and I sought her guidance only in so far as it impacted on the other negotiations. . . . I have got no criticism or adverse comment in terms of the advice and information she gave me. It was very frustrating to find that the solicitor wasn't able to give more information, but in terms of the dealings that I was having with the CSA, it didn't surprise me. So I certainly wouldn't criticise her. If I couldn't get it, she wouldn't be able to get it."

Whilst most solicitors acknowledged that they had had only peripheral involvement with the Agency, we came across a few practitioners who had developed a special expertise in the area. This usually arose from their role as legal adviser to a particular group of employees—for example, the Police Federation. Solicitors who had this kind of responsibility were often extremely knowledgeable.

The only other circumstance in which a solicitor felt the need to become expert in this field arose where she had a client who took the Agency to court in order to resist a threatened attachment of earnings. This is what happened in the case of Michael Seeley (case 54). The outcome here was instructive in that, it being one of the earliest such applications, the Agency found that it had not followed the correct procedure. Accordingly it sought to withdraw the threatened attachment of earnings and vacate the court appointment. Mr. Seeley's solicitor would have none of it, pointing out that it was her application, so the Agency could not simply withdraw. On the day of hearing there was no attendance by the Agency, the order was overturned and costs were awarded in favour of the applicant. This case involved a very determined rearguard action against the Agency, fought with the assistance of the solicitor—but this level of lawyer involvement was exceptional. In general solicitors did not expect to deal directly with the Agency as they would a court. This is because most Agency decisions are not open to review. They can be subject to appeal on the basis that there has been a miscalculation or some significant oversight, but solicitors cannot apply general legal principles to a particular set of circumstances as they would in ancillary relief negotiations conducted with another lawyer.

It should also be emphasised that there is no presumption of Agency contact with legal advisers. Solicitors do not have privileged access to Agency staff: if they want information about a particular case they are liable to experience the same frustrations as do parents. The following jaundiced comments were typical:

> "I've written countless letters to the CSA and I've had real problems. This lady's file there, I got the file out the other day to review it and I've seen that I've written four or five letters and I have not had any reply. You hear horror stories about sackfuls of mail disappearing at one of their offices." (Solicitor for Surbinder Lamie, case 36)

> "I've helped some people fill in forms—not that we get paid for that. But clients tend to phone the CSA themselves and they become resigned to the fact that nothing is going to happen. Therefore it's pointless for solicitors to intervene. Partners in the firm who have written to the CSA on behalf of clients get standard undated letters back." (Solicitor for Kirsty Smith, case 12)

The fact that solicitors do not get paid for their attempts to communicate with the Agency is doubtless a disincentive to becoming too heavily involved, but an equally fundamental problem for the solicitor is that the Agency's line of communication is directly through the client. It does not behave like a court, or a fellow practitioner, each of whom would normally act on the assumption that correspondence should go via the solicitor. It is not surprising that solicitors feel ill-equipped to advise in these circumstances: they may have a better *understanding* than the client, but they are not running the case, and in certain respects they may be less well informed than the person whom they are seeking to advise.

9. THE IMPACT OF THE CHILD SUPPORT AGENCY UPON SOLICITORS'
WORKLOADS

A related question is whether the creation of the Child Support Agency has meant more or less work for solicitors. The minority view was that, at least in the early days, the Agency had led to more work rather than less. A few solicitors pointed to the transitional arrangements and the need to incorporate an assessment according to formula into each case:

> "In some ways it has added to my workload. Working through the calculations is time-consuming, and putting that into the equation when looking at the capital settlement takes time. . . ."

Meanwhile there was no less need to secure financial disclosure or to review the full financial history of the marriage. The negotiations had, if anything, become more complicated. Other solicitors told us that they had to deal with queries concerning assessments which in themselves created additional work:

> "The main issue I find is how to deal with women who have to cope with the delays and how they are treated by the bureaucracy. That is the principal effect on my work: at the first interview I have a litany of forms having gone missing, being recycled, sent to the wrong address, very mixed responses to enquiries."

There might also be queries from people who were thinking of applying to the Agency, and from absent parents seeking advice on how to complete the form. So there was some reactivating of old cases, now subject to assessment by the Agency, plus additional work attributable to Agency involvement. However, the dominant view amongst solicitors was that there was now less work for them to do in the average divorce case because there was less to negotiate about. Some solicitors had anticipated a flood of queries relating to the Agency, but for the most part this had not happened. Amongst our sample of 123 cases, absent parents had sought advice from a solicitor in eighty-four (68 per cent). But for the most part legal advice was *not* sought in respect of the Agency. It has always been the case that the (typically) male respondent is less inclined to seek legal advice than is the (typically) female petitioner, and this pattern is now being repeated with respect to the Agency. Solicitors are not seen as providing a solution to the 'problem' of the Agency—mainly because most absent fathers have absorbed the message about the inflexibility of the formula.

Most solicitors appeared to accept that the child support assessment was something best left to parents to sort out. As we have seen, they might try to anticipate the calculation to enable them to negotiate the other elements of ancillary relief, but cost considerations precluded their doing more than that. The following comments were typical:

> "Mr. Wade's done it all. In fact I don't think I have ever had any contact with the CSA. The problem is that people like Mr. Wade—privately paying clients— if they can do it themselves, they will do, which is quite reasonable. Just point them in the right direction, give them the paperwork—I think I probably gave him my calculation pack—and they are able to do it." (Solicitor for Tim Wade, case 56)

> "I offer them advice under the Green Form, but it is limited obviously. We do our best to do a calculation and check once they've got the assessment, but it's so complicated that it's very time consuming I find, despite the fact we bought a computer programme to try and assist with the calculations. But it's still not something I can do in ten minutes." (Solicitor for Richard Timms, case 60)

Given that there is pressure on solicitors to anticipate the Agency assessment, the question then is whether these calculations, which can take time, are covered under a Legal Aid Certificate for ancillary relief. The answer seems to be that the calculations are included within the scope of Legal Aid but the solicitor will not be paid for dealing directly with the Agency on the client's behalf.

As to the green form, the problem is that advice on the formula, or on any other aspect of dealing with the Agency, takes up so much time that there is very little left over to enable the solicitor to do anything else for the client. We can see from this that the impact of the Agency upon solicitors' workloads in part reflects limitations in the scope of the Legal Aid scheme, and in part it reflects declining eligibility.[20] One solicitor told us that she believed that her firm would have to devise a scheme of discretionary rates, somewhere between Legal Aid rates and their standard client charges. (Her private client rates were twice those of her Legal Aid clients.) As it was, she was finding that, taken together, reduced Legal Aid eligibility and the maintenance demands generated by the Child Support Agency were having a significant impact upon clients' approach to using solicitors:

> "People don't just plonk everything on my desk and say 'do it for me'. They're much more attuned to. . . . 'Do you offer a free half hour?' [laughs] and things like that. People are much more sussed about that. More people are refusing offers of Legal Aid because the contributions are so much higher. If they're already being knocked out with this massive assessment from the CSA, they're not particularly keen to give solicitors another three hundred pounds to sort it out for them, when actually the prospects in most cases are that you won't be able to do much about it. So it is affecting the work. . . ." (Solicitor for Carl Mullaney, case 52)

It has always been the case that some men have chosen to struggle on without legal advice, or else have consulted solicitors on a very occasional basis, but that tendency has become much more marked since Legal Aid eligibility was tightened. Many men will consult a solicitor and then go their own way again, trying to employ whatever advice they had received in the course of the one appointment. Alternatively they will consult a solicitor from time to time when they became concerned about a particular issue. This is now the standard pattern, in marked contrast to the protracted, lawyer-led negotiation so characteristic of ancillary relief proceedings.[21] Lynn Enderby (case 65) was typical in this respect, as her solicitor explained:

> "I would normally have advised on maintenance, but Mrs. Enderby was a privately paying client and did not ask me to, and she would not have thanked me for running up costs. My experience is that since eligibility for Legal Aid has been cut back a lot of people who are privately paying are not in a good position to pay substantial fees, and so I am very mindful of not running up unnecessary costs. In a case like this I would proceed very carefully. In a case

---

[20] According to Lord Chancellor's Department estimates, eligibility for legal aid in respect of a civil matter (including Family and Matrimonial) declined from 68% of the adult population in 1989 to 53% in 1992, and thence to 48% in 1997. These figures relate to civil legal aid eligibility with or without a contribution (personal communication).

[21] Davis, Cretney, and Collins (1994).

involving more affluent people, for peace of mind both parties accept there should be an order and are prepared to meet the expense of that. With legally aided cases, clearly even the Legal Aid Board accepts they should be resolved. But the Enderbys were caught in the middle, and there are more and more of such cases these days."

Likewise Carl Mullaney (case 52) took advantage of a free half-hour consultation which he saw advertised—and that was the last his solicitor saw of him. This was not because he was dissatisfied with the service which he had received—on the contrary, he had found it very helpful. If he had not had to pay for her time he would have wanted the solicitor to check his assessment and, since there were many matters which he disputed, he would have wished her to enter into negotiation with the Agency on his behalf. But because he knew how expensive a solicitor's time could be, he preferred to do these things himself. This was a clear example of a man of modest income and limited educational attainment who felt that he had to skimp on legal advice in circumstances where he was clearly out of his depth. The solution which he eventually hit upon— giving up his employment—was one which occurred to him following the coverage of the Agency in the news media.

Some solicitors presented a cogent case against the present trend towards requiring parties on modest incomes to conduct their own financial negotiations on divorce or separation. They argued, and we think fairly, that the practice of family law has improved in recent years as it has become more specialised and, furthermore, as it has been accepted that it is a reasonable field for bright young lawyers to enter. The evidence of *Simple Quarrels*[22] was that specialist matrimonial practitioners deliver a much better service than do non-specialists.[23] Many firms had resolved to provide a decent service to ordinary people, inevitably with heavy reliance on Legal Aid. That philosophy is now under threat. As one solicitor put it to us:

> "The culture of my firm has always been one where . . . 'why should it just be Lloyds Bank or XYZ plc who have people with brains and commitment?' I don't see any reason why ordinary people shouldn't have the right to that, and I don't see why there should be this kind of discrimination over 'well, if you're on Legal Aid, you have our most junior member of staff.' We have never actually organised ourselves in that way. But there are firms that do, perfectly understandably."

The implication of this solicitor's remarks was that even his firm might have to submit to these pressures in time, although his own practice was notably successful. It is indeed ironic that this level of threat to the matrimonial practitioner is being experienced even as the degree of special-

[22] Davis, Cretney, and Collins (1994).
[23] See Genn (1987) for similar observations in respect of personal injury litigation.

isation increases.[24] It is important to ensure that effective, principled solicitors are not driven from this particular market place, whether for economic reasons or—amounting to much the same thing—through the creation of an intolerably pressurised work environment.

10. KEY COMPARISONS BETWEEN THE CHILD SUPPORT AGENCY AND LAWYER-LED NEGOTIATION

The focus of this chapter to date has been upon the impact of the Child Support Agency upon the residual elements of ancillary relief and upon the role of matrimonial practitioners generally. We shall end by making some direct comparisons between the way in which the Agency operates and the way in which lawyers and courts have tackled these same issues in the past. We shall focus in particular upon problems in securing full disclosure and, secondly, upon the issue of effective case management or, as we term it, 'responsiveness'.

(i) Disclosure

One potential inequality which is not always redressed by the legal process lies in the parties' capacity to manipulate or conceal resources.[25] The discretionary model is effectively a settlement model. This does not always work as intended, one reason for this being that to settle cases requires a reasonably comprehensive knowledge of the parties' financial circumstances. In practice a settlement is often negotiated despite there being significant gaps in this knowledge. It is usually the woman who seeks an order, while the man may be prepared for the stalemate to continue; and it is likewise more commonly the man who is being pressed to give a full account of his finances, the woman's circumstances being comparatively straightforward. Given the pressure on the parties to reach a settlement, the discretionary model favours whoever has the greater capacity to withhold information. Considerations both of cost and of the need to limit delay may lead courts (and opposing legal advisers) to tolerate some degree of concealment. At the same time they have the option of pursuing full disclosure through interlocutory applications and, in theory at least, the court has draconian powers to enforce its own procedural orders. So either party may be able to get away with some measure of concealment, but solicitors will claim that whilst it is unrealistic to attempt to turn over every stone, for the most part they succeed in exposing (and remedying) any flagrant attempt to conceal resources.

[24] See the growth in membership and influence of the Solicitors' Family Law Association.
[25] Davis (1994).

If we accept this to be the case, how does the Child Support Agency compare? This is a matter concerning which critics of the legislation have consistently expressed grave doubts, the argument being that it would be impossible for the Agency to match even the limited effectiveness of courts in securing full disclosure from obstructive parents.[26] This is because there is neither the will nor the resources to enable the Agency to go behind the figures presented on the maintenance application form or the maintenance enquiry form. It is therefore placed in the position, at least in the first instance, of accepting each parent's version of his or her financial circumstances. It is almost as if there were no adversarial element in these proceedings, and yet anyone familiar with divorce would have been able to inform the government that financial statements on relationship breakdown are commonly—indeed, routinely—highly contestable and bitterly contested.

We must assume that the reason why there appears no inclination to challenge parents' initial accounts of their financial circumstances is that this would be both expensive and time-consuming. Indeed, it is expensive and time-consuming within the legal framework, and not necessarily very effective either. This is an important point to acknowledge: solicitors and the courts quite commonly come to the end of their capacity to investigate a man's earnings well before the solicitor for the wife feels that a true account has been achieved. Nonetheless more can be done than appears to be possible under the Child Support Agency. For the most part solicitors seemed resigned about this. As one put it: "They don't even have the time to write to you, let alone carry out investigations" (solicitor for Ravinder Jivraj, case 123).

Our research has confirmed that the Agency is ill-equipped to test, and if necessary to challenge, information provided by absent parents—especially that which is provided by the self-employed absent parent. Agency practice, on the contrary, is to take the self-employed parent's account at face value. Were it to do otherwise this would no doubt lead to an impossible number of reviews and appeals. This picture was confirmed for us by solicitors, several of whom claimed that it was easier to pull the wool over the eyes of the CSA than it had been to deceive the court. For example, Lynette Bass's solicitor (case108) was convinced that her client would have had a better prospect of getting to the bottom of her husband's earnings as a self-employed labourer had she been operating within the framework of ancillary relief:

"Certainly I think he would have been required to pay something in maintenance even if he were unemployed. First of all there would have been discovery and financial documentation. And I think if a solicitor were acting on Lynette's behalf she would have required him to produce—though he might

26 Cretney (1992), 184–94.

not have had accounts—trading ledgers, expense sheets, to get a full picture. It is not a number or a name, it is a person you tend to know, and the incentive is there to discover for your client. You are under a duty to do that, so I think that is a lot easier than when you have a load of clerks who are sitting there with computer-generated stuff. They are also undermanned. We are all under pressure of work but there are few who would deny that the CSA have just too much to cope with; so things which take a lot of time and investigation, they have not got the resources to do it."

In theory a parent who believes that her former partner has not supplied accurate information about his earnings can appeal. But how effective is a tribunal in these circumstances? As we have seen, tribunals have limited capacity to ensure full disclosure of the parties' finances.[27] In many of the tribunals which we observed there seemed a lack of clarity concerning whose responsibility it was to pursue such further investigations as might be required; both the Child Support Agency and the tribunals appeared to lack the resources to pursue an effective investigation. Certainly there appeared no mechanism to assist Agency staff to identify clearly fraudulent statements, so that the onus lay entirely with the other parent to challenge the assessment and pursue a remedy. It seems therefore that the system relies, just as courts rely, upon the *parties* to identify deficiencies in the information supplied. But the Child Support Agency is not designed to be driven by the parties: as a government bureaucracy it is meant to do its own driving. Courts, on the other hand, are geared to *respond*. They rely upon energetic and determined legal advisers to drive the case along. Nonetheless, on the basis of our research evidence it would seem that courts, for all their deficiencies, operate their party-driven model more effectively than the Child Support Agency operates its bureaucratic one.

(ii) Responsiveness

On the basis of earlier research into the negotiation of ancillary relief[28] it was observed that for solicitors faced with a workload of 200 cases it is almost impossible to initiate or to monitor progress; the solicitor can only respond to immediate demands. The authors referred to this as the responsive mode, arguing that few cases were really "managed" in any meaningful sense of that term. The system was characterised by settlement, but not necessarily by a purposeful settlement seeking; instead it was characterised by delay, with much depending upon the knowledge, determination, and negotiating skill of the respective legal advisers. Payment by item of chargeable work encouraged low-level activity on a

[27] See Ch. 7.
[28] Davis, Cretney and Collins (1994).

large volume of cases, so that each case tended to last a long time, although most were settled in the end.

The parallels between this account of financial negotiation in the hands of lawyers and the Child Support Agency's approach to case management—as we have observed it and as it has been conveyed through a variety of internal and external reports—are not hard to identify. Of course the Agency has had to deal with a lack of co-operation from many parents. But the same might be said of solicitors trying to advance a contested application on ancillary relief—they too are faced with all manner of resistance. The question to be asked of either 'system' is: can it overcome these obstacles? Many of the solicitors whom we interviewed were highly critical of the Agency, comparing its performance unfavourably with what they would have been able to achieve within the court framework. For example:

> "In the old days, you could get a court order for child maintenance. Now the CSA is onto it, you send off the forms and wait months and nothing happens. The CSA sit on it, arrears build up, and of course they are never recoverable."

The problem with such accounts is not that they exaggerate the failures of the Child Support Agency, but that the performance of solicitors and courts under the former discretionary regime is presented in an unduly favourable light. The latter was reliant upon the applicant (or rather, her legal adviser) making proposals for settlement and thereafter, should it prove to be necessary, advancing the case to trial. It also relied upon courts to enforce their own procedural orders. All too commonly, neither of these things happened. This picture was confirmed in the course of our current study. Many of the cases which we followed saw solicitor negotiations running alongside the Agency assessment. The comparisons were not always unfavourable to the Child Support Agency: for example, in case 94 Sue Williams' solicitor failed to reach a financial settlement over the course of two years' desultory negotiation; the Agency, by contrast, did at least secure her some maintenance. Several of these cases manifested the style of solicitor case handling reported in *Simple Quarrels*—that is to say, negotiation entirely through correspondence, with each letter eliciting in due course a letter in reply, but neither solicitor getting to grips with the fundamental issues in the case and formulating proposals for settlement.

If the applicant (or, in Agency terms, the parent with care) has an ineffectual solicitor the costs to her lie not only in increased anxiety and delay, but also in the likelihood that she will fail to secure a substantial part of her capital entitlement. This is what happened to Maureen Hyde (case 49). She eventually settled for £2,500—a sum that her solicitor conceded was far from satisfactory given that her husband had received a substantial redundancy payment shortly before they separated. But by the time the Legal Aid Certificate was secured and affidavits filed—some twelve months later—the redundancy money had all been spent.

It was not untypical of the cases which we followed that even as Maureen Hyde failed to obtain a satisfactory lump sum settlement in the course of ancillary relief proceedings, she was equally unsuccessful in obtaining even token child maintenance through the Agency. Her financial salvation lay, as it happens, in forming another relationship and moving in with her new partner—still the most effective route out of poverty for the lone parent.[29] That particular solution is neither available to nor desired by all, but the Hyde case was instructive in that it involved unsuccessful attempts to resolve the other elements of ancillary relief alongside equally unavailing efforts by the Child Support Agency to complete a child maintenance assessment and enforce payment.

But whilst both the Agency and legal advisers might fail to achieve the money transfer which they are seeking, certain features of the two performances are very different. An advantage enjoyed by solicitors is that they are at least *contactable*, even if this is a bit of a struggle sometimes. It was commonly asserted, contrary to popular wisdom, that "courts have a human face"—human, that is, compared with the faceless Child Support Agency. So from a communicative viewpoint the Agency bureaucracy is not favoured, whilst solicitors and courts, even if they fail to deliver, fail to deliver in person.

The court system is also more flexible than the Agency: a section 18 review deals only with the facts as they were at the time of the original decision—and it is quite common for this to have been taken a year or two prior to the review. Solicitors may be slow, and prior to the introduction of the Agency courts routinely ordered maintenance payments that fell well short of the true costs of child care, but at least when a further application was made courts brought their decisions up to date.

Blame for this lack of responsiveness should not be placed at the door of Agency staff—they must operate the legislation as they find it. But the Agency was meant to advance these cases to assessment and, if necessary, to enforcement in the face of predictable parental resistance—and it has not managed to do this any better than the lawyers. There was meant to be a fundamental difference between court resolution and the Child Support Agency. The former relies on whichever party actually *wants* something bringing the case to the court door and demanding resolution. The process is understood to be dependent on the parties and their lawyers. The critical difference between the courts and the Child Support Agency is that the Agency accepts responsibility for bringing each case to a conclusion. More than that, it undertakes to carry out periodic reviews. In theory this should be preferable from the point of view

---

[29] Eekelaar and Maclean (1986); Maclean (1991).

of the applicant. Unfortunately, as was predicted, the Agency has in a great many cases proved unable to secure the necessary information upon which to base an assessment; it has failed to enforce the assessment; and it has failed to review the assessment at the time stipulated. The Agency was not meant to operate in responsive mode—and yet, as we have described, that is what it has ended up doing. An under-resourced bureaucracy has proved more random in its effects than the discretionary court system (the lawyer-led/party-driven system) which it in part superseded.

11. CONCLUSION

One characteristic of our legislative process—and certainly a characteristic of the introduction of the Child Support Agency—is that important social legislation can be introduced at great speed and with a minimum of consultation, essentially because there is a strong political motivation behind it. In general the government is wary of consultation where the presumed 'experts' are known to be hostile to the broad thrust of the reforms proposed. In the case of the Child Support Agency the government paid scant regard to the people who were most knowledgeable about the operation of the pre-existing system (many of whom were lawyers) because it was assumed that the introduction of the Agency was at odds with lawyers' interests and that their arguments were based on self-interest rather than on a dispassionate view of the then existing procedures. Of course lawyers may not have been dispassionate, but they were at least in a position to provide an account of why the court-based system had developed in the way it had, with all its acknowledged deficiencies. It is largely as a result of this failure of consultation that the Child Support Agency gives every impression of being yet another example of policy-making on the hoof gone badly wrong.

At the same time it is easy to forget—and to be dismissive of—the cost implications of our longstanding reliance upon state benefits to support separated families. Some parents, especially fathers, looked back nostalgically to a pre-Child Support Agency golden age when they paid a few pounds per week maintenance per child, topped up by some additional (and undeclared) contribution for holidays, clothing or pocket money. The modest court orders for maintenance which were made at that time were very acceptable to these fathers, several of whom persuaded themselves that they were being generous in paying slightly over the odds, or in making the occasional additional purchase for the children. If the parent with care was in receipt of Income Support she had no incentive to seek an increased maintenance figure. Some parents simply could not understand why this arrangement need be disturbed, if both were happy with it.

Parents with care had a less sanguine view of the former discretionary system, accompanied as it was by the lack of any effective system of enforcement. The accounts provided by those who had experience of both regimes were consistent with the evidence gathered in the course of earlier research, namely that many men got away with paying little or nothing, that they were quite content to let the State meet the cost of maintaining their children, that they were reluctant to pay even the modest sums required of them by the courts, and that there was no effective means of enforcing these often token payments.

Solicitors whom we interviewed in the course of this study frequently claimed that, had they been given a free hand, maintenance would have been arranged expeditiously and non-payment would have led to immediate enforcement action by the court. Despite such claims the reality of the operation of the discretionary model was that its effectiveness—both in securing orders and enforcing them—was extremely mixed. Nonetheless it was free of some of the most severe handicaps suffered by the Child Support Agency. The system was driven by lawyers, one of whose motives was to make a living out of it, and given that matrimonial lawyers were—and largely still are—paid by item of chargeable work, it is not difficult to see the potential inefficiency in that particular funding arrangement. But solicitors at least have a direct relationship with their clients. They also have direct access to the courts. They were, and indeed remain, individually accountable. The system was not cheap, but it was controlled by the parties and their representatives. At the same time it was not particularly effective in overcoming resistance and intransigence at whatever stage of the process these were experienced, including non-compliance with court orders.

This acknowledged weakness had led some solicitors to advocate the setting up of an administrative authority, but one whose role would be limited to that of enforcement. Others had had the same thought, but their experience of the Agency had led them to lose faith in even this limited conception of its function. The lack of direct contact with the parties and the reliance on essentially formulaic communication were viewed as undermining this, as every other element of the Agency's operation. Of course we have to be careful not to take these strictures entirely at face value. As a group solicitors prefer principles to formulae, and they do not favour standardisation. It is in the nature of administrative systems to slot people into boxes, and some achieve this with reasonable efficiency. But it is doubtful if there have been many attempts to do this in the context of failed personal relationships, against the background of continuing reliance upon state resources, whilst at the same time seeking to respond, and to keep on responding, to changes in either party's financial circumstances. That was a tall order indeed.

It is by now evident—and this study has confirmed—that the advent of the Child Support Agency has led many separating and divorcing couples to feel more threatened and more beleaguered than under the previous discretionary regime. The reason for this lies not only in the predictable failure of the Agency to achieve the money transfers which were envisaged, but in the multi-faceted attack upon the role of lawyers in divorce. The decline in Legal Aid eligibility has led many parents to soldier on alone when badly in need of authoritative advice and support. The government's answer, it would appear from the Family Law Act 1996, is increased resort to mediation. The Child Support Agency regime is based on obligations rather than rights, obligations imposed without much subtlety and without reference to what many parents argue are valid distinctions. Mediation is not about rights either: it is reliant upon the effective pursuit of compromise and consensus. Lawyers, even operating within a discretionary framework, represent a rights-based approach. This has now been repudiated and largely replaced by an uneasy combination of obligation and consensus—an unsubtle obligation and what may yet turn out to be spurious consensus.

9

Relationships and Negotiations

The determination of financial issues on relationship breakdown is always liable to be contentious. This is so whatever mechanisms are involved. We must not attribute all disagreements between parents over money to the advent of the Child Support Agency: divorcing parents have always argued over these things. This has to be borne in mind when reflecting on the many painful, difficult quarrels which we observed in the course of this study. Otherwise there is a risk of naïvely attributing effects to the Agency when these have in fact been observed in the course of previous studies of ancillary relief in the hands of lawyers. This is far from saying that the Child Support Act has not made any difference—or even, in certain circumstances, that it has not made things significantly worse.

In this chapter we shall try to assess the impact of the Child Support Agency on the relationships between ex-partners, between parents and children, and within second families. We shall also look at some of the ways in which parents have tried to use the Agency for their own purposes—to improve their bargaining power, or to redress what they regard as wrongs done to them. We begin with the story of Lynn and Brett Enderby, a couple who struggled initially to come to terms with the impact of the Agency upon their already fraught relationship, but who eventually achieved resolution of a kind.

2. THE STORY OF LYNN AND BRETT ENDERBY

Lynn and Brett Enderby (case 65) had been married for eleven years when they separated in October 1994. They had two children, aged eight and four at the time of our research, both of whom lived in the former matrimonial home with Lynn and her new partner, Peter. Lynn and Brett had been separated for almost a year when we interviewed them, he having "thrown her out", as she put it, when he discovered that she was having an affair. Initially Lynn went to stay with her mother, but then Brett found a new partner and moved in to her local authority accommodation. This enabled Lynn to move back in to the former matrimonial home where she took up residence with Peter and resumed care of her two children. This case is noteworthy for the fact that Lynn Enderby had at least as much power in the subsequent negotiation as did her husband: she was in full-time employment, as was Peter, and she earned at least as much as Brett. Lynn was, moreover, the more articulate and forceful personality. It was she who had brought the marriage to an end, whereas Brett would have preferred for it to continue.

We interviewed Brett after he had moved to live with his new partner, Iris, and her eight-year-old daughter. He worked full-time as a shift supervisor, while Iris worked part-time as a cleaner. Iris had come off Income Support when Brett moved in. She had increased her working hours, but calculated that she was still worse off than before she met Brett. She did not get any maintenance from her ex-husband, and indeed did not want to approach him as she regarded him as a violent drug user and not someone she wanted to have contact with her daughter.

Lynn's new partner, Peter, was in financial difficulties. He was being asked to pay maintenance for his two children. The situation was complicated in that he still co-owned *his* former matrimonial home, on which there were mortgage arrears. His former wife was in receipt of Income Support and the building society was refusing to transfer the home into her sole name. This meant that Peter was unable to negotiate a joint mortgage with Lynn—which was unfortunate given the pressure upon Lynn to buy out Brett's interest in the former matrimonial home. Peter had nonetheless stopped paying the mortgage on *his* former matrimonial home, as he explained to us:

> "I stopped paying the mortgage about two months prior to leaving, and that was basically because of the CSA. They do not take the mortgage into account unfortunately. I had no option really."

> Lynn: "That's why it gets hostile. Because if he says he can't pay the mortgage she is up in arms about it. But the reason you can't is that you just can't afford to pay it. Surely a roof over your children's heads is more important than the amount of money coming into their hands . . . because he was willing to pay the mortgage plus £60 a week. But the CSA don't see it like that."

Brett meanwhile had entered into a "voluntary agreement" with Lynn to pay her £50 per week. This just about met the cost of Lynn's childminder. She did not consider that the amount was adequate:

> "I don't think it is fair because £50 a week for the children is nothing in my opinion. I know he earns quite a substantial wage, not colossal, but I felt that he could give them more."

Brett on the other hand considered that £50 was ". . . not bad for two children . . . I can manage that."

Despite feeling that £50 was parsimonious, Lynn told us that she would have been prepared for this level of maintenance to continue. But unfortunately Brett reneged on at least one payment. As he recalled:

"The first time I bounced a cheque on her. There wasn't enough money there. But I paid her the next day in cash. But she put that to her solicitor and said I was paying it erratically, which I wasn't. I know I shouldn't have bounced a cheque on her, but I didn't mean to and I paid her the next day."

Lynn however alleged that there was a *pattern* of irregular payment and concluded that decisive action was called for. As she explained:

"A month after he moved out he stopped paying the mortgage, saying he couldn't afford it. He said he could afford to give me £50 a week, take it or leave it basically. So obviously I took it. But I had cheques bouncing, irregular payments and all the rest of it. And it was a worry for us because we didn't know where we stood financially. We had quite a lot going out for Peter's children, and not enough for mine. So after a lot of umming and aahing we decided to go to the CSA—not from malice, but because I thought it was the only way of sorting out the finances because he wouldn't play ball. If he was making regular payments I wouldn't have gone to them and he wouldn't have got into this situation."

Brett's account of the build-up to Lynn's approaching the CSA was somewhat different from hers:

"She said she couldn't manage the mortgage. I was giving her £300 at first, but I told her I couldn't manage it and I dropped it down to £200. I couldn't afford to pay it. I said to her I couldn't manage it and she didn't say any more about it then."

Brett claimed that Lynn's decision to approach the Agency had damaged their relationship, but Lynn was more sceptical:

"Yes [it affected the relationship] to a certain extent . . . but because of his financial position it probably would have come anyway. I think he used that as a scapegoat. He was in financial difficulty already . . . it hasn't helped."

Brett was assessed by the CSA as having to pay £77.61 per week in child maintenance (or £330 per month). He told us that he was "devastated" by this, particularly as he had debts amounting to £4,500—partly, he said, as a result of a loan incurred jointly with Lynn.[1]

The CSA had further calculated that Brett owed arrears of £1,097. Brett disputed this, claiming that it did not take account of the voluntary payments which he had made. He was also dismayed at the assessment fee, pointing out that he had not asked to be assessed, and furthermore he was not "the guilty party". He told us that he had tried on a number of occasions to telephone the Agency, but the number was always engaged. Brett told us at this stage that he was contemplating becoming bankrupt, and also that he was considering giving up his job as he could not afford to pay what was being asked of him.

---

[1] As we shall see, Lynn denied responsibility for this loan.

He also began to put pressure on Lynn to agree to the sale of the former matrimonial home (in which she was now living with Peter and her two children) in order that he might have his share. Both Lynn and Peter interpreted Brett's attempt to force the sale of the house as a response to the Agency assessment, particularly the demand for arrears. Lynn resolved that she would tell Brett not to worry about the arrears: "If that is what is really bothering him, forget it, and I will forget it. I would rather have the regular payments of £330 a month, knowing that it is coming in regularly, so that we know where we stand." But Brett did not think that he could afford to pay £330 per month. He was labouring under a strong sense of injustice:

> "They don't take anything else into consideration. The idea is to save money for Social Security, isn't it? I saved them money by moving in with Iris. It would be cheaper for me to move out . . . and another thing, I'm not the guilty party. Obviously if it was the other way round it would be different, but I wasn't the guilty party in the first place."

Brett and Iris claimed that their relationship was affected by the financial pressures upon them, and that they were contemplating having Brett move out in order that Iris might once more claim Income Support and have her rent paid by Housing Benefit. But, she said, this would probably lead to their breaking up:

> "It nearly split us up three weeks ago, with this £1,000 arrears. We've just had one thing after another. The council tax as well . . . we had problems with that. We just thought it was best we split up. If he moved away and we saw each other say three nights a week then eventually that would have split us completely because I don't think it's fair on me or my son—because he's accepted Brett as his father and he's never really had a father. It would upset him and would cause problems again. But it might come to that."

Lynn and Peter meanwhile resented the pressure from Brett for them to sell the former matrimonial home. Lynn told us:

> "He's blaming the CSA, but he's not making any contributions at the moment so the CSA don't come into it. He's blaming them because of the assessment, but he's in financial difficulties anyway. It's his fault as far as I'm concerned. He's got loans, but I don't know what for. A car I think. But not loans that I've left him with."

Peter was even more hostile:

> "Quite honestly, I think for somebody to get into financial difficulties because of his own incompetence . . . it is totally unfair that our home should have to be sold because of his financial commitments."

Brett was unrepentant:

"It's because of the debts that I've asked my solicitor to get her to buy us out. I obviously don't want the kids to go on the streets, but if she won't sell the house the courts automatically take it anyway."

Brett reported with some satisfaction that following his solicitor's letter about the house, Peter had come to see him in an effort to negotiate. He began to think he could see a way out of his financial problems:

"He's panicking now because they might have to get out . . . originally I wanted her to buy me out and she said there was no way. And now the situation has come that I have to clear my debts and the only way they can be cleared is by taking collateral out of the house. If she buys me out it should be about £6,000, and that would clear my debts. If she won't, then the court will automatically take it . . . the mortgage is £40,000 and the house is worth about £52,000 or £53,000, so what's left is split between the two of us . . . I should be entitled to half of it."

In this period the relationship between Lynn and Brett became extremely acrimonious. Iris told us:

"She [Lynn] keeps coming: she comes every week, knocking on the door, causing trouble, shouting and bawling every day. We've had to change the phone number. We keep getting phone calls and if I pick the phone up, she'll put it down. Even Brett's family have had phone calls."

Following the change of phone number Lynn was able to contact Brett only at his work. This she did frequently. This was how she explained the deterioration in their relationship:

"I've been up to his house a couple of times when I've had to, for solicitor's reasons, and she's got abusive to me, so I won't go up there any more. So it's very very hard to get in contact with him. The only place I can do that is at his work. If anything happens to the children, I can't get in contact with him other than going up there."

Interviewer: "Have you tried to negotiate directly with him over money?"

Lynn: "Yes. But he just says he can't afford it. I think basically his commitments to his relationship are more important than his commitment to his children . . . as times have gone on I get the feeling that he is being manipulated from the other side. I think her child, because she is living with them, gets whatever he has to give."

Interviewer: "And Brett goes along with that?"

Lynn: "Yes. He's soft."

In fact the story of Lynn and Brett has, by the standards of the Child Support Agency, a happy ending. Brett had found the one tactic—pressure on Lynn to agree to a sale of the former matrimonial home—which was likely to bring him some relief from his financial problems. When we spoke to Lynn and Brett some four months later we found that a resolution of sorts had been achieved. Lynn told us that she and Brett had "come to an agreement without the CSA". The Agency assessment had been for £77 per week, but Lynn had talked this over with Brett and they had come to an agreement that he would pay £60. This was effectively a bargain between the two of them. We asked Lynn how the agreement had been reached (given that when we last spoke to her the relationship between her and Brett had completely broken down). She told us that Brett had come round to talk to her. He said that he was worried about his debts, but that if the maintenance figure were reduced he would not have to require Lynn to sell the home: "I was in a position where I could help him, and he could help us because of the house." Lynn also told us that she and Peter had resolved that as soon as they could they would raise a loan in order to buy out Brett's interest in the home. Then they would not have to worry any more about being put under pressure to sell.

We asked what would happen if Brett went back on his agreement and either stopped paying maintenance or tried once more to force a sale. Lynn said that if Brett did this she would simply go back to the Agency:

> "I'm using them as a lever. . . . I don't have to keep pressurising him for money because I know that if he doesn't pay me I will go to the CSA and say he is not making regular payments and they will sort it out for me."

Brett confirmed that his involvement with the Agency was now "stopped" as he and Lynn had agreed a lower maintenance figure. He attributed the agreement to his solicitor having written to Lynn's solicitor seeking a sale of the former matrimonial home. Brett told us that he was now "just managing to cope" with the various financial burdens which he carried. He was keeping his creditors at bay, and Lynn had accepted that there was no need for him to pay the arrears. Brett told us that "I can't see anything changing unless she decides to go back to the CSA". He was still living with Iris.

At the point when we last had contact with them, Brett and Lynn Enderby had emerged from a turbulent few months with a financial agreement which they had themselves negotiated and which both were satisfied with. Their relationship was not warm but they were no longer at loggerheads.

3. NEW FAMILIES FOR OLD

In over 40 per cent of cases in our study one or both parents claimed that their relationship had suffered as a result of Agency involvement. Other researchers have reported similar findings.[2] The Enderby case demon-

---

[2] Clarke *et al.* (1994).

strates that it can be extremely difficult to disentangle the specific effects of Agency involvement from the various disagreements and unhappinesses which might have existed in any event.[3] The process of obtaining ancillary relief through the courts was productive of its own tensions, in the course of which some divorcing couples would blame their unhappiness on the legal process.[4] Once this litigation was concluded, however, most people gradually came to terms with their new situation and with each other. This became more difficult for some parents following the introduction of the Child Support Agency. Some men seemed to be obsessed with the Agency and its perceived iniquities, blaming it for just about everything that had gone wrong in their lives.

Forcing parents to give more money to an ex-partner with whom they are on bad terms is likely to exacerbate the ill-feeling between them. This is fundamentally different from the pre-CSA pattern when divorce would commonly involve property adjustment, but *not* substantial on-going maintenance payments. Many solicitors and district judges whom we interviewed alluded to problems which arose from the fact that, in a great many families, money no longer followed the bonds of affection. Most people accept financial responsibility in respect of those with whom they have a continuing relationship—even if that relationship is attenuated through divorce or separation—but they tend not to accept it otherwise.

The question of which of two families—the 'new' or the 'old'—we expect separated fathers to support is well ventilated. At its simplest it can come down to a stark choice between two principles: to uphold the obligations of marriage—that is to say, first marriage—and the power of the blood tie; alternatively to accept the power of a current relationship and the needs of children living in the same household. This issue is complicated by the interests of the State, and specifically the Thatcher administration's belated recognition that it was paying a high price for permitting men to walk away, leaving their children a roof but precious little in the way of daily bread.

The Child Support Act 1991 was intended to make absent parents worse off. Ancillary relief orders made prior to the introduction of the Agency had downplayed the element of child maintenance in most cases. This was done in order to maximise parents' call on state resources through Income Support and the associated mortgage interest payments.[5] The whole point of the Child Support Act was to make divorce settlements less 'benefit-efficient'. It is hardly surprising in the circumstances if we witness a degree of parental conflict which can be attributed to the introduction of the Agency. Furthermore, given the dependence of so many separated parents upon Income Support, and

[3] Ahrons and Rodgers (1987); Davis (1988); Davis and Murch (1988).
[4] Davis, Cretney and Collins (1994).
[5] These questions are explored in greater depth in Ch. 3.

given also that there is no 'disregard' of maintenance payments, the Agency was bound to confer pain upon absent parents without any compensating benefit for the carer and her children. In the great majority of cases, and certainly in all Income Support cases, the Agency assessment either made no difference to the caring parent or, if she found herself just above Income Support level, she might be worse off in real terms.

Separated parents still need to co-operate with one another. Experienced solicitors understand this, and prior to the Child Support Act the entire ancillary relief negotiation was coloured by a sense of what the children's interests required. A common objective was to preserve the home, and the absent parent might be prepared to assist in this, for example by paying half the mortgage interest for the period before the Department of Social Security would take this over entirely. Or he might be prepared to pay the instalments on the endowment policy. This kind of 'deal' was frequently done. Solicitors regarded it as routine in cases involving mortgage arrears. Following the introduction of the Agency this kind of co-operation is less evident. One solicitor told us how he now found himself approaching the building society, having to concede that there were already arrears, and saying to them, in effect:

> "Look, we're very sorry about this, but there's going to be another two months' arrears by the end of the next four months; we've got no proposals to pay this off. And by the way she's on Income Support. She's got her club book still to pay off. She can't pay the endowment policy either. . . ."

In this sense the pressure on the man to pay significant amounts of maintenance inevitably undermined co-operation between former partners. The man would realise that from the time he got his first letter from the Agency his financial liability was increasing. One solicitor told us of a case where a father had been paying the mortgage and generally keeping things going; he was then sent a Maintenance Enquiry Form. He showed this to his solicitor, who advised him: "Look, stop paying what you've been paying. Put that money aside, because you're going to get a bill from the Agency." His client did as he was told, but that meant that mortgage arrears started to build.

The introduction of the Child Support Agency also challenged the assumption—perhaps the rather cosy assumption—that second families must be adequately supported before absent fathers could consider paying anything towards their former partner and children. Lynette Bass (case 108) was one mother who complained bitterly that her ex-husband, Perry, paid nothing for their daughter whilst devoting all his resources to his new partner and her two children:

> "It really used to drive me to distraction that he would refuse to accept responsibility for her, and I think what made it worse was when he married: she has two children, and she doesn't claim anything from her ex-husband for those

kids. I fully accept he's got to support them, they're part of his life, but what I do dispute is that *all* his money should go to two children who are nothing to do with him blood-wise while his own flesh and blood daughter gets nothing. He should at least make a contribution to his own flesh and blood."

So we can see that Lynette endorsed the Child Support Act principle that biological parents should retain a life-long financial responsibility for their children. Perry's view was different however: he held that his first responsibility was to the family with whom he lived. He had no compunction about not contributing to his daughter's maintenance. A similar case was that of Nathan Banks and Amelia Radcliffe (case 114). Amelia complained that Nathan's contribution had become much more erratic after he met his new partner, while the informal help which he used to give to her and their daughter Katie had ceased:

> "When he met her, that's when the problem started . . . 'she'll have it when we've got it' sort of thing. Sometimes I'd have to go for about two months without the money. Everything was going all right until he bought a house and moved in with her. If Katie wanted clothes or anything, he would buy them. If she was short of anything all I had to do was phone him and we'd go shopping. There's nothing now, nothing at all. Since he met her he hasn't bothered . . . he doesn't want to know."

Equally, the maintenance demanded of separated fathers could increase the financial pressure on second families—deterring some couples from forming a stable, cohabiting (or married) union, and in other cases generating tensions which contributed to the breakdown of that second relationship. Nathan Banks's new partner, Bryony, was concerned that Nathan was able to give less to *her* daughter since the CSA became involved:

> "The relationship between me and Nathan and Laurie is a bit different, because we can't give her the things you want to give a child. It's no help at all, the CSA. I think the only person who loses really is Laurie, my little girl."

The hardship experienced by Nathan and Bryony was unrepresentative to the extent that Nathan was being significantly *overcharged* by the Child Support Agency following an assessment error. But there were other cases, currently assessed, in which absent parents felt torn between the demands of two families. Where the carer was an Income Support claimant, and so unlikely to benefit financially from any payments made, resistance to the Agency's demands was almost inevitable.

As we have seen, the Child Support Act was intended to stimulate applications from the parent with care against the absent parent, and this in turn was intended to stimulate applications by the new partner of that absent parent should she have children of her own. There is a presumption that each maintenance assessment will ripple out into other relationships, requiring parents who would prefer to reject the principle entirely to apply to the Agency because they (or their partners) are on the receiving end of those same demands. But for some parents the social costs of claiming maintenance through the Agency are too great—even when a member of their household is an absent parent required to pay substantial maintenance: it follows that the so-called 'domino effect' does not always work as intended. This can lead to substantial financial inequity between families who, had the legislation been accepted and implemented universally, would have been placed on a more-or-less equal footing.

There are a variety of reasons why a parent with care may be loath to apply to the CSA even when her new partner is himself paying significant sums to the children of his first family. It may be that the mother does not wish to have any further contact with the father and fears that a maintenance demand would bring him back into her life and into the lives of her children. Alternatively, she may know that he is himself in financial difficulties and be sympathetic. As a consequence one couple—perhaps just one earner—may be required to support two sets of children. The financial pressures can be enormous, and may well contribute to tension in the reconstituted family. Nadine and Angus Bailey (case 85) provide one example. They had married two years prior to our contacting them, and Nadine's children lived with them. Angus's three children lived with his ex-wife, Jill, but visited regularly. Maintenance payments were minimal until Jill, who was claiming Family Credit, was contacted by the Agency. In due course Angus received an assessment of over £100 per week. In the circumstances Nadine felt bound to apply to the Agency for maintenance from the fathers of her two children. One successfully stalled the application, and the other was assessed as having to pay only £2.20 per week. According to Nadine, her relationship with Angus went downhill in consequence:

> "Angus has become depressed, withdrawn . . . he is grumpy all the time. We had mortgage arrears and other financial pressures already. It's just added to it. Our marriage isn't anything like it was for the first 18 months and I don't foresee it continuing. It's one thing losing your home for a good relationship, but to be in an iffy relationship and lose everything, I'm not prepared to do it. It sounds terrible, but it has definitely had a serious impact on our relationship."

By the end of the research fieldwork the Bailey marriage had broken up—in Nadine's view, partly as a result of the pressures generated by the Child Support Agency:

> "The CSA played a part. The marriage wasn't good enough to withstand the pressures. It was a factor . . . it wasn't all of it. Financially, we just couldn't make ends meet."

4. RE-VISITING THE PAST

Another feature of the CSA legislation, much commented upon, is that it operated retrospectively. It is true that under the former court-based system either parent retained the right to apply to the court for a variation in child maintenance payments; in practice however such applications were seldom made, and if they *were* made they tended to result in only very small changes to the amount of maintenance ordered.

Some two-thirds of the couples in our study had separated more than two years before we first contacted them, and a third had separated over five years previously. Only one in ten had separated within the last twelve months. This suggests that the Child Support Agency, at least in the early years, was dealing with a great many cases where the parents had viewed their finances as settled. Within our sample of 121 cases, seventy-nine absent parents had paid some maintenance—albeit this may have been modest or irregular—prior to the involvement of the Agency. Of these seventy-nine, forty-three (54 per cent) were subject to a court order for child maintenance. So well-entrenched patterns of payment (or non-payment) were revisited, and at the same time these revised assessments were generally to the detriment of the absent parent whilst conferring no benefit upon the carer. The lack of any 'disregard' of maintenance payments when calculating Income Support entitlement has always acted to deter payment whilst inviting the carer to collude in non-payment.[6] This lack of inducement has continued post-CSA, but it is following the introduction of the Agency that it has become an issue for parents (as distinct from the Exchequer) because the level of payment demanded is usually appreciably more, and parents with care who are on benefit have no discretion about whether to make an application.

5. SOMETHING ELSE TO QUARREL ABOUT

It is important to bear in mind when trying to assess the Agency's impact upon parents that it is an *additional* element to the pre-existing structure based upon lawyers and courts. To that extent it was almost bound to create new problems, if only because child maintenance discussions had previously been something of a backwater in ancillary relief. In theory, since the Child Support Agency operates by means of a formula, it should not readily be employed to generate the delays and various other frustrations which have always comprised a large element of the divorce experience for many couples; in practice however the Agency can indeed be used in this way—principally by the absent parent, in not responding

---

[6] See discussion in Ch. 3.

to the Agency's requests for information, or, having responded, in not paying the amounts ordered. If separating people wanted to make life miserable for one another they were always able to do this through lawyers and courts; now they can do it through the Agency as well. Of course, viewed from the other side, these gambits and irritations may appear perfectly justified. What one parent perceives as manipulation may, viewed from the point of view of the prospective payer, be regarded more sympathetically as an inevitable response to straitened financial circumstances.

Many of the tensions and frustrations which we have described were a feature of pre-CSA negotiations, but a vital difference prior to the introduction of the Agency was the role of legal advisers.[7] Solicitors were almost routinely involved in the management of ancillary relief. There is no such mediatory figure between parents and the Agency. One might be critical of the way some solicitors managed their cases, but there are many competent matrimonial practitioners, and they were often able to persuade their clients to do the right thing. They were a controlling influence. This support and advice is not available to most parents in their dealings with the Agency.

Solicitors also require their clients to tell the truth—or at least, they will not collude in the transmission of blatant untruths. From the perspective of the parent with care it is galling, to say the least, that the Agency appears willing to accept whatever account of the absent parent's income is presented to it. Wages slips will be required, if available, but even they can be misleading. In effect it is up to the carer to contradict the absent parent's account through the provision of other evidence. It is unrealistic to expect parents always to tell the truth in these circumstances, and the court-based system has an array of procedural responses which can be instigated where one side's version of income and outgoings is not accepted. The Child Support Agency on the other hand is heavily reliant upon parents to supply correct information. The fact that this is not how people tend to behave, particularly when under grave financial pressure, has undermined the Agency's whole operation. It has also heightened the distrust which may already have existed between separated parents.

The Child Support Agency requires parents to perform a number of tasks; for many, these are unwelcome tasks—completing assessment forms, arranging payment, and so on. We know from earlier research[8] that when parents operate strategies of avoidance, or when they otherwise attempt not to meet requirements imposed upon them, this induces a sense of frustration on the part of the former spouse who has to suffer through these stratagems. Prior to the Child Support Act parents

[7] See Davis, Cretney and Collins (1994).
[8] *Ibid* .

relied on solicitors to compile and present their evidence. Now, as far as the demands of the Agency are concerned, they must do this themselves. We noted in Chapter 7 that the appeal process, in particular, could put parents in a position where they felt bound to conduct their own investigations. One example is the case of Stuart and Doreen Mullins, whose story we have already recounted at some length. It will be recalled that Doreen had taken it upon herself to photograph Stuart's new house so as to provide some measure of his lifestyle. Both Stuart and Doreen identified this as having exacerbated the tension between them. Doreen told us:

> "Our relationship is even worse than it was before after what happened in that court [tribunal]. . . . I know the photographs I took of the house really annoyed him. He told my daughter: 'I'm going to put man-traps in the garden so your mother can't get in and photograph my house.' But I didn't need to go on to the property to take those photographs because I've got a long lens."

Long lens or no, if parents feel bound to turn themselves into private detectives it is to be expected that this will give rise to a certain antagonism.

6. MISUNDERSTANDING THE CHILD SUPPORT AGENCY

Misunderstanding concerning the role of the Child Support Agency, and in particular an imperfect understanding of the role of the parent with care in initiating Agency involvement, exacerbated conflict between parents. Whether or not they had been given prior warning, absent parents sometimes blamed their former partner for the arrival of the maintenance enquiry form, suspecting that he, or more usually she, had acted out of malice. Some appeared unaware of the link between the application to the Agency and the carer's benefit status; and some of those who were aware of this link appeared to believe that if the parent with care had not wished to involve the Agency then she could somehow have avoided claiming benefit. For example, Gavin Field (case 92) insisted that his former partner, Delia Shearer, had wanted the Agency to become involved:

> "I thought it was a ridiculous move. I was paying her £40 and then they came along . . . I thought she was quite happy with the financial arrangements as we had them. I didn't see the point in getting the CSA involved."

In fact Delia had likewise seen no advantage in applying to the Agency. As a long-standing Income Support claimant she had been sent the maintenance assessment form. She had little choice but to complete it. She tried to explain this to Gavin, but he remained sceptical. This reaction was common to a number of absent parents. It did not help matters that at the time of our fieldwork the letter sent by the Agency did not distinguish between cases in which its involvement was dictated by the mother's benefit status and those other cases (a tiny minority in fact) where the application had indeed been initiated by the parent with care.

In practice some parents with care welcomed the element of compulsion which enabled them to disclaim responsibility for initiating a process which they knew would upset their former partners but from which they might ultimately benefit. They may also have thought it right in principle that the absent parent pay whatever level of maintenance he could afford, even if this did not benefit the carer (or her children) directly. For example, Tania Burford (case 39) believed that her ex-partner could afford more than the £27 a week ordered by the court:

> "The problem was he wasn't paying enough. And when the Child Support Agency came up at first I thought it was a good excuse to get some more money off him. I knew he could pay more. But as soon as they started writing to him, he was coming back at me on the phone and saying: 'Why have you got them on to me?' He thought it was my fault they were after him. Then I explained to him that it was just done automatically. . . . When he realised it wasn't me, he was alright."

Other areas of misunderstanding concerned the so-called "carer's element" in the maintenance calculation and, secondly, the part played by the earnings of the absent parent's new partner. The latter seemed particularly troublesome. We noted several cases in which *apparently* taking into account the new partner's earnings created a sense of grievance which was then visited upon the carer. Many couples misunderstood the purpose of questions about the income of a new partner and concluded that in some way the Agency was holding both partners responsible for maintaining the children of one of them. As we have explained,[9] this is not the case. The income of a new partner is taken into account when calculating the level of protected income below which a household's resources are not meant to fall. Thus it can reduce the maintenance assessment, but it cannot increase it. Perhaps unsurprisingly, many absent parents and their new partners were unable to appreciate this distinction. They responded angrily, or not at all, to this element of the maintenance enquiry form. Patrick Beamon (case 118) was typical:

> "The money [new partner] was earning, it was going to my ex-wife. That didn't go down very well, and you can't blame her. Why should she pay for my son? And for my ex-wife to get the benefit from it. . . ."

Patrick's partner gave up her job, apparently in protest, but the couple were disappointed to discover that the assessment was unchanged.

---

[9] See Ch. 2.

Cliff Shilton's new partner was another who refused to provide the Agency with any information about her earnings. In fact she claimed that she did not even tell Cliff how much she earned lest he inadvertently disclose it. It appeared from our interviews with this couple that the Agency's insistence on knowing the details of the new partner's income contributed to tensions within their relationship. They broke up shortly afterwards.

7. ADMINISTRATIVE FAILURE

There is little doubt that the inefficiency of the Child Support Agency has created tension between parents which might have been avoided had the Agency been adequately resourced. In theory the Agency should act as a buffer between warring parents, but in practice any lack of trust is likely to be exacerbated. For example, some parents found that payments made by the absent parent at the beginning of a month were not credited to the carer for another two or three weeks. As we have seen, it was exceptional for maintenance to be paid regularly and in full, but even where the absent parent was paying as ordered there might still be tension because the Agency was slow to hand over the money. The Agency seemed to regard a two-week delay as not unreasonable, whereas the parent with care, struggling to balance her budget, took a different view.

Other failures were more flagrant. This can be illustrated by reference to the case of Nathan Banks and Amelia Radcliffe (case 114). An assessment error led Nathan to overpay maintenance to the tune of £1,000. When he sought repayment he was told that he would have to recover the money from Amelia. But in fact the overpayment had not benefited Amelia at all; she was claiming Income Support, so the money which Nathan paid went straight into the state coffers. It does not take much imagination to see the damage which could have resulted from this incorrect information being casually relayed to Nathan over the telephone. Thankfully he was aware of Amelia's benefit status and so appreciated that the Agency must be responsible for making good the overpayment. Many of us have struggled at one time or another to cope with bureaucratic failure, but the shortcomings of the Child Support Agency are particularly damaging because they typically involve two people rather than one, a conflict of interest between the two of them, and what may already be a fraught relationship.

8. THE CHILD SUPPORT AGENCY AND VOLUNTARY GIVING

In the past some men felt able to make payments in kind because the amount of maintenance which they were ordered to pay by the court verged on the nominal. They were able to 'top up' these modest child maintenance payments through purchase of clothing, pocket money, and so on. Even before the assessment process was completed, some absent parents had decided to cut back on these payments when advised by their solicitor that the assessment would be backdated. According to one Bristol-based district judge:

> "That's causing an awful lot of upset in Stoke Bishop [upmarket district of Bristol] . . . lots of rows apparently . . . wives not talking to husbands . . . yes, there's all hell to pay."

Of course it is likely that some of these accounts of previous generosity were exaggerated. Also, where there is a relationship of some trust, and common sense, one might have expected parents to come to terms with the fact that a higher maintenance assessment would constrain the absent parent's ability to contribute in other ways. But many separated parents do not have a trusting relationship, and they did not always think through the implications for their former partner of the increased maintenance burden now imposed upon them. As a result some parents held that the goodwill which they had formerly enjoyed, and which had been reflected in various acts of generosity, had been damaged through the intervention of the Agency.

At the same time we have to be clear that this was precisely the pattern of post-separation child support that the Agency was introduced to circumvent. The arrangement whereby an absent parent supplied goods rather than money may well have been satisfactory for all concerned: the children received the additional items that they needed, the absent parent was able to behave 'generously', and the carer continued to received her benefit payments without deduction. Now, instead, both households might be reduced to subsistence level. Robert Howell (case 46) was one vehemently critical absent father:

> "My children say 'We've got the best daddy in the world . . . he looks after us and buys us our clothes . . . he's a wonderful daddy'. But does it matter to these people? Not a bit. Once I have been assessed properly, that will be all my wife will get. They will get nothing else, nor will the children, because according to the CSA that money is to pay for everything for those children. That's what they've told me, so as far as I'm concerned I will be doing my duty to my children through the CSA."

Robert was not entirely consistent in his approach to these issues, but that was not unusual amongst absent parents who struggled to reconcile a number of different strands in their thinking: a sense of responsibility towards their children; resentment at having to make any financial contribution towards their former partner; and a rather ill-thought-through conception of where their responsibilities should end and those of the State, through the benefit system, should begin.

9. MAINTENANCE AND CONTACT

The relationship between payment of maintenance and the absent parent's expectations regarding contact with his or her children has always been problematic.[10] Or rather, it has been problematic for the court to insist that these two matters should be regarded as entirely separate, given that parents for their part have been stubbornly inclined to insist that they are linked. The advent of the Child Support Agency has highlighted this issue, and it has also introduced a new twist, much touted in the media, this being that high levels of maintenance ordered by the Agency have limited the capacity of absent parents to maintain the contact with their children which they had previously enjoyed. Frankly, we saw little evidence for this latter assertion. A few parents did indeed claim that the increased amounts of maintenance now required of them would mean that they would be unable to visit their children as often as in the past, or perhaps even at all, but none of the absent parents who claimed this were actually at that stage paying any more maintenance than they had been paying previously (although they may have been subject to a significantly increased assessment). Indeed, one of them, at the point we last had contact with him, had managed to avoid paying any maintenance at all. So whilst we acknowledge the possibility that absent parents' ability to maintain contact with their children may be affected by the amounts demanded of them by the Agency, we are not convinced that the level of maintenance demanded has had this effect other than, perhaps, in some men's imagination.

But as for the observation that absent fathers make a link between payment of maintenance and the expectation of a continued *relationship* with their children,[11] the answer is that, yes, they do indeed make this connection. To that extent both parents with care and absent parents implicitly challenge the "maintenance should follow blood" thesis in that both make the link between money transfer and the continuation of a relationship between the absent parent and his children. This was Polly Fookes's account (case 119):

"I went to Europe for six months and he stopped paying maintenance then. He seemed to think that the amount he paid was for access. So he actually thought

[10] For a thorough discussion of this point see Maclean and Eekelaar (1997).
[11] *Ibid.*

he was buying time with the child . . . not that he is supporting his daughter, he's buying her time. So now he's paying £35 a week he reckons he should get her for two days and she should stay overnight. That's how he is. . . ."

Despite criticising her former partner for this attitude, Polly had herself responded to his request that he be allowed to start seeing their daughter again by asking for more maintenance:

"I got a letter saying he was taking me to court for access. So I spoke to him and said 'Well I want extra money. You can either give it to me in my hand, which would be better for me and Kerry, or we'll go to court over it'."

Polly was not unusual in contending that "if he wants to see them, he should pay".

The link between maintenance and contact is made everywhere other than in the Court of Appeal. Thus we interviewed absent parents who resented the fact that, as they saw it, the demand for maintenance through the Child Support Agency was not accompanied by an opportunity to have a relationship with their children. Parents with care on the other hand tended to view the matter differently, seeing in the increased level of maintenance demanded of the absent parent an incipient threat that he might demand to see his children again—or demand to see them much more frequently following what may have been years of intermittent contact. This prospect might be viewed with considerable alarm. In some cases the former partner had been violent or otherwise abusive; in others the parent with care feared that the stability of the family unit might be disturbed by erratic visits from the absent parent. This was Kim Atkins' account (case 35), the father in her case having never previously seen the child:

"We didn't speak until earlier this year, when he got a letter off the CSA saying he had to pay all this money, and he got on the phone to me straight away. He wasn't very pleased, but he was saying 'I know it's not your fault, but by the way I'd like to see him now' and I said 'What's made you suddenly want to see him?' and he said 'I've always wanted to see him'."

Janice Vaughan (case 27) had even more reason to worry, her ex-partner having previously attempted to abduct their son. This was how Janice expressed her concerns:

"Once he pays maintenance he knows he's got a right to see James. Then I'll have no chance. If he says he's taking him out, I'll always be wondering whether he's bringing him back. But at the minute it's my say-so."

There is no legal basis for these particular fears, but it is entirely understandable that the parent with care should be concerned lest an increased maintenance burden on the absent parent will lead that parent to seek a greater measure of control over the child's life. Equally, it is important to acknowledge that not all absent parents wish to maintain contact with their children—and that this can be extremely hurtful both for the children and for the parent with care. It is not uncommon for the carer to do everything in his or her power to *encourage* contact, and for this to elict either no response or else erratic, unreliable visits which simply upset the children.

Denial of paternity is a powerful weapon which can subvert the assessment process for months or even years. Whilst undoubtedly there are some cases where the man identified as the father of a child may doubt his biological paternity, there are others—perhaps the majority—in which this is a stratagem employed cynically to subvert the assessment process. As such it is used only by a minority of fathers, some of whom may have been inspired by correspondence with one of the anti-CSA pressure groups. It is certainly one of the more destructive manifestations of the anti-CSA protest movement.

Denial of paternity did not feature largely in child maintenance cases prior to the introduction of the Child Support Agency.[12] Whilst child maintenance was set at a modest, even a nominal level, there was not the same financial incentive to deny paternity. Indeed some men were content to be acknowledged as the child's father even where they harboured doubts about the blood tie. But the child support legislation links biological fatherhood so strongly with financial obligation that this kind of free-and-easy acquiescence is no longer an option.

The approved procedure for challenging paternity is to deny responsibility from the outset. One of the first questions on the maintenance enquiry form is: which of the children named in the enclosed letter do you accept that you are a parent of? The options are all, none, or some (with a space to specify which children are accepted for the purpose). If paternity is denied then the man may simply sign a declaration that the information which he has provided is correct, and return the form to the Child Support Agency for further investigation. This usually leads to an interview with both the parent with care and the presumed absent parent in which each is asked to provide details of the circumstances surrounding the conception (or the denial of conception) of the child. If the man's argument is not accepted by the child support officer then the case may be referred to the magistrates' court, who may order a DNA test.

There is scope for ambiguity in that 'parent' is not defined on the form. Many men regard themselves as 'parents' when they are not so in a

12 Collins and Macleod (1991).

biological sense. They may therefore feel themselves to be in a dilemma, not wishing to deny paternity of the child and yet not wanting to find themselves liable to increased child support. This is one possible explanation for the pattern which we observed of some men apparently accepting paternity at the outset, only to challenge it later. Those who apparently change their minds during the course of the application may have genuinely misunderstood the purpose of the question; or fresh information may have come to light; or they may have been engaged in a deliberate ploy to delay the assessment process for as long as possible. Certainly those fathers who waited until the tribunal stage to raise the issue of paternity could succeed in delaying the assessment, and thereafter enforcement, for eighteen months or more.

There were six cases amongst our sample in which paternity was disputed at some point. Miles Saltford (case 66) was typical in that his assessment was held up for over a year whilst his denial of paternity was investigated:

> "I had some grounds, although the CSA wouldn't see it that way. It wasn't that I didn't have any doubts before. But I was quite happy, even if I wasn't the father, to accept that I was. But when you're going to be stitched up for thousands of pounds a year for the rest of your life, you want to be sure it's right. If it was true that she had had an affair, and it was somebody else's child, she wouldn't admit it . . . she would lose a lot of money, over £3,000 a year."

Miles denied that his disputing paternity would have any adverse effect on his daughter. At the same time he did acknowledge that his relationship with her, and with his ex-wife, had been damaged through the assessment process and that he now had scarcely any contact with them. This dispute was not resolved by the time our fieldwork came to an end. It seemed implausible, on the information supplied to us, that Miles would win his case; indeed there seemed little basis upon which to order a DNA test. His daughter was born within the period of the marriage and there was no suggestion at the time that his wife was having an extra-marital relationship. Thus one would expect a presumption of paternity to apply.

Someone who appeared to have rather better grounds for challenging paternity was Roy McLellan (case 107). He claimed that there had always been a question mark over his daughter's conception: he had had but a brief affair with the mother, Sue Cannon, who was in a long-term relationship with another man whom she planned to marry. On Roy's account Sue had shared his doubts and acknowledged them at the magistrates' court hearing where the maintenance issue came to be decided. He told us that he had been prepared to act as 'social' father of the child as long as the maintenance required of him was set at a nominal level: "The doubts had been there since day one . . . but I signed the declaration because she carried my name."

Prior to the advent of the CSA it is unlikely that either Roy McLellan or Miles Saltford would have challenged paternity. In both cases the man's relationship with the child whom he had accepted as his daughter suffered in consequence. The Child Support Act, in elevating biology above social bonds, has given new impetus to one of the most damaging weapons that warring ex-spouses, or ex-partners, can use against each another.

11. THE COSTS AND BENEFITS OF AN ARM'S-LENGTH SYSTEM

One of the arguments against discretion in the divorce context has always been that it permits one partner, generally the man, to impose a variety of pressures, often quite illegitimate pressures, upon his former spouse in order to secure a favourable settlement. Earlier research[13] had revealed flagrant attempts to prevent one spouse pursuing a legal remedy. In theory the Child Support Agency should be free of that particular problem. Where the parent with care is in receipt of state benefit the Agency should initiate the application and, the application having been made, follow it through. All that momentum—which requires a huge amount of energy in the context of divorce or separation—is meant to come from the Agency. Lifting responsibility for pursuing an application for maintenance from the shoulders of the parent with care ought in theory to limit the potential for conflict. Although, as we have noted, there is ample scope for misunderstanding, the fact is that the parent with care is not in these circumstances responsible for the Agency's involvement. Thus the Agency can be presented as a neutral mechanism for determining the level of child maintenance: the separated parents need have no contact with one another. As such the Agency stands in contrast to the more directly adversarial form of proceedings represented by an ancillary relief application to the court.

Earlier research into the conduct of these applications revealed a preference on the part of many women for negotiations to be conducted through their lawyers rather than directly with their former partner.[14] One might have anticipated that the formula-driven Child Support Agency would be attractive for much the same reason, and indeed there was some evidence of this. Marie Calderdale (case 79) told us that her husband "got a bit aggressive" when she mentioned her need for more money, so she was pleased to have the Agency deal with it. Likewise Yvette Henderson (case 26) had felt unable to ask for more maintenance from her ex-husband until the advent of the CSA. As she explained:

[13] Davis, Cretney and Collins (1994).
[14] *Ibid.*

"It's a good thing, because it means that if as in my situation you don't get along with your ex-husband and you don't want to meet face to face, then it's a good way of getting it sorted and making it fair. I filled in the form and someone has done the horrible work for me . . . I haven't had to sit and argue it out with him."

That was also the view of Lynn Enderby (case 65), whose story we told at the beginning of this chapter. As Lynn put it to us: "It's out of my hands now, which is what I like. . . . I don't have to worry about confronting him all the time." But this lack of direct communication between parents can be two-edged. Experience of divorce disputes suggests that the parties' ill will towards one another can dissipate over time. Indeed, some parents come to have an amicable relationship having been completely at odds in the period immediately following their separation. In so far as the advent of the Child Support Agency removes responsibility for negotiating the level of child maintenance from parents, it may limit the potential for quarrelling; but it may also limit the potential for reasonableness, decency, even for generosity, and thence for repair. In other words it is possible in some cases that the Agency has made it more difficult for men to choose to behave well.

12. NEGOTIATING IN THE SHADOW OF THE CHILD SUPPORT AGENCY

Although we have characterised the Child Support Agency as limiting the scope for negotiation between parents, we must not exaggerate the extent to which child maintenance assessment is now entirely formulaic. There is some basis for asserting that parental input, and discretion, is almost as great as when child maintenance was just one element within ancillary relief. Parents can still be subject to pressure from their former partner not to apply to the Agency (if it is a non-benefit case), or to come off benefit and accede to some private maintenance proposal. Of course the character of the negotiation is likely to be somewhat different because the level of maintenance imposed by the Agency tends to be higher than that ordered by a court. This strengthens the hand of the parent with care. It is not clear whether this makes for more or less conflict overall, but it certainly alters the balance of power. In the course of our fieldwork we often observed the Agency being employed as a lever (to quote Lynn Enderby) in what were essentially private negotiations.

The role of the Agency in these negotiations was generally not revealed to the court, and it was often not apparent to legal advisers either. One circumstance would be that in which the absent parent would try to persuade a non-claiming parent with care to drop her application to the Child Support Agency. Alternatively, a parent claiming Income Support might come under pressure to withdraw her claim to benefit—or, if that were not feasible, to claim 'good cause'. In either case she might be offered financial compensation in the form of undeclared maintenance payments.[15] This strategy was adopted by at least five absent parents in our sample. For example, Joe Nixon (case 48) persuaded his wife to accept a privately-negotiated "ten-point deal" under which he retained his pension and paid her an agreed £40 per week. She meanwhile was expected to abandon her claim to Income Support and undertake not to seek further maintenance through the Agency. This was Joe's account:

> "She has already fulfilled part of the bargain: she has come off Social Security and is actively looking for employment. I've increased my money to £40 a week. Obviously there was a load of bitterness, but we had to talk because what the DSS gave her, it was not a realistic amount so she could adequately clothe the boy, send him off to the school trip to France, and things like that. . . .We agreed a ten-point deal because she could see that the way the CSA was going, what was happening to me, it would absolutely destroy anything for the future . . . it would destroy my life . . . and I would never have any contact with my kids again because I couldn't afford it."

Michael Seeley and Alison Pringle (case 54) reached agreement on the basis of a manufactured claim of 'good cause'. This was Michael's version of events:

> "I went to see Alison and told her about the withdrawal of consent, and at the time it seemed that there were several bases for withdrawing consent, including threatened violence, which is not something I have ever done, but the main one we were talking about was the distress thing, which is there in black and white in the legislation . . . it says 'undue distress to the parent with care of the child . . .'. She was worried about doing it, because she is frightened of the powers-that-be, but in the end she went down and saw them and she told them I'd been beating her up. So they said 'Right, we're not going to do anything'. What I agreed to do was to pay her another £50 a month. She's going to be getting that on top of her Income Support, so if she gets caught that's her lookout. She didn't want the CSA, but she didn't really want the hassle of dealing with the withdrawal business either. That is why it took so much persuasion to get her to do it, because it just seemed so much effort to withdraw consent—and there was this worry that she might lose her Income Support."

In fact this couple subsequently fell out and Alison refused to accept the extra money. It is probable—although we were unable to contact her to confirm this—that she became frightened of the possible consequences were the Department of Social Security to discover that she was making a fraudulent benefit claim.

An arrangement such as this carries considerable risks for the parent with care—not something to be entered into lightly where the relationship may already be characterised by a good deal of mistrust. Kim Atkins

---

[15] See also the discussion in Ch. 3.

(case 35) was one parent who did not trust her former partner to deliver on the superficially attractive package which he offered her:

> "He suggested that I say to them that I don't want this maintenance any more, and he said they would stop £13 or something out of my money and he'd give me more to make up for it . . . but I can't trust him to do that."

An element of collusion was almost inevitable given that the child support scheme offers no 'disregard' of maintenance paid to the benefit claimant. It is unfortunate if the legislation has encouraged a culture of dishonesty, but that would seem an inescapable conclusion. Certainly it has fostered private negotiation between separated parents in a rather unexpected way. We observed a great many cases in which parents were in effect bargaining in the shadow of the Agency. Where the parent with care is in receipt of Income Support it will seldom be in her interests to accede to any suggestion that she withdraw from that safety net and instead rely on private maintenance negotiated directly with her former partner. However, where the carer has some alternative source of income, and where the level of maintenance liable to be paid by the man is considerably in excess of that which he may have been required to pay under a court order, then it may be the parent with care who finds herself in the driving seat. The case of Lynn and Brett Enderby provides an excellent example. Brett was subject to what he considered an unreasonable assessment by the Child Support Agency. The Agency's refusal to compromise led him to approach Lynn with a view to negotiating a private deal. This suited Lynn as she felt that the Agency had made little progress (no payments had been made) and she had the prospect of regular child support, albeit at a lower rate than that set by the Agency. What is more, Brett was prepared to withdraw his threat to force the sale of the matrimonial home. She knew that she could always re-involve the Agency if Brett were to renege on the agreement which they had reached.

In due course Brett did experience difficulty in making the payments which he had agreed with Lynn. He had moved in with his new partner and had accepted responsibility both for her and for her child. As we saw, Lynn therefore decided to go back to the Agency. Brett's initial response was to demand what he took to be his share of the former matrimonial home. Eventually they reached agreement once more and Lynn allowed Brett to pay her rather less than he had earlier undertaken to do. She also agreed to write off the arrears—again secure in the knowledge that she could re-apply to the Agency if Brett once more fell behind with his payments or if he tried to put pressure on her to sell the home.

The Enderby case is instructive in that it reveals that the Child Support Agency is not some monolith which has taken over all of child support. It is commonly used as a lever, or threat, with both parents calculating the advantage for them in coming to some private arrangement over maintenance. In making these private arrangements there remains ample scope for the kinds of pressure, particularly pressure imposed upon parents with care, with which we have become familiar through earlier studies of the lawyer-led, court-based system. Child maintenance is now meant to be decided according to a formula, but to a very considerable extent it is still being bargained, with all that that implies—both positive and negative—for post-separation family relationships.

10

Conclusion

"It has been evident for some time that the task set for the Agency has proven to be more difficult in practice than had been anticipated when the scheme was devised. In particular, I do not think it was fully appreciated that the Agency's intervention into the most personal and sensitive areas of people's lives would make such a negative impact; nor was it realised how many people would actively resist or reject prioritising child maintenance above nearly all other financial commitments." (Miss Ann Chant, then Chief Executive of the Child Support Agency, quoted in the Report of the Parliamentary Commissioner for Administration (1995), page 1)

1. INTRODUCTION

In general, just as one would expect, our research presents a predominantly negative picture of the Child Support Agency. In part this may be because we were researching a very public phenomenon: overwhelmingly negative coverage of the Agency over the past five years must have had its effects. Nonetheless, even given this inevitable bias, the disenchantment of most of the parents we interviewed must be emphasised.

This disillusionment has to be set alongside more objective measures of the Agency's performance. All the available indicators point to the Child Support Agency having become, in effect, an arm of the benefits system, and an arm which is largely failing to cope with its ever-expanding caseload. We know, for example, that the number of 'live' and assessed cases in the child support system rose from 484,600 to 609,800 between May 1996 and May 1997.[1] The latter total included 530,000 full maintenance assessments. Seventy-two per cent of these parents with care were recorded as being in receipt of Income Support, while a further 15 per cent were claiming Family Credit.[2] A mere 13 per cent were 'private' cases.

The dominance of benefits-related work within the Agency is also reflected in the number of absent parents on its caseload who are them-

[1] Department of Social Security (1997b), 1.
[2] A tiny fraction of the latter group may have been claiming Disability Working Allowance rather than Family Credit.

selves benefit claimants. In 1997 some 260,000 absent parents were in employment; 24,000 were self-employed; and 217,000 were in receipt of some form of benefit, with 178,000 of these on Income Support.[3] The single most common method of payment of child maintenance is direct payment from the absent parent's Income Support, with the result that a substantial part of the Agency's operations are devoted to "churning": transferring money from one part of the benefits system to another. Nevertheless the Agency's focus on benefit cases has produced some savings. In 1996–7 it was calculated that £268 million, some two-thirds of the £400 million collected or arranged for payment by the Agency, went to the Exchequer in the sense that that it represented an equivalent saving in benefits expenditure.[4] A further £201 million was said to be saved as a result of benefit claims being withdrawn following the Agency's involvement.[5] This is still well short of the original prediction of annual benefit savings of £900 million. At the end of 1996 the Social Security Select Committee reported that the cumulative savings achieved by the Child Support Agency in terms of social security expenditure amounted to £1.74 billion.[6] Against that should be set the administrative cost of the Agency, amounting to some £660 million in its first four years.

The sums which absent parents are required to pay, at least if taken as an average, are somewhat lower than might be inferred from some media accounts. For example, the average value of full maintenance assessments was £21.14 per week in May 1997. This figure reflects the impact of nil assessments, principally assessments made in respect of absent parents who are themselves on benefit.[7] We should also note a considerable disparity between the average weekly assessment for employees (£38.99) and for self-employed absent parents (£23.68).[8]

Meanwhile, as we know, the Agency's record in securing compliance with these assessments is unimpressive to say the least. Of those fully assessed cases in which the absent parent was supposed to pay maintenance via the Agency's collection service, 31 per cent were paying the full amount due, 36 per cent were paying part, and the remaining third were

[3] The remaining 29,000 are mysteriously described as "other"; Department of Social Security (1997), 32, Table 3.8.
[4] Hansard, HC Debs., Vol. 297, col. 454, 8 July 1997, written answer.
[5] Hansard, HC Debs., Vol. 297, col. 375, 7 July 1997, written answer.
[6] House of Commons Social Security Committee, *Child Support*, 5th Report, Session 1996–7, (1997) p.vii, HC 282, London: Stationery Office. The conventions for calculating benefit savings only take into account cases where claims are withdrawn within 4 weeks of the Agency's involvement. It is then assumed in respect of these cases that the family in question would have remained on benefit for a further 51 weeks.
[7] Department of Social Security (1997b), 38, Table 4.1. We refer to final assessments only and not to interim assessments since the latter are artificially inflated.
[8] *Ibid.*, 39, Table 4.4.

paying nothing.[9] At the end of March 1997 the Agency estimated that absent parents owed £513 million in unpaid maintenance, of which less than half was thought to be collectable.[10] Faith Boardman, the Child Support Agency's Chief Executive since April 1997, has admitted that a significant backlog remains from the Agency's first two years of operation. [11]

2. JUSTICE BETWEEN PARENTS

We have noted that before the advent of the Agency the absent parent could rely upon the divorce court not to be unduly concerned about his paying very little maintenance. Courts routinely made orders for maintenance which verged on the nominal. This practice, coupled with the almost moribund state of the liable relative section of the Department of Social Security, meant that child maintenance was accorded very low priority. That is not to say that absent fathers are, in general, content for the State to support their children. Most, in considering the financial consequences of divorce, bear in mind questions of need and of fairness as these are reflected in their own experience. In considering need, they take into account the element of state support available to their former partner and children. In considering fairness, they take account of any capital element that they may have been obliged to forego. Within these constraints the predominant view expressed by absent parents, as well as by parents with care, is that parents who are not living with their children should indeed continue to maintain them.

We interviewed only two absent parents who objected in principle to paying any maintenance at all, largely on the grounds that their wives had chosen to leave and so should be responsible for the financial consequences of their actions. Both these men had an enormous sense of grievance and both would have preferred their children continue living with them. But otherwise we became used to absent parents expressing their commitment to their children and to doing what they could to support them. The fact is, however, that in their own particular circumstances they had concluded that what they could contribute was limited. In other words: "It is right for men to pay maintenance, but unfortunately I, in my particular circumstances, am able to pay very little." This reflects the findings of the attitudinal survey conducted by Maclean and

[9] *Ibid.*, 40. This suggests some improvement in the Agency's initial performance in that the compliance rates for Nov. 1995 were 22 per cent (full), 34 per cent (partial) and 44 per cent (nil).

[10] Child Support Agency (1997), 71. In February 1998 the House of Commons Committee of Public Accounts (1998), v, reported that outstanding debt owed by absent parents totalled over £1,127 million.

[11] House of Commons Committee of Public Accconts (1998), Minutes of Evidence, 2].

Eekelaar.[12] Their results show a strong commitment by mothers to a support obligation based on natural parenthood, whereas fathers relate that obligation much more to social parenthood: thus two-thirds of men felt that the fact that a father is living with stepchildren should affect the amount he gives his first family, while only a minority of mothers felt the same.

Whilst it is possible to be cynical about absent fathers' protestations that they cannot afford to pay more for their children, many men in our study had indeed lost a great deal. They felt very hard done by even without the Child Support Agency. This was particularly true of those who had not sought divorce. They were left feeling that not only had they lost their marriage, they had also had to accept reduced contact with their children, they had lost the right of occupancy of the family home, there was no realistic prospect of a sale in the short term, and now they were faced with a heavy maintenance obligation courtesy of the Agency.

It is tempting to conclude from this that the Child Support Agency is a blunderbuss introduced into what was previously a delicate balance of fairness and welfare considerations. There was general agreement amongst solicitors that some change had been needed, but some of the policy objectives reflected in the Child Support Act could have been achieved without root and branch reform of the mechanisms for determining child maintenance—that is to say, without the creation of a parallel bureaucracy alongside the court system. For example, one set of concerns, which had to do with the cost in social security payments of the high divorce rate, could have been addressed simply by altering the rules of benefit entitlement—most obviously in respect of assistance with mortgage payments. In fact this has already happened, independently of the Child Support Act 1991. Certainly the government did not need the Agency if the object was simply to cut the social security budget. The same point applies in relation to Legal Aid. The government has for some time been worried about the rising cost of the Legal Aid scheme. But here again we have seen steps taken to cash-limit Legal Aid, something which has happened quite independently of the Agency.

Given that savings could have been achieved—and have been achieved—by these other means, why create a separate, parallel system? It would seem that the main reason (apart from overconfidence and chronic miscalculation) is that the government wished to give expression to the ideological principle that separated parents should continue to support their children no matter what. This accounts for the insistence that even Income Support claimants must pay something for their children's upkeep. In other words the Child Support Act 1991 can be seen as the re-assertion of the view that responsibility for children does not end

---

[12] Maclean and Eekelaar (1997).

with the breakdown of the parents' relationship. There are two obvious problems with this. First, it flies in the face of the principle upon which benefit entitlement upon relationship breakdown has been calculated hitherto, with its insistence upon imposing *de facto* maintenance obligations upon *current* partners. Secondly, to the extent that it requires men to devote their resources to former rather than to current partners, it flies in the face of human nature—or at least it flies in the face of what many people, in this age of serial relationships, take to be human nature.

This problem is exacerbated because the redistribution which was intended to be brought about by the Child Support Agency rests principally upon a calculation of the absent parent's income and outgoings: the income and expenses of the family to which he is required to contribute are largely removed from consideration. Eekelaar has suggested that redistribution on this principle will command support only up to a point; that the more the absent father is required to pay, the more that principles of 'commutative' justice-taking *both* families' finances into account—will be considered relevant.[13] Eekelaar contends that once an attempt is made to impose child maintenance at higher levels—as in the UK scheme—the demands of commutative justice become overwhelming. This has traditionally been the responsibility of the courts. The question then becomes whether it is reasonable to expect the State to underwrite, not just the cost of bringing up children, but the cost of achieving commutative justice between parents. Eekelaar argues that the UK government drew the line between commutative and (much cruder) 'distributive' justice in the wrong place. Equally, commutative justice is expensive to administer. To go down that road would render the Child Support Agency even less cost-effective than it is at present—particularly in respect of low-paid absent fathers who can afford to pay little in any event. At the same time, the fact that there is no commutative element to the justice administered by the Agency has certainly contributed to parental resistance.

3.   WHAT IS THE RIGHT BALANCE BETWEEN STATE AND PRIVATE RESOURCES IN
SUPPORTING CHILDREN FOLLOWING RELATIONSHIP BREAKDOWN?

Aside from questions of distributive or commutative justice between parents, there is the equally fundamental question whether we should expect separated parents to give priority to maintaining the children of earlier relationships or whether we concede an element of state subsidy for serial relationships and serial parenting. The relative ineffectiveness of the Child Support Agency in part reflects its failure to secure parental

[13] Eekelaar (forthcoming).

acceptance of the former principle. As Lister has observed, there seem to be two distinct approaches to child welfare following the breakdown of the parental relationship: an Anglo-American model in which market-driven public policies have depressed family benefits and placed child-rearing firmly in the private domain; and a more supportive European model in which governments have strengthened rather than weakened safety nets for families with children.[14] As Lister puts it :

> "The low level of child care provision, minimal maternity leave arrangements and absence of any statutory right to paternity or parental leave, or leave for family reasons, exemplify the philosophy which treats the costs of caring for children as a private rather than a public responsibility."

The Child Support Act 1991 was not concerned with achieving an effective integration and rationalisation of public and private support for separated families. It was ambitious in the amount of financial responsibility it sought to transfer from the State to the private sphere. In that respect it was rather unlike the Australian scheme.[15] The model was essentially one of offsetting benefit payments. Welfare expenditure was to be reduced by imposing a greater part of the burden of child support upon absent parents. The fact that the Agency was conceived as a means of cutting the welfare budget explains why the original formula took no account of *past* arrangements in respect of property and capital;[16] after all, social security entitlement is calculated on the basis of *current* finances—it takes no account of what has gone before. The fact that the focus was exclusively upon the parent with care's claim to benefit probably explains why there was little appreciation of the difficulty which would be involved in extracting money from absent parents. It was as if the Agency was conceived as a calculating machine, computing the extent of the transfer of responsibility from the State to absent parents. The fact that this had to involve *collection* was seen as unprob-lematic.

International comparisons illustrate the ambitious nature of the goals set for the Child Support Agency. The Agency's 1993–4 target was a benefit saving of £530 million, whereas the total amount of maintenance collected under the Australian scheme in 1991 was £111 million, three years after the scheme was set up.[17] Whiteford estimates that this is the equivalent of £25 million if account is taken of the value of the currencies and the different size of the populations. He suggests that this contrast explains much of the difference in the strength of adverse reaction to the introduction of the new regime in the two countries.

[14] Lister (1994). See further Lewis (1997).
[15] Whiteford (1994).
[16] John Eekelaar, personal communication.
[17] Child Support Evaluation Advisory Group (1992).

There is a stark contrast between this determination to reduce state spending on separated families—a one-dimensional benefit-cutting agenda—and the Finer Committee's proposals in the early 1970s for a Guaranteed Maintenance Allowance (GMA) for lone parents, a measure aimed at giving *choice* to those parents whilst lifting their income substantially above subsistence level.[18] Finer's aim was to put lone parents in a position where they could choose whether to take paid employment or stay at home and take care of their children. The GMA proposal, which would have involved positive discrimination in favour of the separating and divorcing population, did not find favour with successive governments. Instead the legacy of Finer was one-parent benefit, the abolition of which was forced through by the new Labour Government in late 1997 as part of its own "welfare-to-work" programme. The GMA was a measure specifically designed to benefit children—something which one is hard put to say of the Child Support Act 1991.

A study such as ours was not designed to determine the precise extent to which the burden of child maintenance has shifted from the State to absent parents, but such evidence as we have suggests a clear intention to bring about just such a realignment of responsibility. As discussed in Chapter 3, we sought to calculate, in all cases in which there was an Agency assessment, whether this was for an amount more or less than the absent parent had previously been paying. The picture was as follows:

Table 10.1 Comparison of Agency assessments and previous payments[19]

Assessment *less* than previous paying	10 (12%)
Assessment *same* as previously paying (which was nothing)	4 (5%)
Assessment *more* than previously paying	44 (54%)
Positive assessment—had paid nothing prior to CSA	24 (29%)
TOTAL	82 (100%)

So at least in terms of *assessment*, although not necessarily in terms of payment, one can see that the Child Support Act 1991 was attempting to increase the private maintenance obligation. The Agency was 'sold' as a means of promoting the interests of children living in poor, one-parent families, but in fact, as all informed commentators on the legislation appreciated, it reflected the UK government's concern to reduce the financial burden of benefit payments to divorced families. It was never likely that lone parents would have more money. The Child Support Act 1991 was a response to the peculiarly British pattern of post-separation dependence on state benefits which had developed through the 1960s and 1970s.

[18] Committee on One-Parent Families (Finer Committee) (1974), Vol. 1, 289–314.
[19] We exclude from this table all cases for which we did not have the relevant data.

The fact that the Child Support Act 1991 was not a child-focused measure is confirmed by the failure to include any 'per child' element. The formula is based purely on the absent parent's income and expenditure, no matter whether he has fathered ten children or one. Obligations are determined by reference to lone parents' entitlement to Income Support. This gives rise to the further problem that it appears to introduce an element of spousal maintenance into the calculation. The Australian scheme, in contrast, is based on the principle of the absent parent's responsibility to continue to share income with his children. The more children an absent parent has, the more he pays by way of a percentage of his gross income, from 18 per cent in the case of one child to 36 per cent if he has five children to support. It follows that it is *children* who are the focus of the formula and the carer is not explicitly taken into account. The UK scheme, on the other hand, produces relatively heavier obligations for parents with one child because of the inclusion of support for the parent with care. The justification for this is that children have to be cared for, and that this is a maintenance cost. In practice a great many fathers, while accepting that they should maintain their children, object strongly to the 'carer' element. They argue that this means paying maintenance for the other parent (and, worse still, for that person's new partner, if any). Some raised the question of how the money would be spent, and whether the children would benefit. These issues were particularly prominent when the child was born of a brief liaison, or when it was claimed that there had been no intention (at least on the father's part) to have a child in the first place.

Further confirmation that the Child Support Act was intended to benefit the Treasury rather than children lies in the fact that while the duty to pay maintenance applies to all absent parents, the legal requirement placed on parents with care to co-operate with the Child Support Agency applies only to those in receipt of Income Support and other specified benefits. The latter group formed 97 per cent of the cases dealt with by the Agency in its first year of operation.[20] In this respect the so-called 'transitional provisions' governing the Agency in its early years were highly revealing. After all, the people who could have benefited most from the Act were those *not* in receipt of Income Support. If the government had been concerned to increase the income of caring parents and their children it would have ensured that the Agency dealt with those cases first. In practice it was the other way round. The Agency did not commit its resources to tracing those absent parents who paid nothing, and it did not chase non-paying fathers where the parent with care was not in receipt of benefit. Our own case monitoring confirmed that

[20] Garnham and Knights (1994).

parents (and children) who were most clearly going to benefit from private maintenance were the ones least likely to receive it.[21]

A further aspect of the government's determination to transfer as much as possible of the responsibility for child maintenance from the public sector to absent parents was its insistence that the legislation operate retrospectively. It is true that so-called 'clean break' settlements have never overridden the obligation to pay child maintenance, but given the way in which capital and maintenance were linked in the course of ancillary relief negotiation there was inevitably a trade-off between maintenance and property. Here again the Australian scheme was less radical, or less unfair, depending on how one looks at it. As previously noted, the Australian legislation applied only to those parents who separated on or after the passing of the Act, or to children born after that date. This meant that many of the thorniest issues affecting child support in the UK were not a factor in Australia. Past property settlements were generally not affected, and liable parents formed new unions in the full knowledge of what they were expected to pay for children of previous relationships.

Another contentious aspect of the formula was the level of so-called 'protected income'. This was initially set at a level which most matrimonial lawyers considered far too low—in other words, too severe a burden was imposed on the payer. Our research has largely confirmed the media story that, at least in the view of absent parents, essential outgoings were not given proper weight under the formula. They cited expenditure such as gas and electricity payments, travel expenses, and even the cost of food. The short answer to these criticisms is that the Agency assessment does indeed make allowance for these items: both the parent with care and the absent parent are assessed as requiring the level of income supplied by Income Support. Notionally that is enough to provide for expenditure on these items.[22] The fact is that with the advent of the Child Support Agency absent parents were required to come to terms with a set of assumptions which have been a fact of life for Income Support claimants for many years. That is not to say that the government calculated protected income correctly. The protected income was set as low as possible. There was no compunction in reducing absent parents to subsistence level.

The final point to make on this theme of the thrust of the legislation being to transfer responsibility from the State to the private sphere con-

---

[21] See Ch. 3.

[22] It may be noted that the former Supplementary Benefits scheme, the precursor to Income Support, prescribed in minute detail the types of normal expenditure on day-to-day living which were covered by basic weekly benefit, including "miscellaneous household expenses such as toilet articles, cleaning materials, window-cleaning and the replacement of small household goods . . . and leisure and amenity items": Supplementary Benefits (Requirements) Regulations 1983 (S.I. 1983 No. 1399), reg. 4(1).

cerns the lack of any disregard for maintenance received when the recipient is claiming benefit. To date the majority of assessments have been made in families where the parent with care is in receipt of Income Support. Yet it is precisely in these cases that private maintenance cannot make any difference to the parent's net income. Maintenance, if paid, benefits only the Treasury. In contrast, the political acceptability of the Australian scheme is enhanced by the fact that parents with care may benefit substantially from an increased level of maintenance: they keep at least half of the maintenance which is paid by the absent parent.[23]

The advantages or otherwise of there being some maintenance disregard have been debated down the years, but the issue has been thrown into sharp relief by the creation of the Agency. The absence of any maintenance disregard, coupled with the decision to concentrate upon benefit cases, has meant a lack of support for the Agency because nobody could see that it was doing anyone any good. To the framers of the legislation it appeared self-evident that the principle of requiring absent parents to support their children was one that would command widespread support. To the extent that this principle was *not* supported, they meant to bring about a cultural change. They did not appreciate that cultural change cannot be achieved simply through the imposition of a new tax. Somebody has to be seen to benefit. If the Treasury interest had not been so dominant, and if parents with care and their children had been allowed to benefit to some degree, it is likely that the Child Support Agency would have attracted greater support. This in turn may have eased its administrative burdens.

We agree with Whiteford that those wishing to improve the operation of the Child Support Agency and build support for it should consider a more comprehensive approach to improving the position of lone parents and their children. There are considerable fiscal and political pressures working against any such fundamental policy change, particularly any change in the direction of devoting additional State funds to the divorcing population and their children. But the relative failure of the Agency should serve to counteract this; the attempt to recoup large sums from absent parents has not worked in practice. Perhaps as a society we had to go through the CSA experience to discover that there was not a lot of money to be obtained from absent parents, many of whom are unemployed or have second families. The financial and political failure of this policy, once it is recognised as such, may pave the way to a more family-minded solution.

Most of the solicitors whom we interviewed conceded that the former practice of trading off child maintenance against the family home, with consequent reliance upon Income Support to maintain separated

---

[23] Whiteford (1994).

families, was a manipulation of the benefit system. But they claimed that this was justifiable in view of the higher social objective of providing a home for the children of separated families. Likewise it has to be borne in mind when evaluating the Agency's pursuit of absent fathers that many of these men have accepted responsibility for other children— either children who they themselves have fathered with a new partner, or step-children whom they have acquired through a new relationship. Often they are displaying what many people would regard as a more than adequate sense of social responsibility.

In the end, despite the severity of the demands placed upon reconstituted families, the question must be asked whether the Child Support Agency has not reinforced a benefit culture. Lone parents' need for a secure income is overriding. They are used to calculating the contribution which they can expect from part-time work, benefit and maintenance. They did their sums in the aftermath of the Child Support Act, and those sums did not add up: they felt they had no option other than to continue to rely on benefits as the main plank of income. Whatever may have been envisaged by government, these parents knew the extent to which they could rely upon maintenance from the absent parent: they knew there was no pot of gold.

4. FORMULA VERSUS DISCRETION

As noted in Chapter 2, one of the assumed benefits of the Child Support Act 1991 was that there would be less arbitrariness about Agency assessments than had characterised court orders for child maintenance. The formula, it was argued, would be able to deliver parity of treatment across individual cases. The reality is that individual claims to justice collide with the rigidities of formulaic assessment. We found that many people are not in supposedly 'typical' situations. The formula approach (quite apart from arguments as to what exactly it should contain) cannot cope with the atypical—for example, people with no income at all, people who do not have straightforward 'housing costs', or people whose contribution to their absent children is made indirectly (such as through the payment of a mortgage, purchase of clothes or private education, and so on).

The model also assumes that a parent either has care or is absent, and will remain in that category, whereas we found even within our relatively small sample that this is commonly not the case. Nor can a formula cope well with people whose circumstances change frequently. The model assumes a fairly static population, with fixed employment and relationship statuses, whereas the reality is that separated parents have frequent changes, in and out of employment and self-employment, in and out of relationships, with accompanying changes of accommodation, and taking on or abandoning responsibility for children or step-children. As a result we observed requests for change of circumstance reviews chasing each other through the system, each one becoming obsolete before it was completed.

It is doubtful whether these problems can be dealt with by means of the element of discretion introduced in the 1995 Act. The Child Support Agency has concentrated on benefit cases. As a consequence, child support has developed the character of a tax. So our comparison should be with the Inland Revenue. It is implausible to suppose that the Revenue should operate anything other than an administrative system, formula-driven; its responsibilities could not pass to judges, charged with taking into account not only obligation, but also fairness and need. Once it is understood that the Agency in effect operates a system of taxation, albeit one that is densely complex and (in aspiration) fine-tuned, the case for adding further discretionary elements appears highly questionable. Of course discretion can always appear appealing in the individual case, but it is the inflexibility of the formula which constitutes the Child Support Agency's main claim to public acceptability. It delivers rough justice, and to be truly effective it probably needs to be rougher yet. Discretion does not provide any kind of answer. The 'departures' system introduced by the 1995 Act was a concession to principles of commutative justice, but to introduce discretion into a formula-based system represents a terrible confusion of purpose. It is not coherent to let some components of an assessment be formulaic and others be discretionary: accordingly we agree with Eekelaar[24] that 'departures' should be allowed to wither on the vine.

In practice the arguments concerning the appropriateness of a formula-based approach cannot wholly be separated from the question of the degree to which the State should be required to support the financial cost of relationship breakdown. Under the old discretionary regime parents were able to manipulate the benefits system to enhance the welfare of their children. Solicitors told us that the touchstone which they and the courts employed over many years was that of the wife's and children's needs matched against the husband's ability to pay. Within that framework there was sufficient discretion to cater for a whole range of circumstances, one of the most obvious being the tendency for one or other parent to have to meet debts which had been incurred for the benefit of the whole family. The options in this and other respects are now much more restricted. This led many solicitors to conclude that the social implications of the Child Support Act had not been thought through. As far as they were concerned it was another Act which had

---

[24] Eekelaar (forthcoming).

been passed with short-term financial aims in mind, without any view to the long-term social consequences. The impact upon their own work-load and practice was quite modest. Their hostility towards the legislation was rooted in their firmly-held conviction that it was socially damaging.

5. ADMINISTRATIVE EFFECTIVENESS

A minority of the parents whom we interviewed were reasonably satisfied with the way in which the Agency had handled their cases. In their experience the procedure had been relatively quick and straightforward and it had achieved its intended objective. But the great majority were dissatisfied. Regardless of the way in which they regarded the *principle*, the Agency's performance in practice had been disappointing, even abject. Delay and error have been rife in these early years—a fact acknowledged by Agency staff.[25] Most of our informants complained about administrative inefficiency in one form or another: non-communication, unclear communication, delays, or contradictory and confusing information. In some cases files were lost, while there were plentiful accounts of letters not receiving replies. Sometimes it appeared from the perspective of one of the parents that the Agency had quietly dropped their case but had failed to tell them so. We were also told about—or ourselves discovered—errors in names and addresses. Parents who had tried to contact the Agency were continually frustrated: it was often impossible to get through on the telephone as lines were constantly engaged. Those who did get through might be passed from one member of staff to another, or be kept on hold for long periods. It is a telling indictment that, within eighteen months of the inception of the Agency, the Ombudsman had decided not to investigate any further claims of maladministration unless they raised new issues or had caused actual financial loss.[26]

The injustices of divorce have always lain in large part with the inefficiencies of the process. This was true under lawyers and it is even more true now that we have a dual system. Our account of the Child Support Agency shows how the pursuit of substantive justice can be undermined by procedural injustice. In order to deliver just outcomes one needs an efficient process. In the case of the Child Support Agency this necessary pre-condition has simply not been met. Even though we now have a formula, the problems continue to lie not only in the calculations, and the principles underlying those calculations, but in relating these to the rest

[25] See Ch. 4.
[26] Parliamentary Commissioner for Administration (1995). The Agency established an Independent Case Examiner in April 1997 to investigate grievances as a new final stage of the internal complaints procedure.

of our hugely complex benefits structure. The problems engendered by the volume of work faced by the Child Support Agency have led to a situation in which it is the vocal, the articulate and the persistent who stand the best chance of success. Perhaps the most glaring illustration of administrative failure is the fact that in the course of our enquiries we discovered that the Agency had moved to a 'post driven' mode of operation. Of course it was never meant to operate in this fashion, but this last resort administrative strategy, introduced to enable the Agency to keep its head above water, has had the inevitable consequence that it is responsive only to parents who badger it. This is how the divorce courts manage their caseload, and for exactly the same reason—controlling workload—but it is precisely how the Child Support Agency was meant *not* to behave. The Agency was meant to relieve the burden of financial support for lone parents carried by the State, and to deliver arm's length 'objective' justice between parents. Excessive government ambition, leading in turn to bureaucratic failure, has resulted in its achieving neither of these goals.[27]

At the same time it is important to acknowledge that parents themselves are important contributors to the administrative failure which we describe. Another way of putting this would be to say that the fact that the Agency has not had the support of parents (in general) has compounded its administrative problems. It is sometimes said (and said by us) that parents feel powerless in the face of the Agency's assessment of their liability, but despite this apparent powerlessness, many parents did manage to find ways to beat the system. For example, they would not disclose relevant information, such as the existence of a cohabiting partner, additional earnings or cash payments from an ex-partner. In some instances parents simply did not respond to the Agency's requests for information. Others tried to do deals with their former partner, the intention being that both parties would thereby be better off. Whilst in some cases these were legitimate strategies, in others they involved an element of dishonesty and potential fraud. So whilst parents complained about the Agency, we have to recognise that many did everything in their power to delay matters or otherwise to frustrate the Agency's operations. Sometimes it was these same parents who complained about bureaucratic inefficiency. In general one can say that the Agency was trying to cope—and failing—with the problems presented to it by parents intent on disrupting its operations.

That is one part of the story. Another part, from the perspective of parents, is that they did indeed feel powerless in the face of what many came

---

[27] As the Children Act Advisory Committee (1997), 25, observed: "It is quite intolerable that delays of this magnitude should occur, and the whole basis of the Agency as provider of a service which is more reliable than that provided by the courts is undermined." See also House of Commons Committee of Public Accounts (1998).

to regard as an impenetrable organisation. They felt that the Agency was faceless, heartless and inflexible. They also resented its draconian powers, for example to deduct payments from earnings. This impression was reinforced by the wording on some standard letters—often perceived as unnecessarily threatening—and by the Agency's failure to respond to queries, or its tendency to ask repeatedly for information which had already been supplied.

There is a considerable body of literature on the key features of a good adjudication system.[28] One suggested characteristic is a sense of participation by the claimant or the appellant in the decision-making process. Our research suggests that the Child Support Agency has to date failed miserably on this score. This must in part be attributed to the fact that parents are seeking to penetrate the Agency without the kind of informed backing such as might by provided by a professional legal adviser. In that sense it is quite unlike most people's experience of the courts. If clients of the Child Support Agency have been divorced they will probably be used to going to a solicitor and being advised about the various steps which they need to take in order to secure court orders. But as far as the Agency is concerned that support structure is not available. Parents are generally struggling to make sense of the Agency's demands without any kind of back-up. It is frustrating enough for solicitors, as we have seen, to be passed from pillar to post, but solicitors are used to dealing with problems of this kind. Most parents have limited experience of administrative systems and it is not surprising that they feel defeated by the facelessness of the Agency.

A very important question here is whether the Agency should be regarded—and regards itself—as providing a *service* to *customers*, or whether—akin to the Inland Revenue—it is assumed to be imposing demands upon people which for the most part can be taken to be unwelcome. Because if the Agency is providing a *service* then one might expect correspondence to be processed and acknowledged and each case to be driven to a conclusion. Otherwise the customer would have every reason to be dissatisfied. But the Agency seems to operate for the most part on the assumption that no-one will be upset if cases are not pursued—on the contrary, they will be pleased and relieved. It is only if we take this to be the working assumption that one can make sense of the practice of shelving cases where there is no persistent pressure for action from either parent.

Comparison may be made here with the operation of the former liable relative section of the Department of Social Security. In theory, non-paying absent parents would be chased by the Department where the carer was a claimant, but in practice absent parents could rely upon the

---

[28] See e.g. Mashaw (1983) and Sainsbury (1994b).

under-resourced nature of the various liable relative sections. This brings us back to one of the main themes of our research, namely that the Agency is grossly overburdened and that this in turn has undermined its effectiveness. This was anticipated by informed observers. Here, for example, is an extract from the Association of District Registrars' response to the government's initial consultation document:

"The only comment we wish to make on the setting up of the Agency is that it must be adequately funded. It is proposed, in effect, to take into the public domain an area which has hitherto been largely a private matter. The public will therefore expect the Agency to act promptly and efficiently. As County Court Registrars we have experience of working in an organisation which is underfunded and understaffed and whose staff are demoralised and inadequately trained. An increasing proportion of our time is taken up in dealing with queries which a properly trained staff would never have put to us and in trying to cope with staff errors. Bearing in mind the potentially emotive subject matter of its work, the Agency will require more support than has been given to County Courts."[29]

The Family Law Bar Association expressed itself even more trenchantly:

"[The White Paper] suggests that the Agency would be able to carry out re-assessment on an annual basis to take account of changes in income and liabilities. We think this statement is staggeringly naive. There are nearly 150,000 divorces annually in England and Wales and in the vast majority of them there are children involved. To suggest that the Agency is going to be able to review each individual case on an annual basis, in addition to dealing with the workload involved in assessing the new ones, seems to us completely fanciful."[30]

Solicitors were likewise sceptical of the Agency's capacity to meet its targets or keep on top of what was evidently going to be a massive workload. They told us that they did not believe that it would be possible for the Agency to review all cases every twelve months, as was intended. This in turn would bring pressure for change. They predicted at the outset of the study—as indeed came to pass—that the Agency would be in no position to take on the backlog of cases in 1996. In short, everyone who had any experience of dealing with ancillary relief recognised from the outset that the Agency's targets were unrealistic. They said this whether or not they were opposed in principle to the creation of an administrative authority. The Agency therefore can be seen as the product of a government that would not listen. It assumed that these were all hostile voices from vested interests, whereas in reality they were the voices of experience.

It is likely that the warning voices would have been raised even more

[29] *Submission of the Association of County Court and District Registrars in Response to Children Come First* (1990), 5–6.
[30] *Submission of the Family Law Bar Association in Response to Children Come First* (1990), 42.

powerfully had critics fully appreciated the rigidity of review mechanisms under an administrative system. A fundamental characteristic of the Agency's mode of operation—a mode of operation which is in complete contrast to that adopted by the courts under the former ancillary relief regime—is that its decisions are compartmentalised. Courts on the other hand consolidate. Typically, they write off arrears. They concertina claims into one. They create a kind of instant (albeit very rough and ready) justice. But the Child Support Agency operates in bureaucratic mode: each decision is taken in its turn, separated from every other decision in that case. This has the strange consequence (strange from the point of view of the parties and of the observer) that appeals are being heard in respect of assessments which are several reviews out of date. Even in these circumstances, as we observed, there will commonly be no attempt to consolidate. This would not matter so much if the Agency were super-efficient and up to the minute. Given that it does not have these characteristics, the effect is one of almost comical rigidity. The assessment process is completely ossified.

The independent child support appeal tribunals cannot remedy this. As we have seen, they operate under the same statutory framework as do child support officers. The tribunals, just like child support officers, focus on the accuracy of decisions which date back many months, if not years. They too must proceed on the basis of incomplete information, and such powers of investigation as they have are rarely used. Moreover tribunals cannot settle a case definitively, but are obliged to remit the matter to the Agency in order for it to implement the tribunal decision. This means that control of the assessment process is left firmly in the hands of the Agency: the 'independent' appeals mechanism has effectively been neutered. This would not matter so much if the Agency were able to bring its assessment fully up to date following the tribunal hearing; but the Agency cannot change its fundamental character: it cannot consolidate.

Reverting to our theme of over-ambition, it is apparent that the government failed to work out the relationship between the Child Support Agency and the rest of the benefits system. It did not think through the issue of how a significant new maintenance requirement was supposed to impact upon other responsibilities which many of these absent parents had acquired. Or if it thought of it, it decided to ignore it. In fact, if the Agency were to work as intended and at the same time avoid imposing impossible burdens upon many reconstituted families, it could only do so by stimulating an avalanche of new maintenance claims. The process of moving from State support to private support cannot be done *en bloc*. It must happen sequentially. Yet there appear to be a great many gaps in the chain, with the result that some men are required to support two families, no matter that they have a modest income. It was difficult for us, given our method of case selection, to monitor the consequences of serial assessment, but it is important to understand that this was in theory how the Agency was meant to impact upon its customers. It was bound to be a huge culture shock to demand substantial post-divorce maintenance payments from men on low-to-middle incomes. But then in addition we have the administrative nightmare of a system which is supposed to operate on a domino principle, with each child being entitled to support from its own biological father. In fact this principle has operated only haphazardly, with the result that some fathers have faced a dual burden whilst others have continued to evade all responsibility.

6. THE IMPACT OF THE CHILD SUPPORT ACT 1991 UPON PARENTS' EMPLOYMENT
PROSPECTS AND EMPLOYMENT DECISIONS

It was part of the policy of the Child Support Act 1991 that absent parents' incentive to work or to go on working should not be removed, and that parents with care who wish to work should be enabled to do so. If we take first the position of the absent parent, there were some cases, albeit a minority, in which the incentive to work was threatened, especially for men on low incomes. We interviewed several absent parents who threatened to give up work in the face of high assessments, although we had only one case where this actually happened. Another absent parent threatened to work abroad, and a third actually did so in apparent response to the assessment in his case. Solicitors likewise told us of men who threatened—although it was not always clear whether they carried out their threat—to give up their job in the face of the Agency assessment. In the words of one solicitor, this was "a fairly constant refrain". At the same time he conceded that he could not tell us that he had a great many clients who were now unemployed because of the Child Support Agency.

A second justification for the creation of the Agency was that it would encourage single carers back into the employment market: it was believed that regular maintenance at a realistic level might offer these parents a way out of their reliance upon Income Support. As it has transpired, the amounts of maintenance actually paid are insufficient in all but a tiny handful of cases to enable parents with care to return to work. In many instances an enormous increase in maintenance would be required in order to achieve this, given all the other obstacles to finding employment. These include the costs of child care and, of great significance to owner-occupiers, the need to cover housing costs which would have been met whilst on Income Support through assistance with mortgage interest payments. But one must also take into account the fact that child maintenance ordered by the Agency is commonly not paid regularly, not paid in full, or not paid at all. It is hardly surprising in these circumstances that the impact upon caring parents' employment prospects has been minimal. We discovered very few cases where payment of maintenance had allowed a parent with care to remove herself from Income Support and return to employment. For the great majority of parents with care the only way they were going to come off Income Support was if they were to embark on a new co-habiting relationship— and that was an option neither available to nor desired by all.

7. PAYMENT AND ENFORCEMENT

Some enthusiasts for the principles which are meant to be embodied in the Child Support Act 1991 have struggled to reconcile their theoretical support with an honest appraisal of its practical achievement. For example, Deech has claimed:

> "Fewer than one in three single mothers received any maintenance at all for their children before the Agency came into existence, and this rate is bound to be improved."[31]

She further observes of the Agency that:

> "Its other successes have been obscured, but are undoubted: mothers, as well as fathers, will know the likely result of an assessment; similar cases will receive similar treatment; divorce bargaining can take place in the knowledge of the likely Agency assessment; the sums assessed can be uprated for inflation; and there should be prompt enforcement."[32]

One of the starkest and, on the face of it, most surprising of our research findings is how few parents with care and their children had actually benefited financially from the operation of the Child Support Agency. In saying this we are referring both to the fact that parents in receipt of Income Support do not benefit directly unless the maintenance received lifts them off benefit altogether, and to the empirical observation that in many cases the maintenance assessment calculated by the Agency did not lead to any payment—or it led to sporadic, unreliable payment rather than to regular payment of the full amount.

We found that the more strongly embedded was the relationship between the two parents, reflected in their having spent a longer time together or having had more than one child, the more likely was some maintenance to be paid. This pattern was even reflected in the degree of engagement with the Agency process—that is to say, engagement with the mechanisms for *resisting* payment of the full amount ordered. Resistance through formal channels, such as applications for review, were associated with payment—at least, with payment in part; the com-

[31] Deech (1996), 93.
[32] *Ibid.*

plete non-payers simply declined to communicate with the Child Support Agency at all.

In general this was not something which appeared to be of great concern to the Agency. In many instances it had no record of whether maintenance was in fact being paid, whether arrears had been paid off, or even whether the parent with care still wished to claim child support. As was confirmed by our conversations with Agency staff, in its early days the Agency seemed to regard its role principally in terms of conducting an initial assessment, rather than in ensuring payment. It made the assessment calculation without having any effective means of ensuring that the figures supplied to it were the correct figures; thereafter it had no means of ensuring that the assessment would lead to payment in those terms. In these two very important respects it is reasonable to conclude that the Child Support Agency lacked investigative and enforcement powers—perhaps not in theory, but certainly in practice.

This threw the onus back on parents to negotiate their own maintenance agreements, the very opposite of what had been imagined at the time the Child Support Act 1991 was introduced. We observed parents being driven to negotiate 'in the shadow' of the Agency. One of the arguments against a discretionary system has always been that it permits one party to impose a variety of pressures, often quite illegitimate pressures, upon his or her former spouse in order to secure a favourable settlement.[33] In theory the introduction of the Child Support Agency should have helped to resolve this problem. The Agency does not require either party to pursue an application. All that momentum—which calls for a huge expenditure of energy in the divorce context—is meant to come from the Agency. Unfortunately the pattern is not as different as was intended. Parents can still be subject to pressure from their former partner—either not to apply to the Agency (if it is a non-benefit case), or to come off benefit and to accede to whatever private maintenance deal is proposed by the absent parent.

One possible response to the problem of enforcement is to make attachment of earnings mandatory in all cases in which the absent parent is in receipt of a salary. This would in effect turn the Child Support Agency into a branch of the Inland Revenue. This was the view taken by the Association of Registrars when the legislation was being drafted. They observed:

"Our only comment as to the machinery (of enforcement) is that experience of debt-collecting in the County Courts shows that attachment of earnings is by far the most effective way of enforcing payment. To avoid stigma we wonder whether universal attachment of earnings (perhaps concealed in some way by

---

[33] Davis, Cretney and Collins (1994).

making it analogous to tax or National Insurance payments) might be the best answer for employed people."[34]

To make attachment of earnings automatic in the case of all salaried absent parents offers one solution to the problem of enforcement, but of course it would be highly controversial given the plentiful evidence of error in the assessment calculations. An alternative approach, and one favoured by some solicitors whom we interviewed, was that the Agency should be transformed into a body responsible for tracing absent parents who could not be located; and secondly that it might function as a collection agency in cases where maintenance ordered by the court was not being paid. Needless to say this is a very different conception of the Agency than the one which the government originally had in mind. While it is possible that the Child Support Agency would have operated reasonably effectively as a tracing and enforcement unit, it has not had much chance to demonstrate its effectiveness in that area because it has concentrated nearly all its energies on making assessments. But if the Agency's brief had been confined to tracing and enforcement then that would at least have been a more manageable task.

8. FINAL THOUGHTS

A Child Support Agency devoted solely to tracing absent fathers and to enforcing maintenance awards might have been a more practical proposition, but it would have offered no solution to the courts' tendency to impose token orders for child maintenance. It would not therefore have contributed to the cultural change desired by government. But a distant bureaucracy is likewise not well equipped to bring about cultural change. Experience of the UK scheme, and comparison with more successful experiments conducted overseas, especially in Australia, has led us inexorably to the view that both the formula and the intended system of reassessment and review are too complex, and that parents lack appropriate incentives to co-operate with the Agency. If a formula-based, administratively run system is to survive, it will require radical surgery.

One option worthy of serious consideration is a move closer to the Australian model. In the first place this would involve simplifying the formula by abandoning the current shadowing of Income Support rates. Instead, the central principle would be the deduction of a specified percentage of income according to the number of children involved. The introduction of a disregard of maintenance payments when calculating Income Support entitlement would also provide a real incentive for mothers to co-operate and fathers to pay. The child maintenance bonus,

[34] N. 29 above.

introduced under the Child Support Act 1995, is a partial and grudging step in the right direction.[35] Such a reform would also entail reviewing the appropriate location for child support work. In Australia child support is administered through the tax system. Admittedly this might prove problematic where some part of the maintenance paid has to be transferred to the parent with care: there is no tradition in the UK of the Inland Revenue acting as a conduit for payments between private individuals. Yet the clear advantages of deducting payments from earnings suggest that this possibility needs to be seriously considered.

Meanwhile the burdens faced by the Child Support Agency in its present form appear set to multiply rather than diminish. As we write (January 1998) the Agency is bracing itself for a 60 per cent increase in workload by the year 2000.[36] At the same time it is expected, in common with other operational arms of the Department of Social Security, to cut its running costs by a quarter. The Agency is doing what it can to meet the burdens imposed upon it, and has just announced a further radical reorganisation. This involves plans to abandon routine work in local offices and instead to offer a seven days per week phone service. Most local office staff will be relocated to regional centres, where they will deal with telephone enquiries night and day, weekdays and weekends. The new strategy will also involve all new benefit claimants being visited and helped to complete the maintenance application form, thus accelerating and increasing the total of child support 'applications'.

It is difficult to regard these developments as other than a further stage in the painful process of modifying a fundamentally flawed design. It has always been a feature of UK government that we have had self-confident civil servants who did not trust experts.[37] Their saving grace was that they were inherently conservative. But in serving a fiercely ideological government these same officials were required to introduce radical change. Naturally they produced one disaster after another. It is time to reintroduce a little pragmatism.

[35] Baroness Hollis of Heigham, at the time of writing a government minister but then leading for the Opposition in the Lords on social security matters, argued that the bonus "will take at least four years to be arrived at, and gives the wrong money to the wrong mothers at the wrong time for the wrong reasons": Hansard, HL Debs., Vol. 564, col. 1195, 5 June 1995.

[36] Child Support Agency (1997), 71.

[37] Thomas (1985).

Appendix
Research Method

We drew our cases from four separate sources. First, we collected a sample of parents who were undergoing the legal processes relating to separation and divorce. The Lord Chancellor's Department allowed us access to divorce files at Birmingham County Court. We selected ninety-four cases from divorce petitions filed in January 1994, choosing only those in which there was at least one child aged 16 years or under. We wrote to both parties and their solicitors in ninety of these cases, in batches of ten or twenty. We sent follow-up letters approximately one month later to all those who failed to reply to our initial letter and, where a telephone number was available, we subsequently telephoned those from whom we had still not heard. These procedures eventually resulted in our securing a total of twenty-two cases, in twenty-one of which we gained access to only one of the parties. This was a disappointing response rate: 60 per cent of parents failed to respond at all, and only 14 per cent of those approached responded positively.

In Bristol we adopted the alternative method of asking local solicitors to invite one or more of their clients to co-operate with our study. We stipulated that the client should be engaged in separation or divorce proceedings and have one or more dependent children. We asked solicitors not to select clients for us, but to approach the first new referral that they came across following our letter. Of the thirty solicitors approached, fifteen gave us the name of a client with whom we subsequently achieved an interview. One solicitor in fact referred two cases, but this still only amounted to fifteen cases in total because two solicitors had referred clients who were in fact parties to the one divorce. Where we achieved an interview with one parent, we routinely asked him or her to pass a letter to the former partner, seeking their co-operation with the study. Six parents agreed to pass on such a letter, but only one former spouse responded positively. However in a further case we met the partner at an appeal hearing and at that point she agreed to be interviewed. Overall, therefore, these fifteen cases included three couples.

Our third method was to approach the Child Support Agency itself. In this we had the co-operation of the DSS social research branch who arranged for case samples to be drawn from the two regional Child

Support Agency Centres (CSACs) at Dudley and Plymouth. In Dudley the cases were taken from one central computer run. In Plymouth the selection was divided between seven business teams and five workload functions. Dudley selected 151 cases and Plymouth 153. These 304 cases generated 627 individuals.[1] All these parents were asked whether they would permit us to contact them. Only when written permission was received by the DSS were names and addresses passed to us. Plymouth sent us the names and addresses of nine 'double' cases and thirty-eight individuals; and Dudley sent us one 'double' case and twenty-eight individuals. There was then some further attrition as we were not always able to obtain telephone numbers or to secure a response to our letters. Of the Plymouth CSAC sample, three out of the thity-eight individual referrals proved to be uncontactable, and we were able to secure an interview with only one parent in two of the double cases—although this did not prevent our securing access to the CSAC file in those cases. A further double case was achieved when one parent volunteered to approach her ex-partner, who agreed to be interviewed. Of the Dudley sample, six people failed to reply to our letters, and a further three proved unavailable for interview. This higher failure rate reflected some inaccuracies in the information conveyed to us by the Dudley CSAC. Thus we achieved nineteen cases referred by the Dudley CSAC (one of which eventually became a double case), and forty-six cases referred by the Plymouth CSAC (including ten double cases). Thus we secured sixty-five CSA-referred cases in total.

Fourthly we sought and received the co-operation of the Independent Tribunal Service (ITS) and with their help secured a further twenty-one cases (ten in Birmingham, eleven in Bristol), all of which had reached the stage of a child support appeal tribunal. The selection was by date rather than by case: everyone whose appeal was to be heard on a specific date was included in the sample. The ITS initially wrote to all parties and informed us of refusals: two parents refused in Bristol; none refused in Birmingham. After we had observed these hearings we approached the parties and sought their consent to being interviewed. In Birmingham we were able to conduct interviews in seven cases (this included four double cases); and in Bristol we were able to conduct interviews in ten cases (including three double cases). Included in these figures are interviews with four people (two at each centre) who had not attended the tribunal but who were approached subsequently.

Our total sample achieved from these four sources comprised 123 cases: twenty-two from Birmingham County Court; fifteen from Bristol solicitors; sixty-five from the Child Support Agency; and twenty-one

---

[1] Some cases involved more than one absent parent or parent with care. When one parent lived abroad—for example in the armed forces overseas—he or she was not approached.

from the Independent Tribunal Service. In twenty of the 123 cases we secured the participation of both parties.

We were able to gain access to Child Support Agency information (interviews with staff and access to files) in nineteen of the twenty double cases. (In the remaining case the parties withdrew from the study after the first interviews.) We also interviewed fifty-seven solicitors, each of whom was advising one of the selected parents. Such an interview could take place only with the permission of the client, and in two cases this was not forthcoming. In a further two cases the parties withdrew from the study before we had arranged interviews with their solicitor. Four solicitors either declined to be interviewed or proved impossible to contact. In the remaining cases there was no current solicitor involvement, usually because the separation had occurred some time previously.

COMMENT ON THE SAMPLE

Each of these sampling methods had strengths and weaknesses. The court and solicitor-based samples enabled us to approach parents who did not necessarily have any contact with the Child Support Agency. These two groups of cases were also the best source of solicitor interviews and therefore of material relating to the interplay between the Agency and the court. The Birmingham County Court sample suffered from a very low response rate, while the Bristol solicitor-based sample likewise cannot be assumed to be representative.

The sampling procedure employed by the Child Support Agency was out of our control, and again the response rate was rather low (at around 13 per cent overall), particularly in Dudley. Nonetheless this sample of cases was extremely valuable from our point of view, enabling us to talk to people at all stages of the CSA process, some of whom may have separated several years previously. It was primarily in relation to this group of cases that we were able to secure access to Agency files and to the perspective of Agency staff. This proved enormously helpful to us.

Finally, the tribunal sample was valuable in affording us insight into the later stages of the CSA processes, as well as generating more double cases than did our other sampling methods.

We believe that the case sample achieved by these various methods, whilst of course it was not random, was adequate in terms of size and representativeness. It included eighty parents with care and fifty-eight absent parents. The strength of the sample lies in its diversity and in the potential which it afforded for the juxtaposition of different perspectives. Those cases in which we were able to talk to both parents, to their solicitors, and to representatives of the Child Support Agency provided us with particularly rich data. We were also able to follow many cases over a significant period of time, thus affording us direct access to the processes involved and enabling us to question the various actors at different points.

Our main concern on representativeness is that we were able to include few parents from minority ethnic groups. Only three sets of parents were of Asian origin and only one was African-Caribbean. The reluctance of members of ethnic minorities to engage in research is well-documented, and our study certainly suffered from this defect—perhaps in part because no member of the research team was of an ethnic minority background. It is also worthy of note that, for reasons attributable to the way in which our CSA sample was drawn, caring parents who successfully claimed 'good cause' did not feature at all.

INTERVIEWS AND OBSERVATIONS

Interviews were semi-structured. We had a list of topics which we would normally hope to cover in the course of each interview, but the wording of the questions and their ordering was left to the discretion of the interviewer. In most instances informants needed little prompting before launching into a full account of their experiences. In that sense interviews tended to be under the control of our informants at least as much as that of the interviewer. The majority of interviews, including our interviews with Agency staff, were tape-recorded.

Initial interviews with parents were invariably conducted face-to-face. Thereafter follow-up interviews might be conducted over the telephone. Occasionally however we would arrange to call to see a parent again.

Most interviews with solicitors were likewise conducted in person, but when this was inconvenient, or if the solicitor had had limited involvement in the case, the initial interview might be conducted over the phone. Many solicitors had strong opinions about the legislation and its effect on their work. They were prepared to reflect on these matters at some length as well as giving us an account of their conduct of the specific case.

As far as the Child Support Agency was concerned we conducted both topic-based and case-based interviews with Agency staff. In the course of our more general interviews we spoke to representatives of as many of the different sections of the Agency as we could, seeking their views of the tasks for which they were responsible, the organisation of their work, and the Agency's practice generally. Case-based interviews enabled us to ascertain the history and progress of the application from the file and computer record and thus provided us with a check on what parents themselves had said. Some child support officers declined to be tape-recorded.

When we attended a tribunal we sought wherever possible to interview the chair of the tribunal, the wing members and the presenting officer. Most of these interviews were conducted under some time pressure as they usually took place at the end of the day or during the lunch hour. We did not always attempt to record interviews in these circumstances.

The tribunal observations form a small but important part of our study. We attended twenty-two tribunal hearings: ten in Birmingham, eleven in Bristol, and one (in a case which we had been following from the outset) in Sussex. In all cases except the last, two researchers were present. This was helpful in enabling us to interview several key personnel in a short space of time, and it gave us time to introduce ourselves to the parties (whom we had generally not met before) and to arrange for follow-up interviews. It also enabled us to compare our separate records of the proceedings.

DATA ANALYSIS

Certain aspects of the case information lent themselves to numerical analysis and we devised a code for transforming some of the interview data into a form which could be analysed with the aid of the SPSS computer package. However it should be stressed that ours was essentially a qualitative research method and we employed SPSS only for the purpose of carrying out simple counts and cross-tabulations rather than for any more sophisticated statistical operations. Most of our data required a much more painstaking process of intensive reading and thematic analysis.

CONFIDENTIALITY

It was of the utmost importance that we maintain the confidentiality of the information vouchsafed to us. The issues were extremely sensitive and we were quite often in the position of talking to two parents who were still in the midst of an on-going personal and legal quarrel. Also, because many of the parents interviewed were dependent on means-tested social security benefits we were sometimes in the position of having information which, had it been brought to the attention of the Benefits Agency, might have led it to seek recovery of an overpayment of Income Support. We gave an assurance of absolute confidentiality regarding all information passed to us. We have kept to this principle and, in presenting our research material, we have given each case a pseudonym and have sometimes changed identifying details.

Bibliography

ADLER, M. and SAINSBURY, R. (eds.) (1998), *Adjudication Matters: Reforming Decision Making and Appeals in Social Security*, (Edinburgh: University of Edinburgh, New Waverley Papers).

AHRONS, C.R. and RODGERS, R.H. (1987), *Divorced Families: A Multidisciplinary Developmental View* (New York: W.W.Norton).

ATKIN, W.R. (1992), "Financial Support: The Bureaucratization of Personal Responsibility", in Henaghan, M., and Atkin, W.R. (eds.), *Family Law Policy in New Zealand* (Auckland: Oxford University Press).

—— (1994), "Child Support in New Zealand Runs into Strife", 31 *Houston Law Review*, 631–42.

BAINHAM, A. (1993), *Children—The Modern Law* (Bristol: Jordan and Sons Ltd).

BALDWIN, J., WIKELEY, N. and YOUNG, R. (1992), *Judging Social Security*, (Oxford: Clarendon Press).

BELL, J. (1994), "Discretionary Decision-making: A Jurisprudential View", in Hawkins, K. (ed.), *The Uses of Discretion* (Oxford: Clarendon Press).

BELL, K. (1975), *Research Study on Supplementary Benefit Appeal Tribunals* (London: HMSO).

BEVERIDGE, W. (1942), *Social Insurance and Allied Services* (Cmnd. 6404, London: HMSO).

BINGLEY, P., SYMONS, E. and WALKER, I. (1994), "Child Support, Income Support and Lone Mothers", 15 *Fiscal Studies* 81–98.

BIRD, R. (1993), *The Child Support Act 1991* (2nd edn., Bristol: Jordan and Sons Ltd).

—— (1995), "Child Support: Reform or Tinkering?" 25 *Family Law* 112.

BRADLEY, H. (1989), *Men's Work, Women's Work* (Oxford: Polity Press).

BRADSHAW, J., DITCH, J., HOLMES, H. and WHITEFORD, P. (1993), *Support for Children: A Comparison of Arrangements in Fifteen Countries* (DSS Research Report No. 21, London: HMSO).

—— and Millar, J. (1991), *Lone Parent Families in the UK* (DSS Research Report No. 6, London: HMSO).

BROWN, J.C. (1989), *Why Don't They Go Out to Work?*. (Social Security Advisory Committee Research Paper No. 2, London: HMSO).

BURGHES, L. (1993), *One-parent Families: Policy Options for the 1990s* (York: Joseph Rowntree Foundation).

CARBONE, J. (1994), "Income Sharing: Redefining the Family in Terms of the Community", 31 *Houston Law Review* 359–417.

CAREY, S. (1995), *Private Renting in England 1993/4* (London: HMSO).

CHILD SUPPORT AGENCY (1997), *Annual Report and Accounts 1996–7*, HC 124, Session 1997–8, (London: The Stationery Office).

CHILD SUPPORT EVALUATION ADVISORY GROUP (1992), *Child Support in Australia: Final Report of the Evaluation of the Child Support Scheme* (Canberra: Australian Government Publishing Service).

CHILDREN ACT ADVISORY COMMITTEE (1997), *Final Report* (London: The Stationery Office).

CLARKE, K., CRAIG, G. and GLENDINNING, C. (1994), *Losing Support: Children and the Child Support Act* (London: The Children's Society).

—— ——and —— (1996), *Small Change: The Impact of the Child Support Act on Lone Mothers and Children* (London: Family Policy Studies Centre).

COLLIER, R. (1994), "The Campaign against the Child Support Act: 'errant fathers' and 'family men' " 24, *Family Law* 384–7.

COLLINS, R. and MACLEOD, A. (1991), "Denial of Paternity: the Impact of DNA Tests on Court Proceedings", *Journal of Social Welfare and Family Law* 209–19.

COMMITTEE ON ONE-PARENT FAMILIES (Finer Committee) (1974), *Report of the Committee on One-Parent Families* (Cmnd. 5629, London: HMSO).

COWAN, D. (1997), *Homelessness: The (In-)Appropriate Applicant* (Aldershot: Dartmouth).

CRETNEY, A. and DAVIS, G. (1995), *Punishing Violence* (London: Routledge).

—— and —— (1996), "Prosecuting Domestic Assault", *Criminal Law Review* 162–74.

—— and —— (1997), "The Significance of Compellability in the Prosecution of Domestic Assault", 13 *British Journal of Criminology*, 75–89

CRETNEY, S. M. (1986), "Money After Divorce—The Mistakes We Have Made?", in Freeman, M.D.A. (ed.), *Essays in Family Law* (London: Stevens).

—— (1992), *Elements of Family Law* (2nd edn, London: Sweet and Maxwell).

DALLEY, G. and BERTHOUD, R. (1992), *Challenging Discretion* (London: Policy Studies Institute).

DAVIS, G. (1988), *Partisans and Mediators* (Oxford: Clarendon Press).

—— (1994), "The Day Before Yesterday", 24 *Family Law* 323–5.

—— CRETNEY, S.M. and COLLINS, J. (1994), *Simple Quarrels* (Oxford: Clarendon Press).

——, MACLEOD, M. and MURCH, M. (1983), "Divorce: Who Supports the Family?", 13 *Family Law*, 217–24.

—— and MURCH, M. (1988), *Grounds for Divorce* (Oxford : Clarendon Press).

DAVIS, K. (1969), *Discretionary Justice: A Preliminary Enquiry* (Baton Rouge: Louisiana State University Press).

DEECH, R. (1996), "Property and Money Matters", in Freeman M. D. A., (ed.), *Divorce: Where Next?* (Aldershot: Dartmouth).

DEPARTMENT OF SOCIAL SECURITY (1990), *Children Come First* (Cmnd. 1263 (Vol. I) and Cmnd. 1264 (Vol. II), London: HMSO).

—— (1995), *Improving Child Support* (Cmnd. 2745, London: HMSO).

—— (1996), *Child Support* (Cmnd. 3449, London: The Stationery Office).

—— (1997a), *Child Support Agency—Quarterly Summary of Statistics, May 1997* (London: DSS Analytical Services Division).

—— (1997b), *Social Security Departmental Report 1997–98 to 1999–2000* (Cmnd. 3613, London: The Stationery Office).

EEKELAAR, J. (1991), "Child Support—an Evaluation", 21, *Family Law* 517.

—— (forthcoming), "Child Support: Judicial or Computerised Justice?", in Oldham, T. (ed.), *Child Support: The Next Frontier*, (Ann Arbor, University of Michigan Press).

—— and MACLEAN, M. (1986), *Maintenance after Divorce* (Oxford: Clarendon Press).

FIELD, F. (1991), "The Future of Welfare Policy", in Wilson, T. and Wilson, D. (eds.), *The State and Social Welfare* (London: Longman).

FORDER, C. (1993), "Constitutional Principle and the Establishment of the Legal Relationship between the Child and the Non-Marital Father: A Study of Germany, the Netherlands and England", 7 *International Journal of Law and the Family* 40.

GARFINKEL, I. (1992), *Assuring Child Support* (New York: Russell Sage Foundation).

—— and MELLI, M.S. (1986), "Maintenance through the Tax System: The Proposed Wisconsin Child Support Assurance Program", 1 *Australian Journal of Family Law*, 152–68.

GARNHAM, A. and KNIGHTS, E. (1994), *Putting the Treasury First: The Truth about Child Support* (London: Child Poverty Action Group).

GENN, H. (1987), *Hard Bargaining* (Oxford: Clarendon Press).

—— and GENN, Y. (1989), *The Effectiveness of Representation at Tribunals* (London: Lord Chancellor's Department).

GLENDINNING, C., CLARKE, K. and CRAIG, G. (1995), "The Impact of the Child Support Act on Lone Mothers and their Children", 7 *Journal of Child Law* 18–25.

GORNICK, J.C., MEYERS, M.K. and ROSS, K.E. (1997), "Supporting the Employment of Mothers: Policy Variation across Fourteen Welfare States", *Journal of European Social Policy* 45–70.

GRAYCAR, R. (1989), "Family Law and Social Security in Australia: The Child Support Connection", 3 *Australian Journal of Family Law* 70–92.

HARRIS, N. (1996), "Adjournments in Social Security Tribunals", 3 *Journal of Social Security Law* 11.

HARRISON, M., McDONALD, P. and WESTON, R. (1987), "Payment of Child Maintenance in Australia: The Current Position, Research Findings and Reform Proposals", 1 *International Journal of Law and the Family* 92–132.

HAWKINS, K. (1992), "The Use of Legal Discretion: Perspectives from Law and Social Science", in Hawkins, K. (ed.), *The Uses of Discretion* (Oxford: Clarendon Press).

HAYES, M. (1991), "Making and Enforcing Child Maintenance Obligations", 21 *Family Law* 105–9.

HOUSE OF COMMONS COMMITTEE OF PUBLIC ACCOUNTS (1998) *Child Support Agency: Client Funds Account 1996–97*, Session 1997–1998, HC 313, (London: The Stationery Office).

HOUSE OF COMMONS SOCIAL SECURITY COMMITTEE (1996a), *The Performance and Operation of the Child Support Agency* (Second Report, Session 1995–6, HC 50, London: HMSO).

—— (1996b), *Child Support: Good Cause and the Benefit Penalty*, (Fourth Report, Session 1995–6, HC 440, London: HMSO).

INGLEBY, R. (1992), *Solicitors and Divorce* (Oxford: Clarendon Press).

JACOBS, E. and DOUGLAS, G. (1995), *Child Support: The Legislation* (2nd edn., London: Sweet & Maxwell).

—— and —— (1997), *Child Support: The Legislation* (3rd edn., London: Sweet & Maxwell).

JOSHI. H. (1991) "Sex and Motherhood as Handicaps in the Labour Market", in Maclean, M., and Groves, D. (eds.), *Women's Issues in Social Policy* (London: Routledge).

KNIGHTS, E. and COX, C. (1997), *Child Support Handbook* (5th edn. 1997–8, London: Child Poverty Action Group).

KRAUSE, H. (1989), "Child Support Reassessed: Limits of Private Responsibility and the Public Interest", *University of Illinois Law Review* 367–98.

LAND, H. (1994) "Reversing 'the Inadvertent Nationalization of Fatherhood': The British Child Support Act 1991 and its Consequences for Men, Women and Children", 47 *International Social Security Review* 91–100.

LEGAL AID BOARD (1997) *Annual Report 1996-97* (London: House of Commons).

LEWIS, J. (ed.) (1997), *Lone Mothers in European Welfare Regimes* (London: Jessica Kingsley).

LEWIS, N. and BIRKINSHAW, P. (1993), *When Citizens Complain: Reforming Justice and Administration* (Buckingham: Open University Press).

LISTER, R. (1994), "Child Support: Boundaries of Responsibility", 11 *Benefits*, Sept/Oct 1.

McKAY, S. and MARSH, A. (1994), *Lone Parents and Work: The Effects of Benefit and Maintenance* (DSS Research Report No. 25, London: HMSO).

McLAUGHLIN, E., MILLAR, J. and COOKE, K. (1989), *Work and Welfare Benefits* (Aldershot: Avebury).

MACLEAN, M. (1991), *Surviving Divorce* (London: Macmillan).

—— (1994a), "Child Support in the U.K.: Making the Move from Court to Agency", 31 *Houston Law Review* 515–38.

—— (1994b), "Delegalizing Child Support", in Maclean, M., and Kurczewski, J. (eds.), *Families, Politics and the Law* (Oxford: Clarendon Press).

—— and EEKELAAR, J. (1993), "Child Support: The British Solution", 7 *International Journal of Law and the Family* 205–29.

—— and —— (1997), *The Parental Obligation* (Oxford: Hart Publishing).

MARSH, A., FORD, R. and FINLAYSON, L. (1997), *Lone Parents, Work and Benefits* (DSS Research Report No. 61, London: The Stationery Office).

MARTIN, J. and ROBERTS, C. (1984), *Women and Employment: A Lifetime Perspective* (London: Department of Employment/OPCS).

MASHAW, J.L. (1983), *Bureaucratic Justice: Managing Social Security Disability Claims* (Newhaven, Conn.: Yale University Press).

MILLAR, J. (1989), *Poverty and the Lone Parent: The Challenge to Social Policy* (Aldershot: Avebury).

—— (1994a), "Lone Parents and Social Security Policy in the UK", in Baldwin, S., and FALKINGHAM, J. (eds.), *Social Security and Social Change* (London: Harvester Wheatsheaf).

—— (1994b), "The State, Family and Personal Responsibility: The Changing Balance for Lone Mothers in the UK", 48 *Feminist Review* 24–39.

—— (1996), "Family Obligations and Social Policy: The Case of Child Support", 17 *Policy Studies* 181–93.

—— and WHITEFORD, P. (1993), "Child Support in Lone-Parent Families: Policies in Australia and the UK", 21 *Policy and Politics* 59–72.

MULLINDER, A. (1996), *Re-thinking Domestic Violence* (London: Routledge).

MURRAY, C. (1984), *Losing Ground: American Social Policy 1950–1980* (New York: Simon and Schuster).

NATIONAL AUDIT OFFICE (1990), *Support for Lone Parent Families* (HC 328, Session 1989–90, London: HMSO).

—— (1991), *Department of Social Security: Support for Lone-Parent Families* (HC 153, Session 1989–90, London: HMSO).

OGUS, A.I., BARENDT, E. and WIKELEY, N.J. (1995), *The Law of Social Security*, (4th edn., London: Butterworths).

OWEN, S. (1994), "Child Support and the Small Business", *New Law Journal*, October 28, 1485.

PARKER, S. (1991), "Child Support in Australia: Children's Rights or Public Interest?", 5 *International Journal of Law and the Family* 24–57.

PARKER, S. (1992), "Rights and Utility in Anglo-Australian Family Law", 55 *Modern Law Review* 311–30.

PARLIAMENTARY COMMISSIONER FOR ADMINISTRATION (1995), *Investigation of Complaints against the Child Support Agency* (Third Report, HC 135, Session 1994–5, London: HMSO).

PARTINGTON, M. (1991), *Secretary of State's Powers of Adjudication in Social Security Law* (SAUS Working Paper No.96, University of Bristol: School of Advanced Urban Studies).

PEARSON, J., THOENNES, N. and ANHALT, J. (1992), "Child Support in the US: Experience in Colorado", 6 *International Journal of Law and the Family* 321–37.

PETERSON, R.R. (1996), "A Re-evaluation of the Economic Consequences of Divorce", 61 *American Sociology Review* 528–36.

PRIEST, J. (1997), "Child Support and the Non-standard Earner—Pass the Heineken, Please!', 9 *Child and Family Law Quarterly* 63.

PROVAN, B., PASCAL, M., JAMES, T. and WHITWORTH J. (1996), *The Requirement to Co-operate: A Report on the Operation of "Good Cause" Provisions* (DSS Research Report No. 14, London: HMSO).

REES, T. (1992), *Women and the Labour Market* (London: Routledge).

RHOADES, H. (1995), "Australia's Child Support Scheme—Is It Working?", 7 *Journal of Child Law* 26–37.

SAINSBURY, R. (1994a), "Internal Reviews and the Weakening of Social Security Claimants' Right of Appeal", in Richardson, G., and Genn, H. (eds.), *Administrative Law and Government Action* (Oxford: Clarendon Press).

—— (1994b), "Administrative Justice: Discretion and Procedure in Social Security Decision-Making", in Hawkins, K. (ed.), *The Uses of Discretion* (Oxford: Clarendon Press).

—— (1994c), "Administrative Review or Tribunal?", *Address to the Conference of Tribunal Presidents and Chairmen*, 22 April 1994, Council on Tribunals, 16–17.

—— and EARDLEY, T. (1992), *Housing Benefit Reviews* (DSS Research Report No. 3, London: HMSO).

—— HIRST, M. and LAWTON, D. (1995), *Evaluation of Disability Living Allowance and Attendance Allowance* (DSS Research Report No. 41, London: HMSO).

SHAW, A., WALKER, R., ASHWORTH, K., JENKINS, S. and MIDDLETON, S. (1996), *Moving Off Income Support: Barriers and Bridges* (DSS Research Report No. 53, London: HMSO).

SMART, C. (1984), *The Ties that Bind* (London: Routledge and Kegan Paul).

SPEED, M., CRANE, J. and RUDAT, K. (1994), *Child Support Agency: National Client Satisfaction Survey 1993* (Department of Social Security Research Report No. 29, London: HMSO).

—— and SEDDON, J. (1995), *Child Support Agency: National Client Satisfaction*

Survey 1994 (Department of Social Security Research Report No. 39, London: HMSO).

SUGARMAN, S.D. (1995), "Financial Support of Children and the End of Welfare as We Know It", 81 *Virginia Law Review* 2523–73.

TAIT, G. (1997), "The Benefits of Childcare", *Adviser*, No. 63, 12–17.

THOENNES, N., TJADEN, P. and PEARSON, J. (1991), "The Impact of Child Support Guidelines on Award Adequacy, Award Variability, and Case Processing Efficiency", 25 *Family Law Quarterly* 325–45.

THOMAS, P. (1985), *The Aims and Outcomes of Social Policy Research* (London: Croom Helm).

WARD, C., DALE, A., and JOSHI, H. (1996), "Combining Employment with Childcare: An Escape from Dependence?", 25 *Journal of Social Policy* 223–47.

WEALE, A., BRADSHAW, J., MAYNARD A. and PIACHAUD, D. (1984), *Lone Parents, Paid Work and Social Security* (London: Bedford Square Press).

WEITZMAN, L. J. (1985), *The Divorce Revolution: The Unexpected Social and Economic Conclusion for Women in America* (New York: The Free Press).

WHITEFORD, P. (1994), "Implementing Child Support—Are There Lessons From Australia?", *Benefits*, No.11, Sept/Oct, 3–5.

WIKELEY, N.J. (1990), "Lone Parents, Maintenance and Income Support", 20 *Family Law*, 458–9.

—— (1995), "Income Support and Mortgage Interest: The New Rules", 2 *Journal of Social Security Law* 168–78.

—— and YOUNG, R. (1991), "Presenting Officers in Social Security Tribunals: The Theory and Practice of the Curious Amici", 18 *Journal of Law and Society* 464–474.

—— and —— (1992a), "The Marginalisation of Lay Members in Social Security Appeal Tribunals", *Journal of Social Welfare and Family Law* 127–142.

—— and —— (1992b), "The Administration of Benefits in Britain: Adjudication Officers and the Influence of Social Security Appeal Tribunals", *Public Law* 238–262.

WOMEN'S AID FEDERATION OF ENGLAND (1994), *Action Against Domestic Violence: 1993–4 Annual Report,* (London: WAFE).

YOUNG, R. (1993), "Social Security Appeal Tribunals: A Fair Inquisition?", 8 *Benefits*, 14–17.

Index